Other Others

Other Others
The Political after the Talmud

Sergey Dolgopolski

FORDHAM UNIVERSITY PRESS
New York 2018

Fordham University Press gratefully acknowledges financial assistance and support provided for the publication of this book by the University at Buffalo, SUNY.

Copyright © 2018 Fordham University Press

All rights reserved. No part of this publication may be reproduced, stored in a retrieval system, or transmitted in any form or by any means—electronic, mechanical, photocopy, recording, or any other—except for brief quotations in printed reviews, without the prior permission of the publisher.

Fordham University Press has no responsibility for the persistence or accuracy of URLs for external or third-party Internet websites referred to in this publication and does not guarantee that any content on such websites is, or will remain, accurate or appropriate.

Fordham University Press also publishes its books in a variety of electronic formats. Some content that appears in print may not be available in electronic books.

Visit us online at www.fordhampress.com.

Library of Congress Cataloging-in-Publication Data available online at http://catalog.loc.gov.

Printed in the United States of America

20 19 18 5 4 3 2 1

First edition

to Helen Tartar, in memoriam

CONTENTS

EARTH ANEW: A PREFACE

How else can one think earth? Does approaching it as either an object (a globe, a piece of land, dust to trample, or soil to clench in one's hands) or as a subject (Fatherland, Mother Earth) or as an affect or a sentiment (patriotic love, fear of a yawning grave) exhaust what earth means? At the junction of classical rabbinic thought and contemporary political theory, this book seeks to expand the horizon for thinking earth in the face of each new challenge and each new responsibility that greets us.

Thinking earth anew is a political and not just an ethical challenge—one that requires a new concept of the political, no longer expressed in terms of sovereignty or democracy, but in terms of engaging extraterrestrial others: those who do not belong to a recognized land. Levites in the Bible and Jews under Nazis are mutually exclusive cases that must be thought anew before we can think earth anew—or perhaps not fully anew, in the ever disappearing and reemerging political paradigm the pages of the Talmud display.

In the dominant account, the political order necessarily denies legal and moral existence to those who do not belong to a land while tolerating the diversity of those who do. Against this core claim of contemporary political theory, this book turns to the Talmud. That late ancient body of text and thought allows a different concept of the political, and with it, a new take on the question of the extraterrestrial other. Philosophical and theological approaches to the political have tacitly elided what the Talmud affords, an elision made legible only by carefully reading the pages of the Talmud through and despite our dominant theologically and philosophically grounded political. This book commits to just such a reading, oriented jointly to the Talmud and its afterlife, and to political theory, so as to think earth beyond the notions of territory, land, nationalism, internationalism, even universe, that have hitherto defined it.

The earth and its relationships to the other others comes to the forefront of the analysis in this book; it also reflects in the book's title as "other others." If books had biographies, this biographer would tell the following short story behind its title.

At inception, a simpler title, "The Political in the Talmud," captured the book's main theoretical and textual frame—a critical exploration of the notion of the political in contemporary political theory, articulated in a bidirectional dialogue between contemporary theory and the late-ancient Talmud and its interpretation and reception through the Middle Ages to modern period. The book's present title, on the other hand, emphasizes not the frame of inquiry but the theme that frame induced: other others, the earthly extraterrestrials who are not and cannot be marked by a recognized land.

This move from frame of inquiry to theme subtly transformed the original title into a subtitle, "The Political after the Talmud." The "after" that supplants the title's original "in" intimates at least three different relationships between the political and the Talmud: "according to," "as a result of," and "post." The book thus addresses three interrelated questions: What notion of the political does the Talmud display? How is the political to be understood and revisited in contemporary political theory as a result of the Talmud? And how are we to contend with the possibility that we live post-Talmud, with the Talmud left behind us even as it still shapes the horizon of contemporary political thought?

Such an imagined book-biography also includes the story about another title, a shorter but captivating phrase that almost captured this project but will need to grace another book instead: "Political Atheology." Such a title would have perfectly expressed this book's central engagement with and crucial distance from the political theology of Carl Schmitt. By extension, it might have intimated a connection to a "political aphilosophy." Different from antitheology and antiphilosophy, "atheology" and "aphilosophy" would indicate an expansion of the horizon of the political beyond what theology, philosophy, and their mutual opposition and their practical implementations in political life afford or allow. Such a title might have renegotiated the traditional (almost dogmatic) aversion of Talmud scholars to both theology and philosophy (informed as this aversion has been by a history of violence in interactions between Christian philosophy and theology on the one hand and Rabbinic schools of the Talmud study on the other). Proposed by Daniel Boyarin when this book was already written, "Political Atheology" does give a name to one of the book's leading motives, and if it isn't quite the proper way to encapsulate what this book pursues as a whole, it promises a direction to which its argument may—perhaps must—lead in the future.

Other Others

INTRODUCTION

Humans, Jews, and the Other Others

The political has been lost, occluded by the industrial, postindustrial, and informational. Entrapped in the centuries-long connection with politics, with the state, and with institutions, even when disentangled from that trap, the political more recently has been effaced by the notions of political theology and political ontology, notions in which that erasure has been masked and suppressed. The effacement of the political awaits discernment.

Effacement is thus one of the central themes in the book. Yet the effacement it addresses differs from the conventional understanding of "effacement" as referring to a simple act of erasing. "Effacement" names a process different from what researchers call "historical shifts," "paradigm revolutions," or "epistemic changes," processes that they "trace." A common denominator between these names is that they all imply a static element or, more precisely, a move from one static element to another in a one-directional progression and/or regression. For example, a new paradigm comes to replace another, and when that is done, the process is over until a newer paradigm comes to replace "the new" one. Similarly, "historical shifts" mark transitions from one historical period to another and normally happen in one direction, just like paradigm changes, from the past to the present, or from present to the past, whichever "the present" means in a given context of a historical investigation or in the development of a science. Similarly, again, "epistemic changes" move from the past to a present or in the other direction, but once a shift happens, things stay still and stable until the arrival of the next shift. These notions—shift, change, and revolution—by definition presume stability that they first disturb and then reinstate. They move from one state of things to another and thus have a beginning and an end.

The notions of trace and tracing are not fully foreign to that element of stability, either. However much different tracing might be from "shifts," "revolutions," and "changes," it can (although does not have to) presume stability or more specifically a stoppage. To trace is in general by definition a way to stop or to grasp things that are gone, things that are no longer or are not here anymore. This stabilizing or stopping element of the trace comes to the fore in an even more important example through which we can differentiate trace from effacement. This example comes come from the work of Emmanuel Levinas, perhaps the most important thinker to have asked about Talmud and philosophy in the last century.

Trace is how Levinas approaches the face of another person. A trace of what neither is present nor ever was, of a time immemorial and/or G-d of the Hebrew Bible, a face limits, restrains, and thus stabilizes the subject's otherwise endless—and false—aspiration for self-sufficiency. It is always already there before the subject, and having always already faced such a trace it makes the subject responsible for what is beyond her control, Levinas argues. Having always already encountered the face—something beyond her control—the subject becomes responsible for treating the face as such, that is, as the face of the other, instead converting it into an object of the subject's power of domination. The face is always already other, a stability and stabilization that therefore restrains and stabilizes the subject as well.

Effacement, in contrast, is neither a one-directional move nor can it be either stable or ever over. Like face and/or trace, effacement is an unfolding that at the same time is concealment. However, there is nothing static, pregiven, let alone stable and/or coherent that would be either unfolding or concealing itself in the process. Rather, effacement entails a dynamic process of the appearance of something at precisely the singular moment of its disappearance. It also forms a series of such moments; it is therefore never over. The effacement creates the effaced, as one comes to appreciate what is being lost precisely at the moment of that loss, not before. The temporality of effacement thus both includes and exceeds the temporality of the trace.

Yet, and precisely therefore, effacement becomes a yet another, dynamic, and much less solitary face of the face. The bidirectional movement of effacement, of appearing disappearance and disappearing appearance, gives a face to what is disappearing, a face to what is being lost, even if and precisely because it did not necessarily exist before the effacement begins.

At this juncture, it is imperative to highlight a sharp distinction between the logic of the question of effacement and that of linear history. More specifically, an analysis of effacement should not be confused with tracing a historical origin. Effacement is a question rather than an answer, a problem rather than a claim. The question of effacement is the question of the appearance of the "origin" at precisely the moment and within the movement of its disappearance. The question of effacement is therefore not an answerable question about historical, let along chronological origins, but rather an unanswerable but necessary and productive question about the appearance of such an "origin" only at a moment of its disappearance. Any claim of an original past presumes an answer or a possibility of an answer—for example, along the following lines: Yes, there was an original state of affairs that disappeared and needs recovery. The analysis in this book does not propose such a linear, historical answer. Rather, effacement strongly gestures toward a methodological distinction between the logic of the question of the effacement and any answers conceivable within a horizon of linear history.

To emphasize that distinction, a further clarification of the question of the relationship between history and "originality" is due. Is a historical claim always a claim for an authentic original past? Different logics of effacement in the following chapters suggest different answers, but a common denominator remains. A claim of an original past, if there is one, is no more and no less than an effect of effacement. If that "original past" appears only at a moment and in the movement of its disappearance, it cannot be original in any linear historical sense. This is why the "intrinsically historical" nature of effacement differs from history in its traditional teleological—that is to say, one-directional—sense, and by the same token from a sense oriented toward an answer to the question, "What is the origin," rather than toward the question why any alleged origin appears only at the moment of its disappearance. There consequently is no need to explain in any detail why the sense and the question of effacement are different from the sense of history as chronology.

The structural role of effacement as posing a question in opposition to any possible answers in terms of historical originality also appears in the book's argument as it is organized into chapters and parts, where the "method" of asking the question of effacement and "history" as a never-sufficient answer to that question come together. Simply put, effacement is a concept defining both the method, that is to say the question, the book develops and the history it unpacks.

A particular move of and a particular form of the question of effacement this book brings front and center is the effacement of the political in the Talmud, or by a necessity that will become clear in the analysis, of the Talmud as the political. The following pages articulate several movements and/or instantiations of such incessant effacement. The logics of that effacement are multiple. One logic articulates a possibility precisely at a moment when this possibility becomes tacitly denied; another constructs an image of the past in order to deny that image any viable future; yet another creates a set of concepts of which one concept becomes tacitly excluded from consideration, thereby making the other elements in the set work smoothly. The chapters below show these different logics of effacement at work as it comes to the ongoing effacement of (the) Talmud as the political.

More broadly, what follows is a series of case studies that collectively respond to the need to recover the political from the conceptual apparatuses that have obscured it. They do so by displaying the political dimension of the Babylonian Talmud against the background of its effacement from the site of the political from the Middle Ages on, when the Babylonian Talmud emerged as a legal document rather than as a prototype, program, and paradigm for a political mode of existence. I look to the Babylonian Talmud and its reception as a way to highlight the erasure of the much broader version of the political of which the Talmud might be the only surviving, or at least the only available, but in no way the only possible example.

From Politics to the Political

Let me first clear a space to establish a viewpoint from which to look at the modern conversation about the political that this book both challenges and advances. The first clearing distinguishes the specific usages of "the political" in what follows from the common usage of "politics," whether that term is taken somewhat ironically, as what politicians do, or approvingly, as what the state[1] has to do to defend the interests of the society.

"Politics" and "the political" are not the same. "The political," as Jacques Rancière has it,[2] refers to the discussion about or acting with regard to justice, liberty, and the common good—as long as the common good is decided on the grounds of justice and liberty, that is to say, not on the grounds of economic "advantage" or "harm," to use Aristotle's distinctions, which Rancière emphasizes in his work.

In yet another way, but still distinct from the commonsense notion of "politics," "the political" is defined by Carl Schmitt not as a particular sphere, whether economic, social, legal, military, or institutional, but as what permeates all spheres, based on an a priori distinction between enemies and friends and the implementation of that distinction empirically, deciding who or what is the enemy and declaring a state of emergency and/or exception when the established legal and social order cannot provide an effective response to that enemy.[3] As is already clear, I thus use and focus on "the political" as a noun, that is, both before (and, perhaps more precisely, after) it became an adjective accepting other nouns, as in "the political sphere," "political life," or "political philosophy."[4]

The second clearing concerns what I will call "the other others," as distinguished from the more traditional notions of the other as sites and sights of alterity, especially in the work of Emmanuel Levinas and Jacques Lacan. An "other other" might suggest Emmanuel Levinas's view of the divine Other, who is neither present nor absent, but whose commandments, in particular, "Do not murder," are always traceable on the face of those others whom the subject confronts—a human, a dog, and perhaps even a snake. Or an "other other" might similarly suggest Jacques Lacan's differentiation between an other as a "petite object"—what the subject confronts as either an image (including the image of oneself) or as a symbol, permitting or forbidding the subject to commit certain actions and/or behaviors, and the real Other, who is never confronted, but who instead arises as the difference between the imaginary behavior of the subject and the symbolic distinctions to which the subject adheres or violates. Yet these two suggestions remain what they are when it comes to a much more dynamic and exterritorial nature of the other others this book aims to articulate.

Despite the verbal connections with these much better known and certainly much better explored sites of otherness, the conception of "the other others" that I address in this book maps a territory that distinctions drawn by Levinas and Lacan can at best only hint at—the territory of and for those who do not have a territory and who therefore help cast a new light on the hitherto prevailing notions of the political.

The other others appear precisely at the moment of their effacement—at a moment, for example, when the Nazi government first denies them their existence or commits a political-ontological act. That denial goes beyond dehumanization, beyond a fantastic reduction an individual to a cockroach. It is a denial of any place in the order of the world to which to belong. Following the logic in political theology of an exception from the law, the Nazis arrived at the political-ontological denial to the other others of any existence at all, proving thereby that existence is always political in the first place. The Nazi state apparatus enacted (or "realized" or, if I may, "cashed"—as one cashes a check) that nonexistence through the system of camps, which were not killing machines, for how can you kill someone who is not simply nonhuman but who does not even exist? It is at this point the other others appear and disappear in this act of effacement.

These other others were not present before the political-ontological denial of their existence began. There surely were others, a variety of them, but not the other others. Before the political act of denying their existence, the others could have been reterritorialized in a "secular" mask of looking, acting, and living as Germans did or else as traditional rabbinic observant communities. In any case, they were "regularly" territorialized others. However, they became other others precisely at the moment of their political-ontological unbecoming.

The Political and the Talmuds

These preliminary distinctions help account for the current state of studies of the political in the Talmud. And when I say "in the Talmud," I mean, first, the political as it is displayed and more precisely to be discerned in the Talmud's folios, but more generally, I am referring to a version of the political for which the Talmud has so far been the only noticeable example, but that, as this book argues, is at work in and is being suppressed in other instances of political life, dominated as that life has been by ontological and theological views of the political. The focus of Talmudic scholars of the political has been, at best, on the state (kingdoms) and monarchy (kings).[5] Yet nearly every interaction of the characters in both of the Talmuds, the Palestinian and the Babylonian, in any sphere of their lives—in the rabbinic academy, in their families, with those in power—is political in a formal sense, a sense that both Rancière and Schmitt emphasize, for as I will show, despite their differences, Schmitt's and Rancière's competing senses of the political are formal, because they refer to no privileged content, that is, to no privileged sphere of life. They therefore open up a view on other formal and therefore foundational senses of the political, in this case, those found in the Talmud.

The omission of that formal political dimension in the Talmuds from the horizon of interests of Talmud scholars has been neither an oversight nor the result of chance. Rather, it has been a function of the predominantly empirical orientation in Talmud scholarship, realized in its exclusive focus on establishing historically accurate texts for the two Talmuds and more recently on the institutional and cultural contexts and meanings that these texts portray or imply. These empirical approaches were developed by advancing an often-artificial separation between empirical and theoretical approaches, as if an empirical orientation does not feature the tacit belief in empiricism as its theoretical foundation and as if any viable theory is possible in abstraction from how texts are read. This artificial separation of the empirical and the theoretical has led to the suppression of any theory except for that of empiricism, which, according to the belief of its adherents, has required no theorization at all. The result has been both the expulsion of theory from Talmudic scholarship and, more recently, its return as no more than a borrowed or applied discourse used to provide rigor where a pure belief in empiricism becomes too apparently naive. However, only the lens of contemporary theory as developed in discussing the formal dimension of the political allows us to discern the formal political dimension of the two Talmuds.

The Political and the Humanity of Humans

The matter goes well beyond the mere application of the theory of the political in the formal sense to the Talmud. Rather, seen in light of the theory of the political, the Talmud has much to contribute to the contemporary theoretical discussion of the political. This is because the theory of the political is currently facing a deep crisis in the face of the extreme fragility of political notions of the humanity of humans, proved, as that fragility was, by what was euphemistically named the Holocaust, but what is in truth still not understood, let alone named properly.

This book therefore addresses a double omission: the omission of the political from the study on the Talmud and the omission of the tradition of the Talmud from current thinking about the political. To compensate for that dual omission and to respond to the crisis in contemporary political theory in thinking about the humanity of humans, this study addresses the political, in the formal sense of the term, in late ancient rabbinical compositions as they arise in and contribute to the modern discussion of the political. It intervenes in the context of contemporary political thought by bringing Talmudic thought, in the scope of its unfolding over the centuries, back into the discussion in order to reconsider the limits of political theology and political ontology by rethinking the area of applicability of the problem of the humanity of humans, or, stated in terms at once broader and more precise, by rethinking the problem of the other others anew.

In this Introduction I only adduce, preliminarily, the relationship between the political, political ontology, and political theology, and elaborate the full structure of that question in Chapter 1. Yet it is important to say up front that by bringing the Talmudic and philosophical traditions of thought in conversation with one another, the book reconsiders the effects that the modern projects of political theology and political ontology have on shaping the currently predominant notions of the political. The linkages between the political and theology and between the political and ontology articulate the gap within each pair, the gap where new possibilities that the concepts of political theology and political ontology have brought forth in thinking the political sphere both occur and are suppressed. The book aims to retrieve those possibilities.

Doing that involves looking at the Talmud and philosophy as two commensurable but mutually irreducible ways of thinking the political that fruitfully can be brought into an explicit dialogue one with another. Facilitating such a dialogue becomes possible—and, as I argue, urgent—because political theology and political ontology have firmly established themselves as dominant on the stage of thinking about the political. Creating a language for a new dialogue means using the contemporary discussions and controversies about the political to shed a new light on the pages of the Talmud, thereby displaying the political in the Talmud in a way one could not before. At the same time and by the same token, that perspective both enables and necessitates bringing the resulting notion of the political in the Talmud back to the context of the modern discussions of the political. The book follows this bidirectional path of inquiry.

Such a project necessarily engages different readerships, which in turn necessitates a discussion of the theoretical stakes that it involves for them and the different approaches that it addresses. The book's rather counterintuitive claim that the political is not about subjects might be particularly helpful and interesting for readers rooted in modern rabbinic responsa (e.g., about organ donation, or about using the seed of killed soldiers who had no children to produce children from surrogate mothers, or about transgender versions of traditional Jewish morning blessings). I must nevertheless emphasize that due to the programmatic distance of this book's argument from theology, the argument cannot be used to recapture the political in the Talmud for theological purposes, if theology means theocentrism or puts a subject, either human or divine into the center of thinking. This step away from the role of the subject in thinking in the Talmud might also have implications for thinking about the LGBT Jewish community, if that community submits itself to theocentrism as justification of its legitimacy. However, in the framework of my argument here, I am able only to gesture toward these implications and limitations.

The book also appeals to other, diverse readerships from disciplines and areas of interests ranging from political philosophy to Rabbinics (the study of Jewish late ancient texts of the Talmud and related corpora), from the history of philosophy and rhetoric in late antiquity to the history of concepts and the intellectual history of the Talmud's interpretation in Middle Ages and modernity, from the philosophical anthropology of neo-Kantian tradition to post-Heideggerian, Derridean, and Lacanian and Levinasian approaches to the problem of human being or its relationship to the Jewish question—which is another instance of other others in modern times, and from contemporary rhetorical and aesthetic theories to the intellectual history and history of concepts of rhetoric and aesthetics.

A unifying factor among these otherwise very different areas of interest is the guiding concern with and stake in the limitations of the modern political construction of "the human" as a would-be common denominator capable of bridging all cultural, ethnic, racial, moral, sexual, and geopolitical differences. It is as if "human being" is a notion capable of bringing together everyone, including the others and the other others. Yet the commonality asserted by the term "human being" proves insufficient when the other others, these nonlinear interruptions of the dystopia of universal humanity, come to the fore. With the advent of the other others at the moment of their effacement, the concept of the human being proves to be both necessary and insufficient. After what the Holocaust names, insufficiently, the human can no longer be automatically granted the status of a common denominator. Neither can it now, after the "Holocaust," be justifiable to insist on such a common denominator by any kind of artificial—imperial, despotic, or any egoistic and/or altruistic—effort.

This book therefore addresses the resulting insufficiency of the notion of "the human" as a figure of political thought in its ontological and theological versions by highlighting intellectual alternatives for thinking about the political that become available by putting modern political thought about the humanity of humans—or, what is the other side of the same coin, the humanity of the other others—and the Talmud's thought about the political in the critical light of each other. That guiding concern with the other others explains the book's even broader appeal to readers interested in the current stage of discussions in both the humanities and the sciences about the humanity of the human, understood in the most general terms, which, as I argue, must be the terms of the other others—those who, as I will explain in the chapters to come, have territory, but have no land, have territorial existence, but have no territorial representation, have indivisible territorialization, but have no divisible piece of land to represent them to others.

By way of that guiding concern with the other others, the book revisits and challenges the hitherto predominant connection of the political with ontology and theology. Articulating the impasses of thinking about the political in terms of ontology and theology, the book reevaluates these impasses for thinking of humans and other possible subjects of reason, asking about the other others by reclaiming for the current debate about the political the late ancient bodies of texts and thought in the Palestinian and Babylonian Talmuds and relevant pagan traditions in their relationships, focusing on the humanity of the human and on the other others as a problem to which the call for the humanity of the humans is a reply, as both necessary and insufficient as this reply is. That leads to two interrelated agendas of inquiry, one in the context of contemporary political theory and the other in the context of the study of the two Talmuds, the Babylonian and the Palestinian.

A Discipline of Remembering

This new book stands in a relationship with my first two books, both in terms of the broad and broadening question of the role of rabbinic tradition in the contemporary intellectual scene and in the narrower and much more specific sense of studying the Talmud.

The three books form a triptych, but the third addresses a much broader question and appeals to much broader interdisciplinary audiences than the first two. The distinction between Talmud without the "the" (a practice) and the objects known as the Talmud(s) was central to my first book, *What Is Talmud? The Art of Disagreement* (2009). The book introduced the question of Talmud without the "the" as a practice, rather than an object. In the second book, the question became "What is Talmud in what is called the late ancient Talmud?" The new book asks: What role does the effacement of that Talmud from the horizon of political thought play in that thought?

The third book thus becomes an exploration of a whole new approach to the "political," thereby addressing much broader audiences than the two books did before. That accounts more generally for a trajectory from *What Is Talmud?* to *The Open Past: Subjectivity and Remembering in the Talmud* (2013) to this new book.

In order to make this trajectory traceable for as diverse readership as this book addresses, it becomes necessary to provide "basic" or rather context-specific background about (the) Talmud. I describe that background where and when it is most needed, that is to say, to an extent and in a form in which that background becomes important contextually.

In much more specific terms of the study on the Talmud, the trajectory of research in this book continues the movement I began in *What Is Talmud?* and *The Open Past* and is in conversation with the most recent scholarship of Daniel Boyarin, Moulie Vidas, Richard Hidary, and Chaya Halberstam, among others. I see that trajectory going backward from the fifteenth-century rationalistic conception of Talmud as the art of disagreement to the late ancient texts of the Babylonian Talmud as distinct from the fifteenth-century perspective on them, as well as distinct from manifestations of the early modern perspective in the modern critical scholarship on the Talmud, toward a new and more precise understanding of the late ancient Talmud as a discipline of remembering. Rooted, as I will argue, not in intersubjectivity of the interlocutors in the Talmud and beyond but in what I will describe in detail as interpersonality, despite the fact that the latter becomes effaced by the former, the discipline of remembering opens up a new way of thinking about the role of the others, and particular of the other others, in thinking itself.

Unlike techniques and technologies of data retrieval, the discipline of remembering is one of the places where the appearance of the other others at the moment of their disappearance and the disappearance of them at the moment of their appearance registers. The process and the discipline of remembering prove to be too dynamic to be accounted for by any static partitioning of territory in which and only in which any stable grasp of the other can flourish. Even failing to remember, one still cannot forget. The discipline of remembering deals with things as elusive as only the other others can be.

In that discipline, animated by disagreement, rational thinking becomes subservient to the task of memory and of remembering, rather than being either coextensive with memory, as in Platonism, or dominating memory (reduced to a database), as in other philosophical schools. In this book,

I take a third step and move even further back from the Babylonian Talmud to begin exploring its relationship to the Palestinian Talmud. That move reveals the political dimension of the two Talmuds. As I argue, contrary to political ontology and its concern with the claims of being versus seeming to be versus nonbeing, and contrary to political theology, with its concern with *theos* as *logos* (or G-d as both word and thought), in the Talmuds, the world-forming political act is remembering—and thereby establishing—the authoritative traditions of the past in the best way possible. The book exposes and structures the complexity of the act of remembering—as an act of encountering the other others and of the effacement of the other others who cannot be encountered on any firm ground. It traces the implications of that act of remembering for the modern discussion of the political in view of the other others, which must proceed beyond either ontology or theology.

In the context of modern political thought, a focus on the act of remembering introduces a series of new distinctions, disjunctions, problems, and/or concepts into the discussion of the political. The first and central one is the distinction between intersubjectivity, understood along the lines of Kant's notion of the subjects of reason (which arguably is the foundation of modern political ontology and theology), on the one hand, and what I introduce as "interpersonality" as the formative element of the political space and practice in the Talmuds, on the other. That distinction between intersubjective and interpersonal helps think the other others with greater precision then the notion of the human subject can help afford. The intersubjective effaces the interpersonal, and that effacement describes the appearing disappearance and disappearing appearance of the other others in political thought.

The second distinction concerns the complex relationship between the modern political figures (or *types*, in the terminology of Philippe Lacoue-Labarthe) of the Jew and the human being that escape the classificatory logics of the linear relationship between species and subspecies, so that neither "human" nor "Jew" relate to each other by the logic of general and particular, thus revealing one of the hidden joints in contemporary political mechanisms. That distinction allows thinking of the role of the "Jew" as modern political figure of the other others.

The third distinction is the disjunction between Kant's transcendentalism as the way out of the dilemma of dogmatism versus skepticism, on the one hand, and a different way out of the dilemma, a solution that arises from the Talmud's programmatic orientation of political thought and action toward a well-structured uncertainty, as opposed to the best attainable certainty, which post-Kantian views of the political keep promoting. Do the corpora of the Talmud and its reception over the centuries afford a different way out of the dilemma? And if they do, what does that mean practically in terms of addressing the vanishing nature of the other others in an interpersonal encounter, which is no longer intersubjective? That distinction is between transcendentalism and what I will call Talmudic irony and/or Talmudic sarcasm, which provides yet another entrance or rather another exit at which to notice the other others at work.

Finally, the fourth distinction is between what political theology and political ontology offer as counterexamples of the political (for example, liberal disputation and ongoing disagreement, for Carl Schmitt, or the suppression of disagreement or dissent by forcing consensus, for Jacques Rancière) on the one hand, and the Talmud's orientation toward self-refutation as a mode of interpersonal action, toward memory as a world-forming activity, and toward well-structured uncertainty as the programmatic orientation in political action, if the latter are to take into account—indeed to welcome—the impossibility of taking the other others into account.

The logic of the question of the effacement of the political in general, in political ontology and political theology, and in particular the effacement of the political in the Talmud, informs both the book's guiding question and the overall structure of its parts and chapters. The text is divided into three parts. The first part, "Modern Impasses," articulates and renegotiates the stakes between political theology and political ontology as two hitherto dominant ways of thinking the political. In application of a critical understanding of these stakes, the first part further addresses the limitations of and intrinsic connection between the modern political constructions of humans, Jews, and the other others these constructions efface. The second part, "The Talmud as the Political," examines the late ancient texts of the two Talmuds, Palestinian and Babylonian, in juxtaposition with—as Christian tradition labeled them—"pagan" late ancient texts, which I read both through and despite the lens of their medieval and modern predominantly Christian interpretations and through the lens of the modern crisis of the constructs and figures of humans, Jews, and their other others in their alleged unity in humanity. The third part, "The Political for Other Others," concentrates specifically on the significance and implications of what the analyses in the second part can contribute to the modern discussion of the political: the interpersonal rather than intersubjective model of the political, the difference between intersubjective dissent vis-à-vis the dominant other and interpersonal disagreement vis-à-vis the vanishing appearance of the other others in the process of disagreement. In doing so, this part tells the story of the construction of the Talmud as "origin" in both secular and rabbinic religious modernisms as they display themselves as a story of the "decline" of the "origin" they construct.

There, a shared implication of these analyses leads to a more general question. This concerns the earth in its relationship to being and to land ("territory") as it most powerfully comes to the fore in Gilles Deleuze and Félix Guattari's last book, *What Is Philosophy?* In that book, the question of the earth is understood as the central question of all philosophy. Navigating the complex relationship between land, earth, territory, on the one hand, and political ontology and political theology on the other proves itself necessary for setting a correct scope for thinking the political in terms of the other others. In view of political ontology, at stake is the question: Is the earth thinkable as being? Or is it, instead, nonbeing, as a certain reading of the biblical verse "and the earth was the emptiness and the void" (והארץ היתה תוהו ובוהו) might suggest? In view of political theology, the question at stake is: Is the earth thinkable as land to divide up among those who partake at the exclusion of those—the other others that is to say—who are denied any part thereof, and thus seen as enemies attempting to control all of it? Or is the earth instead an indivisible—or if you will, a liquid—abyss, a never firm foundation from which both land and humans first erupt and which humans then mistake for the dry land to control, as a certain reading of the biblical verses connecting humans (אדם) with the land, dirt, clay, or ground (אדמה) but not with the earth (ארץ) is suggesting? If neither being nor land, does the earth require another horizon of thinking? Working through instantiations of the thinking about the political in political theology, political ontology, and in the Talmud, the series of inquiries undertaken here ends by addressing the question of the relationship of Talmud and philosophy as corpora of thought about the earth. Who are those other others who appear only at the moment of their vanishing, and who therefore invite us to think beyond the types of humans and/or Jews among the rest of territorial types behind which both the earth and the other others disappear at the moment of their appearance or appear only through their disappearance in the depths of the earth?

The question of the earth is the question of the other others. This question calls for a much more fluid and dynamic ways of thinking the political, and therefore the earth, than have been afforded by the traditionally static territorial distributions and redistributions of solid and stable land among either recognized or denied groups—such as sovereigns, humans, and/or Jews in both political theology and political ontology. Unlike these static (ex)territorial types, the other others and with them the earth vanish at the moment of their appearance and appear at the moment of their vanishing by the logic and by necessity to which the argument in this book aims to attend.

PART I

Modern Impasses

CHAPTER I

The Question of the Political: Back to Where You Once Belonged?

A formal element prevails in the question of the political as it is articulated in the philosophical discourses of political theology and political ontology. That element is neither dualistic nor oppositional. Nor is it cast in terms of the difference between friend and foe or in terms of the disagreements of what is in conventional terms called "politics." Rather, it is tripartite. Beyond any bipartite opposition between elements—between each other's other, which is an opposition that always can be recuperated—the political always involves a third term that has no place in that opposition: other others.[1] This can be seen in the discourses on the political in the work of philosophers as different as Carl Schmitt and Jacques Rancière. For both the theorist of National Socialist dictatorship and the populist post-Marxist philosopher, the foundation of politics occurs not just on the basis of inclusion and exclusion, but on the basis of what cannot be included in that dynamic. That tripartite element is an essential formal characteristic of the way in which the ontotheological has been conceived in the classical philosophical tradition.

For Carl Schmitt, the specific content of political claims is not as important as their ontotheological form. In an early work, *Roman Catholicism and Political Form* (1923),[2] Schmitt lays the conceptual foundation for his later and more widely known theory of the political as the friend-enemy grouping, including the theory of sovereignty as based on the proclamation of a state of exception from what otherwise would be the universal rule of law administered by the state. In this work, Schmitt distinguishes between the general ontotheological form of a political office and the content that any particular person can bring to it.

Schmitt argues that as a particular person, an official of the Catholic Church represents the truth of G-d's existence, both through and as opposed to representing the official's own personhood. Representing G-d takes precedence.[3] As a result, the personal vices or virtues of a Church official do not directly interfere with the efficacy of his office. What matters is his status, not his personhood, either vicious or virtuous.[4] According to Schmitt, in other words, political power is attainable due to its ontotheological form—the performance of the existence of G-d on earth, regardless what particular content advances that claim to power. Both the official and his words or acts represent the Church better than any external reality reflected or implied in those words or acts.[5] This form, when it is looked at from the outside Catholic Church, is a "representation of representation,"[6] as Schmitt perhaps bitterly characterizes it. As contrasted with other, more familiar forms of representation, in the "representation of representation," what is represented is the act of representation itself, not something that differs from and is external to the representation. In the ordinary sense of "representation," the Church might be understood as a representation of Christ and a Church official as a representative of the Church. Thus, there is a chain of antecedents external to such representations. However, the Church claims to be the mystical body of Christ on Earth and thus is not different from, let alone external to, what it represents,[7] and a Church official is thus part and parcel of the Church as the body of Christ, rather than a representative of something different. He does not represent either himself, or the Church, or any other external entity. Rather, he represents the fact that he represents.

Whether Schmitt considers Roman Catholicism to be a "political form" or only models that notion after the Church in application to modern national state is not at issue here, and he does find paradigmatic examples of the "representation of representation" leading to "political form" not only in Roman Catholic Church, but also in other medieval corpora—in professional guilds of craftsmen and university corporations of scholars, as well as in the religious orders of monks and in the military orders of knights in the Middle Ages. What is important is that viewed from a point of view external to the Church's own ontotheological conception of itself as the mystical body of Christ,[8] the representation of representation necessarily appears as an "empty form"—"a representation of [the idea of][9] representation," a form that is "the political" per se for Schmitt precisely because fundamentally and primarily, it represents no intrinsic content, even if there always is *a* content. And it is that notion of "political form" that leads Schmitt to his later and more most widely known notion of political theology—a theory describing how the theological concepts operate outside their proper context of theological-juridical representation, that is, in the proper register of "political form," both inside and outside the content of any particular law or any particular theological claim.

Schmitt thus ventures to say that the Roman Catholic Church is the only historically surviving genuinely political institution and that all other modern institutions, including modern nation-states, even if commonly called "political," are in fact of merely a "techno-economical nature." In what Schmitt calls "techno-economical" forms of rationality, means must match ends. In techno-economical rationality, one may have any desires, goals, or ends whatsoever. Realistic or not, these desires do not have to be rational; the only requirement is that the means to satisfy them must be "rationally calculated." For Schmitt, techno-economical rationality involves no politics, although of course it might involve the state and its institutions. Political rationality, in contrast, requires the "rationality of goals" or a selective approach to ends to differentiate worthy ends from unworthy ones. In *Roman Catholicism and Political Form*, he sees the celibate bureaucracy of the Catholic Church as the only surviving example of that rationality, which is a genuinely political form.

In his later work, as an example of a rational goal, Schmitt uses Hobbes's notion of *conatus*—in Schmitt's terms, the preservation of one's existence or ways of life at all costs. That goal is achieved through an a priori political form that is empirically filled by a sovereign deciding who or what is an enemy, who is a friend, and whether or not dealing with the enemy requires suspending the otherwise purely techno-economical rule of law, which governs, as it otherwise does, the relationships between friends. The law, in other words, still represents only the techno-economical rationality of goals, which might have been irrationally established. Yet in the face of the enemy threatening one's way of life or existence, the *conatus*, the rational goal to survive, takes precedence over the techno-economical rationality of the law.[10] At this point, the sovereign proclaims the state of legal exception and thereby becomes a political figure. The power of the sovereign to declare the state of exception is prior to any specific representation of friends and enemies that the sovereign makes in each case, when an emergency is declared.[11] It is the power of the representation of representation.

It follows that the decision on the exception in the face of perceived emergency can generate any content as long as it generates *a* content. That content includes indicating who, or rather what the hidden enemy is and who is a friend.[12] This is why, after *Roman Catholicism*, Schmitt can say, "The specific political distinction to which political actions and motives can be reduced is that between friend and enemy."[13] Making such a decision follows the logic of immanence in the political form of the representation of representation, because the form relies on no external factor—neither on a group of "formed interests" nor on the figure of any particular leader. Because the logic of political form does not depend on any external reference and/or content, it can produce any reference and/or content. That enables the representative of representation who is performing that form to make a decision, rather than to apply or create a rule. It also leads to an immanent legitimization that precedes, suspends, and supersedes any positive legality of the law as a set of rules.

In these terms, the political decision on the state of exception is not dictatorial, because it does not abandon any positive laws but suspends them until the state of exception is lifted, and that can be done only by a someone who does not depend on any intrinsic external factor, not even on his own personal will, and who therefore can act only "properly." Such a representative of representation by definition acts independently of any positive legal regulations because he or she decides on the exception from them.

The power to decide on a state of exception produces a tripartite division: first between "us" and any particular "them," a distinction that in these terms is merely techno-economical and empirical, but in addition, a formal distinction between those who can be included in that distinction and those absolutely excluded from it.[14] That second, fundamentally political distinction excludes all other others from the distinction between us and them, friend and enemy, a distinction that is operative at any given moment and that can change over time. Three groups thus emerge from this tripartite division: those whose power derives from an ontotheological source as the representation of representation, those whom it identifies as having the appearance of others, and those other others who are ontotheologically excluded from being by the decision on the state of exception.[15] It thus is also a distinction based on the distinguishing of three ontotheological qualities: being (the ontological source of power), appearance (the contingencies of otherness in the mutable friend-foe distinction), and nonbeing (the essential otherness of the other others). In Schmitt, the political figure of the sovereign is thus predicated on the exclusion of the other others from the order of being.

As for Rancière, he identifies an even more radical element at work in the constitution of the political—not the exclusion of the ontotheologically other, but the exclusion of politics itself, properly understood, from philosophy, an exclusion that nevertheless is made on the same basis: the formal character of the ontological foundation of philosophy and the tripartite distinctions of being, appearance, and nonbeing.

"What is called 'political philosophy,'" Rancière argues, is in effect "the set of reflective operations whereby philosophy tries to rid itself of politics, to suppress a scandal in thinking proper to the exercise of politics. This theoretical scandal is nothing more than the rationality of disagreement (*mésentente*)."[16] Disagreement, for him, is a mode of orientation toward being—being together or being with people and groups who are irreducible one to another.

In incompatible ways, different parties draw rational distinctions between what is and what merely seems to be, resulting in *mésentente*, the unavoidability of different groups talking past each other in matters of the common good, including what is just and what is not.[17] These disagreements remain despite any assumed shared understandings of words, their meanings, and the things these words address. This is because without knowing it different groups can see radically different things expressed by identical words. What is more, no group can notice the discrepancy until a philosopher speaks powerfully enough to draw attention to it. As Rancière puts it, "Where philosophy runs up against poetry, politics, and the wisdom of the honest merchants" when talking about justice, it has to borrow the other's words in order to say that it is saying something else entirely: "It is in this that disagreement lies, and not mere misunderstanding, which can be resolved by a simple explanation of what the other's sentence is saying—unbeknownst to this other."[18] There is disagreement, *mésentente*, not misunderstanding. Philosophers can attempt to put things in their true light, as it were, but even in this light, one still cannot overcome disagreements. The result is that any agreement is always temporary and illusory, and disagreement is the political reality of society.

Thus, disagreement "is less concerned with arguing than with what can be argued, the presence or absence of a common object between X and Y. . . . An extreme form of disagreement is where X cannot see the common object Y is presenting because X cannot comprehend that the sounds uttered by Y form words and chains of words similar to X's own. This extreme situation—first and foremost concerns politics."[19] If X uses certain words to present a certain thing, and Y uses the same words to present a different thing, then X, believing as she well might, that things and the meanings of words always correspond and that there is only one thing, not two, cannot comprehend that the words of Y are the same words with a different meaning.

For Rancière, this political discourse of unavoidable—and in the extreme case, uncontrollable—disagreement is prior to and grounds any discussion about what is economically "useful" or "harmful." The same applies to discussions of what is morally right or wrong or aesthetically beautiful or ugly.[20]

On the basis of the unavoidability and uncontrollability of disagreement, Rancière criticizes classical philosophical thinking of the political. The terms "useful" and "harmful" are from Aristotle, and Aristotle is included because he insisted that ontological claims about what is versus what seems to be are able to ground agreement between citizens in a society and that any other ground for agreement is false, immoral, and ugly.

It is here that political ontology gets its name—from the understanding of the political as the ground of the possibility and impossibility of agreeing based on the claims of being versus seeming. Although Rancière rethinks the classical political ontology of Plato and Aristotle, submitting that there can be no genuine agreement achieved on the ground of the difference between being and seeming, he continues to maintain that the distinction between being and seeming is the only available basis for political life in a city-state, because only the difference between being and seeming can support the discourse of disagreement.

That in turn sustains the discourse of justice, without which there is no sufficient ground for Aristotle's seemingly purely economic distinctions between the "useful" and the "disadvantageous." Uncontrolled disagreement controls the "fairness" of economic exchange, and it is the task of a philosopher to make this clear. This alone allows the discourse of justice to operate and be operated in its full power, instead of slipping into the despotic rule of established "positive" law. Instead of the classical political ontology of agreement, Rancière thus advances a new political ontology that cannot eliminate disagreement from the core of political life, but that still maintains the rhetoric of being versus seeming as the foundation of the political.

Rancière further insists that even in Hobbes's model of modern political life in a nation-state, which—as Rancière understands Hobbes—arises from the fear of "confrontation" and the hope of a "forming of interests," disagreement continues both to underlie and to undermine the economic (or, more broadly, pragmatic) order of "interests." It does so because the latter can never suffice to hold the state together in a "national" unity against the attacks of another nation-state. Uncontrollable disagreement, in other words, continually threatens nation-states, no less than it constantly threatened the classical city-state.

The difference between the classical and the modern thus concerns the new role of fear in the nation-state. For a citizen in a classical city-state, freedom is supposed to be more important than the preservation of life, even if that is so only as long as the citizen remains within the city. This is how a citizen differs from a slave, who strives for life at all cost. For a modern nation-state, as Rancière understands it, according to Hobbes, life is a "natural value" for all, a goal in itself, whether one is a slave or not. By the logic of natural law, that goal, to preserve life, therefore justifies any means. In turn, it leads to the "forming of interests" in the nation-state. What for Aristotle was a feature of slavery for Hobbes becomes the character trait of all citizens and conditions their being together.

Rancière therefore argues that however drastic it seems, the difference between excluding slaves and considering all humans as behaving like slaves in preserving their lives is not as consequential for political ontology as it seems. What is common prevails over difference. The discourse of justice, grounded in the distinction between seeming and being, serves the new situation of nation-states, as well as that of city-states, as long as the "fear of confrontation" leads to the "forming of interests." The forming of interests cannot be based on simple fear. It requires a discourse, and the ontology of being versus seeming supplies that discourse for all parties involved, a discourse in which there can be no genuine agreement achieved on the ground of the difference between being and seeming.

Since the origins of philosophy, Rancière thus argues, irreducible disagreement has disrupted philosophy's project of establishing an ontological basis for itself. "Philosophy's atomic project, summed up in Plato, is to replace the arithmetical order, the order that more or less regulates the exchange of perishable goods and human woes, with the divine order of geometric proportion that regulates the real good, the common good that is virtually each person's advantage without being to anyone's disadvantage."[21] However, the demos, identified as that part of the whole of society that is characterized only by what characterizes all in society—freedom—"appropriates the common quality as their own."[22] This "dividing of society into parts that are not true parts" and in which the demos is the "part that has no part" is the ontological origin of the political.[23] Because "the people appropriate the common quality as their own," they expose as mere appearance "the sheer contingency of the social order,"[24] the order of oligarchs, aristocrats, technocrats, and the demos itself. Consequently, "Politics is the sphere of activity of a common that can only ever be contentious, the relationship between parts that are only parties and credentials or entitlements whose sum never equals the whole"[25] In that whole, "there is no part for those who have no part."[26]

Thus, here, as in Schmitt's account of the political, a tripartite structure emerges. In addition to an apparent internal division of society, where "there are only *parts* of society—social majorities and minorities, socioprofessional categories, interest groups, communities, and so on,"[27] there is a fundamental division, an exclusion that constitutes the political, the exclusion of the political itself as the locus of irreducible disagreement.

And philosophy's exclusion of politics—of the political, understood in this way—entails a further exclusion for Rancière: the exclusion of those who do not exhibit a certain kind of subjectivity, the exclusion and by the same token presupposition of the symbolic position of the slave, either real or imagined, who can perceive reason (in particular the geometry of the common good), but cannot understand it. This is based on classical philosophy's distinction between "human beings endowed with the logos and animals restricted to sole use of the organ of voice (*phônê*)," between those whose articulations involve "the profitable and the injurious" and hence "the just and the unjust" and those whose articulations involve only "sensations of pleasure and pain," or comprehension without understanding (slaves, the position in between humans and animals.) It thus entails a distinction between those who are human, those with logos, who distinguish between truth and falsehood, being and nonbeing, and those who only appear to be human, those without logos—between "those who really speak and those whose voice merely mimics the articulate voice to express pleasure and pain,"[28] or only mimics human, rational speech.

The political claim to power thus remains effective regardless of varying and even mutually exclusive designations of who exactly "is" and who only "seems to be," and who is blatantly "nothing," beyond seeming. The common denominator that Schmitt and Rancière share is thus an understanding of the political as assigning being to certain groups of individuals and denying it to others—to the other others. The formal structure of the essentially ontological dimension in the theories of the political that Schmitt articulates and that Rancière analyzes critically moves the discussion beyond any empirical distribution of particular and contingent political designations of social, economic, or pragmatically political identities and roles, determining in addition who truly is and who simply is not.[29]

The common denominator in these so diverse understandings of the political, Schmitt's, and Rancière's, is Kant's older figure of "*vernünftige Weltwesen überhaupt*," which can be translated as "the subject of reason" and which implies the intersubjective community of the subjects of reason.

What is at issue here is Kant's conception of the humanity of humans as developed between the *Critique of Pure Reason* and the *Critique of Judgment*, because the definition of the human in the *First Critique* does not coincide with the definition of the human in the *Third Critique*. In the *Critique of Pure Reason*, Kant envisioned an a priori way to discriminate and identify entities: "The concept 'dog' signifies a rule according to which my imagination can delineate the figure of a four-footed animal in a general manner, without limitation to any single determinant figure such as experience or any possible image that I can represent *in concreto*, actually presents."[30] A dog is what appears to be a dog. The same would of course apply to the concept of "the human"—the human is what appears to be human. Such "schemata" "serve only to subordinate appearances to universal rules of synthesis, and thus to fit them for thoroughgoing connection in one experience."[31] Yet this mode of identification and discrimination is not enough when it comes to the definition of the human in the *Critique of Judgment*. There, what defines the human is action in accordance with and within the limits of reason alone—that is, along the lines of the categorical imperative, which is not limited to the conformity of appearances, that is, to those who look like humans, in the terms of the *First Critique*—but is inclusive of any and all subjects of reason.

Excluded from that inclusion are the other others, those who have no schematic representation fitting a concept, except by way of the sublime, which is precisely a feeling that there something does not fit in schematic representation. The other others thus are neither humans nor, for example, devils, for the latter still have an image and are acceptable to Kant if they are indeed subjects of reason.

In Kant's sense, Reason, *Vernunft*, is Understanding, or *Verstand*, that understands its limits. In his sense, then, the subjects of reason, although they are known empirically via the form or schema of the human, need not be human. Rather, the community of the subjects of reason potentially includes those who do not fit the schema of the human, as distinct, as in Kant's example, as a dog is distinct from a cat. By extension, a subject of reason can be distinct not only from a dog, but also from an anthropoid. Conversely, those who are schematically human may also be excluded from the subjects of reason if they do not understand the proper limits of their understanding and instead of acting according to the categorical imperative of Reason, act only in terms of the positive law, either by complying with it or violating it, whether acting dogmatically or skeptically or acting in accordance with or in revolt against "positive" morality conceived of as a set of norms in society. In turn, those who are schematically nonhuman may be included in the intersubjective community of the subjects of reason.

This broad inclusiveness of the humanity of the human thus excludes those humans who are not the subjects of reason. Who phenomenally appears to be human need not be a subject of reason. In turn, whoever is a subject of reason does not have to appear to be human. In that sense, humanity could include Martians, but excludes anyone who is human in form, but does not act like a subject of reason. In particular, it excludes anyone who obeys "positive law," not the moral law within, the categorical imperative. Mere appearance becomes the place of the other others.

Kant's view of humanity thus produces and is produced by a tacit theological exclusion of the other others as would-be humans who forfeit their subjectivity of reason in favor of obeying the imposed laws and/or rules of Christianity, Judaism, or other "positive religions."[32] I term this "theological," because ironically, in replacing the "positive religions"—Judaism, Catholic Christianity, and others—this move tacitly follows the traditional Christian figure of supersession, replacing the "Old Testament" with a "New" one, with a "religion of reason" replacing the positive religions.

Viewed more broadly, however, the consignment of the other others to nonbeing extends back to the classical origins of philosophy. For Plato and Aristotle, everything first of all merely seems to be, and only then, through either a judgment or a decision, some appearances turn out truly to exist, to be, while other appearances turn out not to exist, not to be.[33] Thus, following out the trajectory of philosophy after Plato, both political ontology and political theology have conceptual access to nonbeing only by first differentiating seeming from being. What merely seems to be may or may not be. Both Schmitt and Rancière remain captured by this trajectory of thought, deriving attributions of nonbeing from seeming. Of course, what only *seems to be* does not yet either exist or not exist, at least not in the strict sense. That is a determination in which even what is determined not to be survives as nonbeing, even when it has been erased as nonbeing.

Thus, at work here is the logic of effacement. By that logic, the effaced never disappears. Still visible, the effaced remains and is a function of the determination that separates seeming into being and nonbeing. In the tripartite structure of being, seeming, and nonbeing, the third term becomes only a derivative of the second; nonbeing is downgraded to only a function of seeming to be. Already in Plato, this structure of thought replaces the pre-Socratic view, which privileged the demarcation between being and nonbeing and worried much less, if at all, about the seeming. A momentary flash of lighting against the temporal and spatial background, the long gloom of night is the image through which Heraclitus introduces what Heidegger in conversation with Eugen Fink would read as a superfast, one-moment-long revelation of the being of things that cuts through their multiplicity without erasing or reducing things to any abstract common denominator.[34] That fleeting moment of lightning, however, is lost in long and slow exposure to a steady light of day. As Heidegger's reading of Heraclitus suggests, in the daylight, one becomes blind to the being of things together, one with another. Instead, one sees things in their crisp and clear distinctions from one another—often at the price of confusing the being of a particular thing or matter with its seeming to be. In the light of day, chimeras emerge.

In contrast to classical ontology, Heidegger's fundamental ontology thus reclaims a "pre-Socratic" view of the being the things—the view of all things being together as revealed in a flash of lightning, as opposed to nonbeing of night or the distinctions of being and seeming arrived at in the light of day, a distinction that for Heidegger applies to the being of each singular thing, as well.

In a positive sense, this move takes Heidegger beyond Platonism back to the pre-Socratics. Yet a negative dependence on Plato remains, for Heidegger's move still depends on the determinations of seeming and being carried out in the light of the day: In order for Heidegger to arrive to such an interpretation of the lightning in Heraclitus, there must already be a certain version of Plato in place. This version must privilege the daylight, even if only in order to be negated in the return to Heraclitus as a pre-Socratic. Heidegger needs the light of the day, at least by denying it, in order to arrive at the primordial power of the night and of nothing, which the lightning highlights and which being confronts. In short, in respect of the night of nothing without seeming, pre-Socratics are only possible *after* and by negating, Plato's philosophy of the daylight.

Both political theology and political ontology not only reduce nonbeing (the night) to a derivative of seeming, but also depend, if only negatively, on the light of the day, even when their determinations consign other others to the gloom of night.[35] With regard to political theology and political ontology, there can therefore be highlighted three ways of thinking about being: a pre-Socratic who bestows nonbeing and being on the entirety of things; a (post-)Platonic philosopher who attempts to separate what is from what seems to be, with what is privileged and nonbeing reduced to seeming; and a (post-)Heideggerian thinker of "fundamental" ontology who "returns" to the pre-Socratic finitude of being in view of nonbeing and thus follows the Platonism in privileging the being over nonbeing. All three translate to, underlie, make necessary, and even coincide with either a political-ontological or a political-theological claim of power. Invariably, in all three, being gives power to those who can connect all things through their being over those who either live in the gloom and the chaos of night or who surround themselves with the bright chimeras of the day.[36]

It is thus that, in all the classical discourses of the political, what is at stake is the exclusion of other others. The other others are politically sorted as having no authentic existence and therefore can never "get back to where they once belonged," because they belonged nowhere. Unlike foes and unlike those who seem to deviate from any merely contingent norm in the realm of appearances, they cannot be recuperated as belonging among "us."[37] They are consigned to nonbeing.

In contrast with the ontotheological tradition of the political as it has developed in classical philosophy, the Talmuds—each in its own way—resist, escape, and thereby reveal and redefine the linkage of the political to ontology and theology, both in ancient thought and today. The Talmuds present an entirely different conception of personhood, of the character of relations between persons, and hence of the political. In place of the conceptions of subjectivity and intersubjectivity, inflecting as they do—but not radically changing—the traditional formal triangle of being, nonbeing, and appearance that has been the defining characteristic of modern philosophy since Kant, the Talmuds produce and perform a conception of personhood and of what I will be calling "the interpersonal" in discourses involving the practices and results of disagreement, refutation, and remembering.

For the concept of the interpersonal that I will be developing here there are no ready-made words that allow for a sufficient gloss. "The interpersonal" refers to a way of thinking and acting in society that both involves a multiplicity of positions and does not involve any rigid connection between any position and any individual who performs it. It thus begins from and always proceeds with a multiplicity of thoughts, both affirmed and denied, with regard to any action. In contrast, the intersubjective begins from a thinking subject and proceeds to a multiplicity of such subjects; it therefore rigidly connects a thought with a subject who both carries it through as an agent and obeys it, as subjects are to obey their king. In the intersubjective setting, the process of thinking is fundamentally solitary, whereas in an interpersonal setting, it never is.[38]

The interpersonal thinking displayed in the Talmuds does not begin from, does not end up with, and does not necessarily include thinking subjects interacting with other thinking subjects, as the notion of intersubjectivity would require. Instead, individuals take part in a dance of thinking that consists of a to-and-fro, strophe and antistrophe, refutation and counterrefutation performed vis-à-vis a tradition, a recorded text of the past around which the dance is unfolding. What is more, the same dance is assumed to have taken place in the tradition itself and in the recorded text, for the text, too, is approached as and is validated by being a thoroughgoing refutation of an otherwise viable position proposed by a dancer in the past, a position that the dancers on stage are to reconstruct and thereby to remember. In such a back-and-forth, no individual subject is in control of the dance, but all participants contribute to and complicate its moves, the strophe and the antistrophe, the refutations and counterrefutations.

The dance thus entails interpersonal relationships, rather than intersubjective ones, as the former unfold either in the script on the pages of the Talmuds or as these pages are performed when the Talmuds are studied in religious schools or other similar settings. While the dance contributes to and leads to remembering the traditions better, the result is not a personal recollection, either individual or collective. In the dance, the refuting and counterrefuting of the record of a tradition contributes to remembering it better by producing an interpersonal memory, which is structurally different from the recollection of a thinking subject or group of subjects. It is the interpersonality of the never solitary participants in the dance of thinking and remembering, rather than the intersubjectivity of fundamentally isolated thinking subjects (who of course are never alone in their engagement in a community of others like them, but still fundamentally solitary in their pursuit of the thinking to which each of these subjects commit). Unlike the subject of classical philosophy, which is prior to and the basis for any form of intersubjectivity, it is the dance of the personae participating in it, not the personae themselves that forms the basis of the interpersonal. The figures in this dance thus present an alternative to what classical philosophy has conceived as the "subject position," an alternative in which that position is not occupied by any individual person, but is produced by the work of remembering itself undertaken by the characters present in the Talmuds.

This inquiry leads to new stakes not just in conceptions of the subject, intersubjectivity, and the political, but also in exploring the relationships between the two Talmuds. In academic scholarship on the Talmud, what I would call a "derivative" approach has recently become predominant.[39] In that approach, the later Talmud emerges as a further development or "derivation" from the earlier—the Babylonian Talmud emerges from and is derived from the Palestinian Talmud.

Highly developed dialectical exchanges between unnamed characters characterize the later Talmud, transforming the divergent opinions of named characters found in the earlier Talmud. In the later Talmud, these divergent opinions reemerge as mutually exclusive contraries, all of which the nameless characters in the Babylonian Talmud attempt to defend. The resulting discussions in the Babylonian Talmud represent nameless and therefore less authoritative characters who argue with one another or in soliloquies in order to attack, but ultimately to defend the pronouncements of the earlier authorities. They do so despite seeing these pronouncements as contrary to each other, rather than merely as diverging one from another, and precisely because they see those opinions as contrary, rather than divergent. In that sense, the Babylonian Talmud can be called "derivable" from the Palestinian Talmud, because it entails converting the diversity of opinions and positions of earlier authorities into a speculatively reconstructed dialectics of discussion about them and on their behalf.

Not totally different from Platonic dialectics, the dialectical discussion in the later Talmud on behalf of the earlier Talmudic authorities, who might have never directly polemicized, targets the ultimate truth of the tradition and its memory, rather than either cultivating arguments for argument's sake or remaining genuinely open to an unknown truth that it is the goal of the discussion to attain.[40] The new Babylonian dialectics contributes to the reaffirmation of the authority of the traditions of the past, despite and even due to their diversity and precisely due to their pastness.

At least, that is the account that emerges in light of developments in the derivative approach to the Talmud. The derivative approach as it has been most recently developed in Daniel Boyarin's work helps to elucidate a subtle, hitherto hidden, but all-important connection between Plato's dialogues as a form through which one makes the fundamentally political truth claim of distinguishing being and appearance from nonbeing and the Babylonian Talmud's dialectics of affirming the truth and the authority of tradition, or, as others argue, of the reliability of its memory.

Boyarin has contested what was the predominant view of the Babylonian Talmudic dialectic as programmatically open, as opposed to the Platonic dialogues, in which the putative openness of the outcome of a dialogue is often tactical, rather than genuine. In that view, ultimately, Socratic irony always wins, whereas the rabbis, it was assumed, keep their conversations in the Talmud open-ended, without a resolution, working, instead, to support each opposing views against each other, because, as the famous Talmudic dictum has it, "these [views] and these [opposing views] are words of the living G-d." Boyarin has argued instead for the absolute, paradigmatic closure of the dialogues in the Babylonian Talmud, in which, as in the Socratic dialogues, openness is only a tactical move, and the defensibility of the Mishnah and other authoritative texts from the past is always maintained.[41] In other words, as in the Platonic dialogues, what occurs is not an open-ended dialectical pursuit of philosophical truth via the discrimination of being from seeming and nonbeing, but the establishment of authoritative positions by rhetorical means.

In the Babylonian Talmud, it is via rhetorical arguments about what is possible, by employing the technical tools of rhetoric, that the ultimate truth and thus the political power of the teachings of the earlier sages come into the hands of those nameless characters who control both the fluidity of the truth and the solid authority of remembering it in the best way possible. In the rhetorical dialectics of the Babylonian Talmud, being, seeming, and nonbeing cannot be distinguished fully. The characters live instead with what Chaya Halberstam calls "uncertainty" about the truth.[42] But hers is an exclusively philosophical use of the term "uncertainty." In the traditional rhetorical sense of uncertainty, in the Talmuds, the uncertain is not merely tolerated, but is actively welcomed and even programmatically required to create room for rhetorical argument about what is possible, rather than for a philosophical-logical discussion about what is necessary or impossible on the basis of what is, what seems to be, and what is not.[43] By revealing the origins of authority in the Talmud in this way, the derivative approach allows us to identify the political in the Talmud beyond and independently from any specific "political," state-oriented themes that are discussed there, such as the status of a king, relationships to surrounding state powers, or relationships with colonizing powers.

In doing so, here, I complement the derivative approach with a deductive one. I employ the term "deductive" in its old usage in the European legal terminology of Kant's time, when it meant determining the rule under which to subsume a case discussed in court.[44] Is the act of X having hit Y with an object followed by Y having died premeditated murder, or an accidental death, or a crime of passion, or caused by negligence, or legitimate self-defense? The list does not exhaust all the options, but what would have been at stake for Kant is the determination under which law the case is to be "deduced"—which law should apply in this instance.

This distinction between "derivative" and "deductive" approaches helps situate the argument here relative to more empirical, philological work on the Talmud. Opposing "deduction" to merely empirical "derivation" helps open up a philosophical (and more specifically, transcendental) dimension of reading and analyzing the Talmud. Strategically, the question of a correlation between deduction and derivation can also help bridge the empirical and theoretical horizons of academic study of the Talmud.

As a complement to the derivative approach, the deductive approach identifies the a priori conditions of possibility for the empirical production of meaning, of writing, of interpersonality, and of authority in both Talmuds. This act of thinking is similar to legal "deduction" in which a case is subsumed under a rule or law, with one but radical difference: that law is not known in advance, but rather is to be deduced as governing the case, explaining it, and making it possible.[45] Such a "deduction" from a case to discovering its governing law is, for Kant, a "transcendental deduction"—the discovery of the rule that makes the case possible, discovering the conditions of possibility of the case. Another—indeed, already implied—difference between the legal deduction of a case under existing law and transcendental deduction as the discovery of a law that governs the case or makes it possible is that the transcendental deduction does not concern a violation of the law of which the case is the case, but instead focuses on discovering the law that makes the case possible. Still, the common denominator between all deductive approaches consists in moving from the case to the law or rule, not the other way around.

In a deductive approach modeled after Kant's transcendental deduction, the question is no longer that of adducing the historical transformation or derivation of one Talmud from the other, but that of the deducing the foundations of the political, that is, how being and appearance are distinguished from nonbeing, in the Babylonian Talmud. However, access to these foundations is possible only in the context, through the lens, and against the grain of current theoretical discussions of the political.

Needless to say, an engagement with Schmitt's, Rancière's, and the Babylonian dialectical approaches to the political entails no conceptual anachronism. It is not about applying modern concepts to late ancient texts; rather, it is about renegotiating modern concepts of the political in terms of and through their differences with political thought in the dialectics of the Babylonian Talmud, thereby reclaiming a role for the Babylonian Talmud in the current discussions of the political. That means tracing, in the

Talmuds, an intellectual and political alternative to the society of Kant's subjects of reason or of its modifications after Kant:[46] an open space of interpersonal action shaped around shared uncertainty and remembering both the distant and the immediate past, personal or collective, a space strikingly different from the intersubjective space centered on being and nonbeing versus seeming to be.[47]

A complication on this path of inquiry is that the interpersonal understanding of the political has been effaced by the modern ontological model of the political and by classical conceptions of the subject of reason and of intersubjectivity based on the ontology of "what truly is" and on the tacit exclusion of the other others, who cannot "get back to where they once belonged."[48] It therefore will be necessary to interrogate the effacement of the interpersonal: to locate the marks of the erasure of the interpersonal beneath the inscription of the predominant modern models of the political. The place to begin to interrogate the erasure of the interpersonal by intersubjective is in the modern figure of the Jew in discourses concerned with the humanity of the human, where the modern erasure of the other others comes to fore in its tacit work.

CHAPTER 2

Jews, in Theory

In this chapter, I further explore the effacement of the other others, their appearance in vanishing and disappearance in emerging, as performed by the currently predominant understandings of the political in terms of political theology and political ontology. A site where this can be detected is the modern theological, ontological, and ultimately political figure of "Jews," in contradistinction from the theological notion of the "Children of Israel" for which rabbinic and Christian communities compete.

Unlike the "Children of Israel," the "Children of Jacob," or other self-characterizations in the rabbinic tradition, the term "Jews" is what the rabbinic literature uses when thinking about Israelites as seen through the eyes of those in domination—Romans in antiquity or Christians as their successors from the Middle Ages on. At the center of attention here, however, is not competition for the name of "Israel," but rather the figure of "the Jews" as an outcome of that competition, which both rabbinic and Christian communities seem to share. I thus focus on the figure of Jews, rather than on that of "Israelites."

Theologically, the term "Jews" is a stepping-stone for Christian identity, ancient and modern alike. The logic at work here is that of supersession. In terms of political theology, Jews defeat any linear definition of others such as occurs in the contingent opposition of friend and enemy, for example, introducing instead the other others that are in play in the tripartite formal distribution of being, seeming, and nonbeing. Jews are not pagans, because they worship the same G-d that Christians do. Nor are the Jews heretics, because a heretic must be a Christian in the first place. Fitting no standard categories of the others of Christianity, Jews defeat any stable placement in the worlds charted by Christianity and its normative others, whether these are seen as convertible to Christianity, as some normative others are, or inconvertible, as some others among them have been considered to be. As the other others who defeat stable classification, Jews theologically cut right to the heart of Christian identity. Theology, that is to say, both produces and is produced by the supersessional logic of anti-Judaism toward the Jews, whom traditional Christian theology must posit and supersede at the same time.

In terms of political ontology, however, modern Jews were fundamentally denied being. The industrial, postindustrial, and informational society initiate the modern transition from the anti-Judaism of the traditional theological anti-Jewish element in Christianity to anti-Semitism, the transition from ontotheology to bare ontology. In the latter, the Jew becomes an ontological figure. Thus, ontologically, in the denial of their being, modern "Jews" can be easily misunderstood as targets of genocide. Yet this is not entirely correct. Genocide implies a group of people murdering another group of people based on a racial, ethnic, genetic, or other criteria. Genocide thus presumes that the targets and perpetrators have the ontological status of "people." People kill people. This is not exactly the case in what is commonly referred to as either the Holocaust or the Shoah. By the force of the power of a national state, a certain target group was denied the status of humans as such. Nor did state power merely reduce them to "subhuman" living beings, such as animals, a reduction that does happen in genocides. Rather, it denied Jews the status of being in the world, refusing to recognize them as having any place whatsoever in the biological, political, or ontological order. It effaced them. But by the logic of effacement, the effaced never disappears. Still visible, the effaced remains and is a function of the determination that separates seeming into being and nonbeing. Thus, the only status that state power gave Jews was the status of apparitions or something or somebody looking like humans, looking like animals, looking like Germans, looking like a man or a woman.

Yet beyond political theology and political ontology, there is a surplus at work in the modern figure of the Jews, a surplus that is a purely political—and as I will argue, formal—element that extends beyond modern versions of political ontology or political theology. In what follows, I attempt to discern this element, which, is not exclusively modern. Rather, as I will argue, it has to do with the effacement of the interpersonal as a mode of political thought and action in and by modern contexts dominated by intersubjectivity, rather than by interpersonality. In other words, in what follows, I will argue that the political dimension of the figure of modern Jews is the effect of an effacement of another version of the political, which I am discerning under the name of the interpersonal found in the pages of the late ancient Talmud.

Effacement and the Return of the Effaced

Political ontology and political theology are necessary, but insufficient ways to discern the political displayed on the pages of the late ancient Talmuds. Political ontology and political theology, as relatively new traditions of thinking about the political dimension of modern Jews, rescued the political from its traditional linkage with institutions (king, state, politicians, policies, and so on) so that the political can now be disentangled from these extrinsic ramifications and recognized as either a theology incognito—more precisely, a theology alienated from itself in the empty political form of the "representation of representation," as in Carl Schmitt—or a version of ontology that, despite philosophy's traditional orientation toward and hope for agreement, admits the necessity of disagreement for political life, as in Jacques Rancière. Yet in the same move by which political ontology and political theology rescue the political from conflation with state apparatuses and institutions, they occlude the political behind theology or ontology. By a logic that I will begin exploring here, the simultaneous emergence and occlusion of the political in political ontology and political theology coincides with erasure of the other others and with the effacement of the interpersonal by the intersubjective.

As a result of the effacement of the interpersonal by the intersubjective, the modern figure of the Jews not only inscribes and is dominated by the notions and practices of intersubjectivity, as theologically, ontologically, and politically charged as these notions and practices are in industrial, postindustrial, and informational contexts, but also and even more importantly shows the return of the effaced in the form of purely formal political action, rooted, I will argue, no longer only and exclusively in representation, but rather in refutation.

Rabinovitch

Let us begin by following a Talmudic tradition that suggests starting a difficult analysis with a joke or an anecdote. In the analysis in this chapter, I will periodically return to and reevaluate the following story's power. It is 1970 in Moscow—Red Square. Rabinovitch, who has a typical Jewish surname, stands there distributing political leaflets.[1] A KGB agent sees what he is doing. Wishing to arrest Rabinovitch, the agent grabs one of the leaflets, only to discover that there is nothing written on them. They are just plain sheets of paper. The agent asks Rabinovitch, "Why do you not have anything written on them?" Now comes the punch line, which I will do my best to translate from Russian: "But isn't it all clear, nevertheless?" (Так ведь и так все понятно!)

Who is Rabinovitch? Does his act of political resistance define him specifically as a Jew or more generally as a human being, or perhaps, by a necessity to be explored in this chapter, as inextricably both, or else, by another necessity to attend to, as neither, or perhaps again in some other way or capacity? To begin addressing these questions, questions of the political element at work in Rabinovitch's action, the focus of a precise theoretical lens is needed. In other words, I will be using the Rabinovitch anecdote as a *topos* to think through the notions that animate the analysis in this book and to afford a language making it possible to formulate its task.

My argument is that Rabinovitch (in Schmitt's terms, outlined in Chapter 1) is a particular kind of representative. In terms of political form, he (or she—the gender is never made clear) exemplifies what Schmitt called the "representation of representation." In terms of content, Rabinovitch exemplifies the universal category "human being," and that the universal "human being," in turn, is inseparably a similar kind of representation of the Jew. Further (in Lacoue-Labarthe's terms, to be introduced and applied later), the inseparable dyad of Jew/human being is a necessary fiction, a "type," that modern political reason, by its very essence, must produce and maintain. I further suggest that both Schmitt's and Lacoue-Labarthe's approaches are necessary, but insufficient to grasp the political act that Rabinovitch commits in the story, an insufficiency that I attempt to redress using resources derived from the notion and practice of refutation in the Babylonian Talmud, which, as I argue, Rabinovitch enacts in his conversation with the KGB agent. Arriving at this understanding of the political as exemplified in the Rabinovitch story and what it can tell us about Jews, political reason, and the concept of the human and the Jew will require slowly working through the argument in several steps, beginning with Carl Schmitt's concept of "political form" and Lacoue-Labarthe's notion of the type.

Rabinovitch's victory over the KGB agent both helps understand the necessity and shows insufficiency of Schmitt's idea of "political form." Rabinovitch's leaflets illustrate both the concept and the power of the "representation of representation." The absence of words shows that the primary representation (the representation of representation) works, even if and precisely because the secondary representation (the referential content of the leaflets) is zeroed to emptiness, or if you prefer, to the fullness of their empty pages. Empty of descriptions, they are still full of powerful political claims, even though Rabinovitch's act seems to be completely irrational from the techno-economic standpoint of the KGB agent. But the empty leaflets and the power of the representation of representation that they wield are only part of the story. However helpful Schmitt can be in differentiating between primary and secondary representation, his approach cannot fully explain why and how contentless empty leaflets work. To explain that, one needs to account for a separate power at work in the story, the power of refutation and of the refutation of a refutation. In other words, and in the first approximation, there, is also Rabinovitch, who argues about the leaflets with the agent. To understand the power of that argument, we need to ask the question again: "Who is Rabinovitch?" Part of the answer is that he is also a part of the representative figuration that the leaflets create.

There is more to the Rabinovitch story than the representation of representation as the invocation of the form of the political. Rabinovitch argues about the empty pamphlets with the agent. But Rabinovitch is also a particular political actor within a specific political context. The story is about more than just the form of the political. So who is Rabinovitch? A woman? A man? A Jew? A human being in general? In which of these possible capacities does Rabinovitch act in the story?

The best way to approach the complexity of the figure of Rabinovitch is via Lacoue-Labarthe's concept of the type, a term he develops in *Typography*. In those terms, Rabinovitch is a very complex interplay of two modern types: the human being and the Jew. In light of this complex interplay, these strange blank leaflets can say or illustrate even more.

Yet, as I will argue at length in what follows, there are limitations to the conceptual apparatus that Lacoue-Labarthe supplies, limits that Rabinovitch seen as a type makes clear. The Rabinovitch anecdote might also seem to illustrate Lacoue-Labarthe's main thesis in *Typography*, which concerns of "fictioning essence of reason." Minimally glossed, *Typography* is a work on Heidegger's reading of Nietzsche, where the notion of the "fictioning essence of reason" appears. The thesis is that reason must create fictions in order to operate and that the way fictions are created changes in the course of history.[2] Viewed in this way, even the most obviously fictive representation, the empty leaflet, is still absolutely necessary for representing and for the reasoning that goes on between Rabinovitch and the KGB agent. Without the leaflet (even if empty, which, as one might say, is the fiction in its fullest), reason and its goal, the political act of protest, would not be available at all.

If we are to decide who Rabinovitch is in terms of Lacoue-Labarthe's concept of a type, the place to begin is with his analysis of Heidegger's polemics with Ernst Jünger, specifically on the central point of the polemics: whether "man," and in particular "the worker," who "bestows meaning" on the world through technology, as Jünger argued, or whether "man" is a product, a fiction—a "type"—produced, as Heidegger claimed, through the "essence of technology." For Heidegger, that essence is "nothing technical," but instead is *Ge-stell*, German for a shelf, *étagère*, and so on. As Lacoue-Labarthe notes, it is much easier to translate this German word than it is to explain how it functions in Heidegger's thought. One reason for this is that Heidegger's notion of *Ge-stell* is articulated in two contexts, the ancient Greek and the modern industrial.

The ancient form of *Ge-stell* is elucidated in Heidegger's reading of Plato's ideas, Lacoue-Labarthe argues. In that context, the "fictioning essence of reason" means that one can encounter reason, in this case, ideas, through and only through fictions. Even true *doxa*, that is, opinions that do bespeak truth, are still opinions, and thus fictions. Additionally, aesthetically, it is only through the looks of things (call these looks "appearances") that one can recognize the ideas that made those appearances possible. That leaves no possibility for encountering ideas directly. Rather, for Plato, the world on which reason operates is mimetic—and doubly so, because it is only a representation of the material, and the material is itself only a shadow representation of the ideal, the representation of a representation. But in terms of the analysis I have been developing, the fictioning essence of reason could be said to involve the act of representation itself: the representation of representation—mimesis as what makes possible the efficacy of reason, regardless of its specific content, not just a chain of external representations. And with mimesis as the basis for the fictioning essence of reason also comes the possibility of misrecognition and confusion, mistaking appearances for reality.

What that means, however, is that if mimesis is necessary for reason to function qua reason, mimesis is not simply the representation of what is represented, but instead the representation of the very act of representing. Mimesis, on other words, is not just the representation of a thing as another thing or a deviation from a norm and therefore a gesture toward what is not there or not there yet, in the sense of *figura*, the core element of mimesis, as Eric Auerbach's essay of that title shows.[3] The fictioning essence of reason thus means not only producing fictions in order to reason but also representing the process of that representation by and through fictioning, so that reason fictions even before and without depending on any particular fictions, representations, and or *figurae* with which reason must always become engaged.

The Jew and the Human Being, in Theory

Facing the inevitability of fictions and the problematics of mimesis, we, together with Plato, first encounter the importance of theory as *theorein*, or the process of discovering the ideas in and through appearances. Such a theory of *theorein* is important in order to eliminate any confusion: if ideas get confused in the process of recognition, it might lead to the mistaking of what seems to be for what is. *Theorein* and the theory thereof therefore have for Plato a moral value, as well: *Theorein* both explains and helps to avoid the nature of evil, because the root cause of evil is mistaking what seems to be for what is. Evil corresponds to no idea, but only to the confusion between ideas. Therefore, even if evil does not truly exist, it has power—the power of confusion. On that view, practicing theory in the form of the philosophical work of the dialogue, in which the philosopher can help the confused interlocutors think through and eliminate their confusion, also helps us to eliminate the evil that confusion creates.

That of course presumes the possibility of avoiding evil by eliminating confusion. If not confused, ideas thus bring forth good and only good, even if and unfortunately only through fiction. Reason must thus produce fictions, "supply" them, make them readily available, as the word *Ge-stell* would suggest. Through these readily available fictions, one could recognize the reason, or for Plato, the ideas, in, through, and behind fictions, even if never leaving the fictions (and fictioning) behind. This path through the fictioning of reason, for Plato, is the only true and ethical way.

However, things change in the industrial stage. There, the fictioning essence of reason works with much greater complexity. According to Lacoue-Labarthe, industrial *Ge-stell* (including postindustrial, and, by extension, informational *Ge-stell*) no longer entails ideas in the Platonic sense and assumes instead a different form. The difference has to do with the even greater role played by confusion in the industrial age. The luxury of eliminating confusion is no longer available in the fictioning reason of the industrial, postindustrial, and informational ages. In contrast to Plato's idea, Hegel's *Ge-stalt*, which is yet another word for an image and/or fiction, entails a confusion that one can at best recognize, but never eliminate.[4] For example, while scientifically understood as an illusion, and thus a confusion, the images of sunrise and sunset do not cease to shape one's experience. A greater approximation of *Ge-stalt* as confusion comes from the example of Marx's political economy of value production. "Scientifically," that is, from the point of view of Marx's political economy, capitalism purchases the productive powers of the workers' labor but pays only for the time of the workers. As a result, the labor produces more value than the cost of the time of labor. The difference (and, if you will, the confusion) between paid time and the productive power of labor, in Marx, is perceived neither by the capitalist nor the worker. However, that difference makes the capitalist-worker economy possible. What is more, failing to notice that difference between time and labor, for Marx, is a confusion practically unavoidable in capitalist society. The unavoidable confusion between the time paid for and the value of labor purchased entails, for him, a number of "inverted forms" in the relationships between the capitalist and the worker. One such "inverted form" is the "form of commodity." In order for the capitalist economy to work, it *must seem*—for all parties involved—that value is an intrinsic property of a commodity, rather than the product of labor. Unlike other commodities bought and sold, which can change in value, gold and silver coins, for Marx, are "inverted forms" of commodity par excellence; their value consists in displaying the value of a commodity, regardless of the value a coin may have as a physical object. (By extension, the coins represent not only the value but also the power to represent that value, which makes the coins into such a powerful form of illusion, the inverted form in its fullest.) These and similar "inverted forms" are specters, appearances that can be theoretically recognized as illusions, but that continue to inform how one practically accesses the world and navigates one's way therein.

The "inverted forms" of Marx, along with other specters, or uncorrectable confusions, exemplify *Ge-stalt* in its role of both fiction (which by Platonic definition is "what is not") and idea (which by that definition is "what is").[5] A confusion that cannot be eliminated is no longer a confusion in the classical Platonic sense, but rather, a *type*. Undermining Platonic distinctions, a *Ge-stalt* is a fiction because it involves confusion, but it is also an idea, because it enables reason. It is, in other words, an illusion that must reside not only in fiction, but also in theory, that is, that must take part in reason and thus have the power of the real.

What is more, the *Ge-stalt* or specter, and thus the type, as well, cannot be recognized as an illusion in practice and/or in experience. Thus, Rabinovitch's leaflets seem to exemplify the concept of *Ge-stalt* well: Their empty pages are specters. The empty leaves of the leaflets do all the work, work that the KGB agent feels in experience, even if he cannot articulate it in theory. This is because the agent has encountered a type and has fallen into its logic of confusion—that is, the logic of the representation of representation, of fictioning, rather than representing any content or any particular fiction—a logic from which there is no escape.

We are now in a position to begin moving slowly from the leaflets to their distributor, Rabinovitch, as a Jew and a human being.

An even greater approximation of *Ge-stalt* is the *Mensch*, "man" or, if disgendered, "the human *being*." (Here the English term "being" in the "human being" affords more than the German *Mensch* or the literary "human," or "person" can.) The logic of functioning (and fictioning) in the *Ge-stalt* of "man" or "human being" has to do with bridging the differences between any two different terms by shaping one of them into the bridge. For example, the difference between man and woman has been bridged in the past by creating the fiction of both of them being "man in general." (And, no, replacing "man" by "[hu]man" does not change much in this fictional logic of bridging.) In this logic of fictioning, any of the bridged terms could be used for the bridging. With "man" no longer politically correct, "woman" ["(wo)man"] or even a "she" ["s(he)"] becomes a possibility, for the language reveals what usage is trying to overcome, the man and the "he" behind the human, the woman or the "she." Along these lines, "gender" comes to be understood as pertaining not only to women, as before, but to men equally well. Yet the switch from "man" to "woman" as a universal only repeats and reinforces the inevitability of a specter, a fiction, that is, the necessity of using one term of the difference to bridge that difference.[6] As a result, the modern *Mensch* or man's/human being in general belongs to the terrain of specters and *Ge-stalts*, rather than that of Platonic ideas.

Following its "fictioning essence," reason must supply these *Ge-stalts* or types. The production of type*s* thus entails an elision and/or suppression of the classical Platonic concept of mimesis as the doubled representation of ideas. And following the industrial age, the types of the postindustrial and information ages can no longer be reached by undoing mimesis, that is, by eliminating its mistakes and confusions. No Platonic clarity about "the human" or "the Jew" can be reached. Rather, even if and precisely because these are no longer even susceptible to the hope of being reached directly, contemporary rational thinking and acting must fight against the specters and types of "the human" and "the Jew," specters and types that thinking also must create.[7]

The Human as Jew

How, then, does Rabinovitch act in the story—as a generic human being, or as a Jew? The modern industrial specter of the human is much more closely connected to that of the Jew than it might seem. The spectral nature of these two modern figures becomes more clearly discernible if juxtaposed to other contexts, contexts in which the Jew functions as an image and/or a concept, but not as a specter. On the way from a territorial and/or tribal or moral and religious designation in the Bible, the term "Jew" in Christian theology emerges as a figure, an image, and if one prefers, an *idea*, but not as a specter.[8] In the early Church Fathers, the figure of the Jew comes to replace/suppress that of the biblical "Israel," which the Church annexed for herself as "Israel in spirit." This both created and left behind the other half of Israel, "the Israel in flesh" or carnal Israel.[9] At this point, "the Jew," was not yet a specter, even if in the theology of early Church Fathers, "Jew" is already *a* figure of exception,[10] if not *the* figure of exception par excellence. Indeed, these theologians could not have placed the Jews among Christianity's others, such as the "pagans" or "heretics." The point is precisely that heretics and pagans are Christianity's (binary) others and that Jews are its third-term other others. Yet in the modern context, where the Jew is no longer a Platonic idea, however complex, but a type, a fiction that cannot be "clarified," the other others become entrapped and erased in that complexity. In a Platonic world, "the Jew" could not be a heretic, for to be a "heretic" one must be a Christian. Nor could "the Jew" be a "pagan," because that would undermine the source from which the Church theologically stems. In a Platonic view, such confusion in the idea of the Jew would perfectly explain why, within Christian theology, the Jew became the figure of evil. Yet to trace the erasure of the other others in the modern, rather then in a platonic world, one has to move beyond Plato, and perhaps even more radically than Lacoue-Labarthe was able to do.

Notably, unlike what either Plato or Lacoue-Labarthe would suggest, the figure of the Jew already possessed something of the character of a specter. Unlike the Platonic version of evil, this new form of evil could not be dispelled by means of a dialogue. Limited as that theological view was by the theological possibility, indeed necessity, of converting "the Jew" to Christianity, the figure of the Jew already had a degree of spectrality, precisely because, as the figure of the other other, the Jew escapes the given stable set of ideas about the others, pagans and heretics.[11]

For Rabinovitch, the degree of this spectrality is intensified, because in Soviet Russia, where, among other places, religious conversion to Christianity no longer even intimates eliminating the status of the convert as a Jew, the Jew is no longer considered a religious figure. And once religion is removed, "the human" emerges.

That is to say, for Rabinovitch, the shift of the type of the Jew away from a religious context happens as the result of the same process that led to the emergence of the notion of the "human being."[12] Such radically different thinkers as the Russian Orthodox theologian Pavel Florensky, on the one hand, and Hannah Arendt, on the other, help us understand the connection between the human and the Jew, as well as its role as the vehicle through which members of rabbinic communities assimilated into the larger society of "secular Christians," who no longer insisted on conversion as *conditio sine qua non* for both social and professional integration.

Employing the anti-Judaic and indeed anti-Jewish reasoning of Eastern Orthodoxy, Florensky diagnoses the modern invention of "the human being" as Jewish.[13] He radically refuses to accept the notion of "the human," deeming it misleadingly egalitarian, and at the same time, he clearly recognizes its political power and "danger" for Russian Christian Orthodoxy. The dual move of refusing to accept and recognizing the danger situates Florensky's notion of *человек*. The word means "human being" or "man," but also "servant" or someone who "mans" a job. *Человек* thus indicates a specter, that is, something that does not exist but that cannot be eliminated either. Florensky insistently warns against the dangers of the specter of "the human." From his point of view, the modern Jew and "man," *человек*, give birth to each other: having created "the human being," Jews, for him, proclaim themselves (and everybody else) human, which explains the theoretical spectrality, including the unavoidable practical misunderstanding, of the spectral character of both the Jew and the *человек*.

From a radically different position, Hannah Arendt illustrates the political danger that the specter of the "human being" represents for her as a Jew. Critiquing, along with Schmitt and Heidegger, the liberal values of techno-economic rationality, she, not unlike Florensky, warns against abusing the notion of the human. She particularly demands, after having been persecuted as a Jew, that she not be respected as a human, a member of "mankind" (a biological and biopolitical notion), but instead insists that political respect be given to her as a Jew, that is, as someone who is both inside and outside "mankind," the only position that, for her, makes the humanity of "mankind" possible.[14] Conceptually insisting on the "human being" as a specter, rather than either an image or a pure idea or concept, let alone as a scientifically discernible object, Arendt approaches the notion of the human as a function of the assimilationist utopia. Thus, in *The Jew as Pariah*,[15] she argues (once again, not totally differently from Florensky) that the idea of basic human rights, such as equality, the right of life, or of having a house, a family, and so on are only assumed to be universal, but in fact are fought for and recognized as universal paradigmatically by Jewish pariahs seeking assimilation.

Both thinkers thus indicate a close connection between the human being and the Jew in the modern context. Following the logic of secularization, the concept of the "human being" makes possible a new, modern operation of disentangling the Jew from any "religious" context. This possibility also turns on racist and nationalist logics of (anti)assimilation. In turn, the Jew makes the "human being" possible by becoming the most concealed and the best-hidden singular beginning of the universality of "man." As a result, the "human being" arrives on the stage as the vehicle of assimilation: The assimilating rabbinic Jews both promote and ultimately fall prey to the modern concept of the human being or *Mensch* as the specter of the humanity of humans.

In juxtaposing these two radically different thinkers, Florensky and Arendt, there thus lurks a new specter. That specter inextricably combines the Jew and the "human being," one as the function of the other. In the example of Rabinovitch, Rabinovitch protests as a human being and as a Jew at the same time. One cannot be separate from the other.[16]

The view of Rabinovitch as a double specter, a human and a Jew, reaches and illuminates the limit of this conceptual approach. I began by noting that Rabinovitch's leaflets illustrate both the concept and the power of the representation of representation, empty of descriptions, yet full of powerful political claims. In order for the fictioning essence of reason still to be "of reason" in such a case, the mimetic aspect of the fiction must be elided or suppressed, even if it can never be fully removed. And in the case of Rabinovitch himself as a type of both the Jew and the human being, it is not just Platonic mimesis that must be elided or suppressed, but the more radical mimesis involved the representation of representation itself. In Lacoue-Labarthe's diagnosis, still faithful to the Platonic *Ge-stell* through ideas, the production or *Ge-stell* through *Gestalts* elides the mimetic (Platonic) part of the fictioning or *Darstellung*, a mimetic form of representation. Lacoue-Labarthe identified the crucial role of that elision in his analysis of Heidegger's *Ge-stell/Idea/Gestalt* complex: the unavoidability of fiction in any deed of reason, which only increases as one moves from classical ideas to modern *Gestalt* and the resulting types and/or specters. The elision of the mimetic representation of either the Jew or the human or both thus establishes the limit in which reason, or rational thinking and acting, can produce fictions, but still remain rational.

Yet the theory of the modern fictioning essence of reason with "Platonic" mimesis suppressed, but never done away with is necessary, but not sufficient in order to understand the full agency of Rabinovitch.[17] There is a question to ask in light of the silent, but salient connection between the types of the Jew and the "human being," seeing it as a political connection in Schmitt's sense. If seen in light of Arendt's, Lacoue-Labarthe's, and Schmitt's engagements with, respectively, the Jew as *a* representation of the humanity of humans, a figure of fictioning or a *type* in modern reason, and the archenemy of the secularized but still theologically driven nation of the Germans, the question of the human being and that of the Jew as two interconnected *Ge-stalts* would have to do with the following: What, if anything, can escape the effacement of the Platonic mimetic representation (*Darstellung*) from fictioning?[18]

What, in other words, can resist the philosophical tradition in which, if not eternal being, then at least being in time allows no role whatever for mimetic representation (*Darstellung*),[19] except for the role of a permanently unwanted factor that causes nothing but confusion, concealment, and ultimately loss of reason behind the fiction? Addressing this question involves a renegotiation of the distinction between *Vorstellung*, or the act of representing, and *Darstellung*,[20] or mimetic representation, as two kinds of representation in their relationship to Schmitt's notion of representation when it comes to approximating the "political form" of the Talmud. The latter form is driven and animated by yet another element, that of refutation, which assumes in the Talmud a status both exceeding and defining that of representation in all of the meanings employed earlier.

If Schmitt views the political sphere in terms of the representation of representation; and for Lacoue-Labarthe, mimesis in representation is the limit of *Ge-stell*, lying as it does at the foundation of modern specters; and if Arendt views the Jew as a specter to be respected if one wants to guarantee the humanity of mankind; and if these approaches can become collectively applicable to or at least heuristically important for addressing the question of the political form of the Talmud, then the question would be: Would political form in the Talmud entail the representation of representation, or, more specifically, representation as *Ge-stalt*, limited by the elision or suppression of mimesis, and would it therefore imply the humanity of the rabbis in the Talmud as Jews, as well (perhaps) as the Jewishness and/or rabbinic character of modern humans? The task of addressing this question consists in mapping out the political form in the Talmud in regard to representation in Schmitt's, Arendt's, and Lacoue-Labarthe's understanding of these terms. That task therefore calls for applying and renegotiating, the concepts of representation, and in particular of type, *Ge-stalt*, in its relationship to mimesis, including their configuration in the fusion of the concepts of the Jew and the human being in Rabinovitch.

The Political in the Talmud

One way to elucidate the political in the Talmud is in comparison with the context of both Aristotle's and Quintilian's rhetoric, taken as a synecdoche for the larger Greek and Latin rhetorical traditions and schools, because in the Talmud, the several parts of classical rhetoric are subsumed by a single practice and theory: refutation.

Aristotle's rhetoric entails three main parts: enthymeme (the "rhetorical syllogism"), character, and example. The first of these can be understood as a shortened logical syllogism. An alternative understanding would be "expressionist," in Gilles Deleuze's sense of the term: The implied, but not expressed part of the enthymeme has a meaning that would be lost when explicated. In that understanding, the fact of something being kept implicit has a meaning of its own far beyond the meaning of what is implied. As I have argued elsewhere,[21] and as I will address further in Chapter 7, the expressionist understanding of the enthymeme provides a better, even if still not sufficient approximation of how the enthymeme as a part of rhetoric is used, de facto, in rabbinic academies.

In turn, Quintilian's arts of rhetoric include character (or delivery), refutation, memory (for words and for things), *inventio* (as simultaneously both "invention" and "discovery"), and example. The art of rhetoric displayed on the pages of the Babylonian Talmud redistributes these categories so that refutation comes to the fore in all aspects of the rhetorical art.

Refutation serves as a vehicle for memory. More technically, it helps both "memory for things" and "memory for words." An attempted and often ultimately failed refutation of the "memory for words" of or about earlier rabbinic authorities results in a better, that is, more precise, "memory for things" involved in the teaching of these authorities. Used as a vehicle of remembering, the process of refutation by the same token becomes the process of invention: the "things" (enthymemes) to be remembered in the teachings or deeds of the earlier authorities are discovered and by the same token invented through heuristic refutation of their given verbal accounts. Refutation thus serves as the driving force of invention. Attempting to refute and ultimately failing to refute an account of a teaching or a deed leads to inventing (discovering) a new memory (and new understanding) of that account. Yet refutation is not only a way to produce/invent a new memory; it is also a criterion for judging the accuracy or truth of the resulting invention: One knows that a memory of a teaching is true if one knows/remembers what that teaching was supposed to refute, or in other words, what it was inventing in the first place. Refutation thus also provides the truth criterion to judge the accuracy of the results: The account is true if there is a valid point or a point worthy of consideration that it refutes. Displayed on the pages of the Talmud is thus a process of *inventio* driven by refutation as both a truth criterion and a protocol of truth production. Finally, refutation also becomes the main feature of character (and its definitive mode of delivery), which therefore is no longer an individual or collective effort, but rather is both the refutation of and the search for refutations implied in the positions of the others.

Memory thus both embraces and exceeds thinking, producing the authority of the open past, which is unlike the Platonic model in which thinking and remembering coincide, thus sending us back not to the past, but to the eternity that Plato defines as "being" opposed to "becoming." In the context developed here, the question would then be how the prominence of refutation (and in particular of the refutation of a refutation) in the Talmudic art of remembering informs our understanding of political form in the Talmud and how understanding that form translates into understanding the connection between the Jew and the human being in modernity, if we think that connection in terms of *Ge-stalt* as a modern form of *Ge-stell.*

To invent or find a novel idea or interpretation in a statement in the Talmud is to find what that statement refutes. The successful delivery of a point to be made is a delivery in the form of an explicit refutation of the position of an opponent, often by presenting the thesis of the opponent as self-refuting. (To reiterate, self-refuting does not mean here self-criticism; rather, it is a form of attack on another person and/or position by arguing that they are "self-refuting" that is, by making them work against themselves.) To remember a given tradition better is precisely to find a novel idea or interpretation in it or to discover what that tradition refutes. Doing so changes the refutation from one in the series of rhetorical techniques to the overarching mode of rhetorical thinking and acting.

That change requires us to move beyond traditionally marginal positions allowed for rhetorical schools within the Aristotelian or Platonic philosophies and academies. This is why any return of the Talmudic refutations on the map of the tradition of rhetoric does not mean subsuming the Talmud into the tradition of philosophy. Instead, it signifies a movement that, using Schmitt's terms, one can define as a movement toward the "political" in the person of a new representative figure, the figure of one who refutes in response to refuting. That means even more broadly that what I have called "Talmud," without the "the," as an intellectual discipline, extends beyond rhetoric, moving toward a theory of the political that is not a philosophy of the political.

If, in that discipline as exemplified in the Talmud, memory both frames and exceeds the philosophical theory of being, refutation subsumes all the elements of classical rhetoric, and refutation operates as a form of remembering beyond the confines of rhetoric, then authority in the Talmud, including political authority, emerges as something different from what it is for Schmitt. Of course, with Rabinovitch's empty leaflets, the representation of representation can still mean that there is no secondary representation—no mimetic representation or techno-economic content. But more is also involved in the example of Rabinovitch.

Rabinovitch's pamphlets refute. They so do not only and not primarily the words, the techno-economic world of the KGB agent, but also, and much more important, they undermine the very possibility of the absence of such content. They are not simply silent and empty. Rather, they make their political point without words. If in the Talmud refutation is a truth criterion, then one is to speak or to write words if and only if there is a point to refute. One therefore is not supposed to say or write the obvious. At least, this is how Rabinovitch explains the leaflets to the agent: they are empty because what they state is obvious. However, he has to talk to the agent, of course, because these things are not obvious to the latter. The leaflets refute the possibility of any representational silence, even the silence of the representation of representation per se. Representation is circumscribed by another operation, that of refutation, so that even silence becomes a positive refutation, rather than merely a representation. The horizon of refutation exceeds the prevalent elision of mimesis in *Ge-stell.* It does so because mimesis and *Ge-stell* operate only in the realm of representation. What Rabinovitch accomplishes with his political action as an example of refuting should not be misunderstood as happening in the realm of representation alone.[22] Rabinovitch's empty leaflets are what Schmitt could not have imagined: the representation of representation of an entirely different kind, representing the political without any mimetic representation at all.[23] Rabinovitch's act takes place on a radically different plane, that of refutation, which conditions both the representation of representation and the techno-economic content that Schmitt discerned.[24]

The prevalence of refutation and remembering in the Talmud does not cancel the importance of representation (including the representation of representation), but instead circumscribes representation within refutation. Perhaps this is why the Talmud shows both a recognition of the possibility of and opposition to the representation of representation: In the Talmud, a sage or other authority should not use his status as a scholar (authority as the representation of representation) to get a gain in a dispute about his private matters, for example to defend himself against allegations in court.[25] More generally, in the Talmud, unlike the case of the Church, ultimately, refutation controls representation, not the other way around.[26]

The Talmudic form of refutation thus is more than merely a rhetorical art or technique, because it informs a way of existence, producing a distinct perspective on being, representation, both political and mimetic, and memory—all matters that traditionally belong to the domain of philosophy. However, that does not make the form of Talmudic refutation a philosophical concept. Talmudic refutation does not lend itself to the confines of the philosophical theory of representation, let alone to Schmitt's representation of representation. Instead, just as in the Talmud memory orients thinking toward the open past (in contradistinction to Plato, for whom thinking orients memory toward eternal ideas and/or being) Talmudic refutations propel memory.[27] Refutations simultaneously produce the outcome of remembering (for example, advancement in remembering the Mishnah), its delivery (for example, the character of the sage and of the sage's student), and its truth (only things that soundly refute other things can be true). Refutation both frames and helps to judge all three of these elements. Talmudic refutation therefore expands beyond the realm of idea in Plato's sense, but, as I will explain, does not take us only and exclusively in the direction of *Ge-stalt*. This is certainly does not exclude mimetic representation (let alone the representation of representation), but it limits its power. Talmudic refutation no longer turns on ideas,[28] nor does it limit itself to types, because the latter are still driven by the representation of representation.

The notion of the representation of representation thus no longer suffices to grasp the scope of political form in the Talmud. Instead, that form has to do with the refutation of a refutation as a way of inventing memory. Because of the multiplicity of its truths, there is no longer an orientation to privileging being (either eternal, as in Plato, or temporized, as in Heidegger)[29] over its mirror image, nonbeing, as well as over what merely seems to be. However, and by the same token, the form of the refutation of a refutation exceeds the distinction between being and mimesis or between "typography," as Lacoue-Labarthe collectively designates the historically changing forms of the fictioning essence of reason, and mimetic representation.[30]

As the form of Talmudic refutation suggests, to get to the broader notion of the political inscribed in the Talmud thus is to reclaim forgotten importance of the past. The forgetting of that importance has itself been "well forgotten," to borrow Chaim Luzzatto's language,[31] by and through recalling the past, either imaginary or "real," in the mode of "what was," as distinct from what "what was" is to refute, as a Talmudic reading of the past would require.

Renegotiation of political form as the refutation of a refutation thus involves reconsideration of the referentiality of representation as the core model of meaning. Beyond its referential aspect, meaning must be understood as always already a refutation. To remember then would mean inventing and discovering (as *inventio* does) what is being refuted in a given speech, text, or any other representation. Refutation becomes essential for understanding any mimetic representation. But what is involved here is not only mimetic representation—mimetic reference—but also the representation of representation.

One way to begin to understand this is in terms of "expression," rather than mimetic representation.[32] Instead of the double of a representation and the represented (or even of *noema* and *noesis*), expression always exceeds its relationship to the expressed by turning on a third element, the difference between what is being expressed, but never reaches full expression, on the one hand, and what is indeed expressed, a distinction that takes us beyond the confines of representation. In these terms, instead of Schmitt's representation of representation, the political is to be understood more broadly as the expression of expression: a political action is possible even if it does not represent, but only expresses.

Such a shift in terminology and perspective is necessary, because it introduces multiplicity: What is being expressed can never fully coincide with what is expressed in any given expression.[33] The open past, which refutation in the Talmud exemplifies, stems from that source. With such a shift, recollection gives way to remembering. Recollection requires a subject who recollects (beginning in the Middle Ages), or at least an agent (in Augustine) of memory,[34] either individual or collective, who recollects and consequently it entails and requires conceptions of intersubjectivity. However, remembering in the Talmud does not entail a subject, because refuting or the refutation of a refutation as a form of memory can never involve a single subject or agent, either individual or collective, because unlike the subject position, refuting must always also involve the position that is being refuted. By the same token, it does not entail intersubjectivity, either.

Instead, in this view of the political, what emerges is interpersonality, not intersubjectivity. In the case of Talmudic practices, the position of an authority must be strong enough to deserve refutation. It must not be obviously wrong, and thus even if it is being refuted, it must have a power to endure. Remembering it is therefore never the concern of a single agent or subject, or of a single individual or nation. Nor does it entail agreement, which implies if not an imposition, then at least a demand for homogeneity in judgment.

In these terms, the story of Rabinovitch not only illustrates but also exceeds the models of the political advanced by Schmitt, and the figure of Rabinovitch also extends beyond the *type* or *Ge-stalt* as the foundation of modern human rational presence advanced by Lacoue-Labarthe. Even if taken as the double specter of the human being and the Jew, Rabinovitch does not necessarily represent, but he necessarily refutes. He therefore escapes the specters or types in which he would remain confined if the framework of the fictioning essence of reason in the suppression of mimesis continued to reign in the political action that he performs. The figure of refuting that he performs reaches places where the intertwining specters of the human and the Jew could not reach: the dimension of the political as an open past beyond the domains of either being or time. The Rabinovitch anecdote thus both illustrates and defies Schmitt's understanding of political form by reinscribing it in a broader view of the political as the refutation of a refutation. On the flip side of the same coin, the anecdote is also a counterexample to Lacoue-Labarthe's analysis of the elision of mimesis from "the fictioning essence of reason," from which stems the complex relationship between humans and Jews as mutually conditioning modern types. Unlike the complex type of Jew-human or human-Jew, which would indeed exemplify the constant erasure of mimesis, Rabinovitch in his action escapes mimesis completely: Rabinovitch is neither distinctly Jewish nor distinctly human. Instead, Rabinovitch is political.

This is because Rabinovitch is a genius of remembering: Memory controls thought and operates where there is neither the *Ge-stalt* of the human, nor the *Ge-stalt* of a Jew, for as the political displayed in the Talmud exemplifies, remembering follows neither time nor being, neither subjectivity nor intersubjectivity. A genius of remembering, Rabinovitch does not speculate on an open future, a notion rooted in the subjectivity of a subject, collective or individual. Instead, he turns to the open past, which he enacts with his empty leaflets. In that past, there is no time, and the difference between mimesis and being fades.

As a result, there, on the Red Square, there is ultimately no *type*, and there is no story. Living, as he does, in the open past, where invention (creating a new thing) and discovery (finding an old one) are the same, Rabinovitch no longer lives in a time container, either naturalist or future-oriented. Instead, the remembering that he shows to the KGB agent no longer coincides with any individual (and by extension collective or inter-subjective) recollection of past, either imagined or real. So, to return to the initial question—Who is Rabinovitch?—we now can answer that Rabinovitch's story has no hero at its center, because Rabinovitch does not represent. Instead, Rabinovitch refutes.

What that means, however is that neither Jew nor human, Rabinovitch is an other other, the one who both simultaneously appears and becomes erased in the conversation with the agent—there where there is no longer a story and no longer a hero, but only the pure political act of remembering through refuting. In the next chapter, I will begin to approximate the complexity of that act of refuting and of the interpersonally it entails through an example of refutation that most readily shows its interpersonal nature: the example of self-refutation.

PART II

The Talmud as the Political

CHAPTER 3
Talmudic Self-Refutation (Interpersonality I)

In the first part, I have detected the political in a new way, as refutation, and in particular as the refutation of a refutation. In the second part, in order to understand the workings of the political power of refutation better, I move back from predominantly modern contexts and modern theoretical concerns to late ancient instantiations of refutation as a formative component of the political. Focusing on the refutation of a refutation, in this chapter, I proceed with a particular example of it, self-refutation, and, in the following one, I analyze a kind of personality or, more broadly, human presence as interpersonal, that the concept of the political in the Talmuds—and more precisely of the Talmud as a version of the political—helps to articulate in greater detail. This chapter focuses on one version of the interpersonal relationship through refutation: self-refutation. This is a relationship in which one party attacks another by showing that the argument of the latter works against itself, or is "self-refuting."

Scholars of the Talmud ask about the nature of conversations among the rabbis in the academy or talks between the rabbis and heretics, emperors, or noble Roman ladies as these figures of a larger society become appropriated in the discourses of the rabbis in the academies. Are these conversations open-ended dialogues, or are they designed to attain a predetermined outcome? "Predetermined" may imply either the design of the discussions to end in a certain way,[1] or the conversations may be "predetermined" by their form, in the same way in which Platonic dialogues are formally ironic or maieutic, leading, as they often do, to the defeat of one party and victory of another. A combination of the two meanings is also possible.[2] Yet, instead of privileging one of them over the other, and more important, instead of insisting on either the predetermined nature of the dialogues in the Talmud as regards the "right" answer (Boyarin) or as open (the more traditional approach), I propose simply to pay close attention to the question of whether these dialogues are predetermined or open. My goal is to demonstrate that no matter how it is answered, that question already introduces the political dimension of the Talmud as permeating and at the same time clearly separate from the legal and/or ethical-homiletic dimensions of the discussions. Comparative analysis of self-refutation in Talmudic and rhetorical-philosophical schools in late antiquity, with an emphasis on self-refutation, offers us a way to detect the political in these discussions.

What follows, then, is a comparative study of self-refuting in the philosophical and Talmudic and literatures of late antiquity. In both literatures, self-refutation in no way implies self-defeat but instead entails proving that the argument of an interlocutor can or does work against itself, thus undermining its own power. I particularly look at the role of self-refutation in interactions between the characters in the Talmud, both among the rabbis and between the rabbis and representatives of the world outside of rabbinic academy, with special reference to the interpretive skills that the Rabbis expect from each other and indeed from any educated person with whom they engage—the ability, as the Psalmist put it, to listen unto the voice of words.

The Voice of Words

Self-refutation is not self-critique; rather, it is directed against another person, or more precisely against the argument that another person or even oneself has proposed. The goal of self-refutation is to prove that the argument refutes itself. That gloss illustrates a difference between the intersubjective and the interpersonal: Self-refutation is the refutation of arguments no matter whose arguments they are. It thus is not a relationship between thinking subjects, but an engagement of arguments performed by individuals, though not rooted in any particular distribution of individuals. Self-refutation can involve one, two, or more parties, but structurally it always is dependent on having more than one party involved. In self-refuting, one is never alone, for in order for the self-refutation of an argument to take place there must be at least an argument and a counter-argument. This means turning the argument against itself, not necessarily against the person who performed the initial argument.

On the technical level, self-refutation must work without introducing additional premises. The argument is to be refuted using the resources and premises already given in that argument.

Understanding the political power of self-refuting inevitably involves the broader question of the kind of interpersonal engagement with the world and with others that is entailed by rabbinic refutations. That question can be approached from a comparative perspective addressing philosophical and other nonrabbinic approaches to refutation.

In this comparative inquiry, I follow the path opened up by Martin Jaffe and others,[3] who have asked not only and not primarily about the characters on stage in either the Talmud or the Platonic dialogues, but rather about what Jaffe describes and what I could paraphrase as the never-passive audience, call it the "master audience," or the audience of the master—the audience implied or, more precisely, constructed by Talmudic discussions and by extension in philosophical and rhetorical encounters in others schools of thought. I am particularly interested in the mastery that the master audience has to perform. That is, I ask what that mastery is in terms of the theory of the political.

The technical term for self-refutation in Stoic, Skeptic, and other Greek philosophical schools is *peritrope*, literally "turning around."[4] One of the rabbinic siblings of that notion is *hilluf*, or changing around another's argument in order to undermine the power of the original version of that argument. Similar to *peritrope*, *hilluf* is a technical term, rather than a mere metaphor, a designation under which self-refutation is not only performed, but also named as such in rabbinical texts.

According to M. F. Burnyeat, as a technical term, *peritrope* appears in the work of Sextus Empiricus at the end of the second and the beginning of the third century C.E., in Plato's critique of the thesis of Protagoras that man is the measure of the being and nonbeing of all things. Yet before getting to that complex example, let me first, following Burnyeat's analysis, look into relatively simpler examples of self-refutation. Thus, if one says, "I am not saying anything," someone else can proclaim that statement to be self-refuting, because one does say something by it. A more sophisticated and therefore more interesting example discussed by

Burnyeat is a claim, "There are no truths," that a Skeptic would make. A Stoic would object: But this statement is a truth claim, too, and thus is self-refuting.

However, would that be the end of the conversation between the Skeptic and the Stoic? Is the Stoic the ultimate winner? If this is an abstract *logical* argument, it would indeed stop there, for self-refutation would have been achieved; the thesis of the Skeptic would be self-refuted and the Skeptic defeated. However, if it is a *dialectical* or genuinely *rhetorical* argument, it might continue. The Skeptic might respond, "Your words only prove my point: Indeed, there are no truths, and even my statement is not true, either."

The difference between pure logical analysis and dialectical or rhetorical exchange is that at the end of the logical process, the parties end up in the same place, with the defeat of the one who advanced the self-refuting claim and the victory for the one who identified the claim as self-refuting. (In modern terms, this would be a scenario based on intersubjective relationships.) However, in a rhetorical-dialectical process, the difference between parties does not disappear but rather is reinforced. No one wins. The Stoic and the Skeptic maintain their positions and even reinforce those positions. The Skeptic continues to maintain that there are no truths, including even the statement that there are no truths, and the Stoic continues to find that claim to be self-refuting. Yet the two parties are no longer indifferent to each other. Instead, their positions can stand only in their mutual contradistinction. This is an interpersonal relationship, not an intersubjective one: The personae involved are now functions of their debate and no longer exist before and independently of it.

The difference between the logical and dialectical-rhetorical registers of self-refutation is important for explaining more complex examples of self-refutation. It is also crucial for differentiating further between the intersubjective and the interpersonal. The default position for the intersubjective response to disagreement is logical argumentation, with rhetorical and dialectical forms as no more than tolerated deviations. The default position for the interpersonal response to disagreement, in contrast, is the rhetorical-dialectical form of argument, which helps strengthen the initial arguments of both parties, making their reinforced positions totally dependent on the success of mutual self-refutation. This is the model of interpersonality rather than intersubjectivity.

In Sextus Empiricus's account of Plato's critique of Protagoras's thesis that man is the measure of the being and nonbeing of all things, to which we can now return, according to Burnyeat, what is at issue is whether Plato's critique is based on the abstract logical argument that the claim is self-refuting or the rhetorical-dialectical form of argument in which self-refutation is mutual. Burnyeat argues that it is the second alternative that is the case, although he does so in terms of subjectivity and intersubjectivity that I will eventually propose to replace.

Let's take a closer look at how Sextus approaches the example in question. "Man is the measure of all things, of those that are, that they are, and of those that are not, that they are not," states Protagoras in his book *Truth*, according to Plato's *Theaetetus* 161c–162a:

> Socrates: In general I like his doctrine that what appears to each one is to him, but I am amazed by the beginning of his book. I don't see why he does not say in the beginning of his Truth that a pig or a dog-faced baboon or some still stranger creature of those that have sensations is the measure of all things. Then he might have begun to speak to us very imposingly and condescendingly, showing that while we were honoring him like a god for his wisdom, he was after all no better in intellect than any other man, [161d] or, for that matter, then a tadpole. What alternative is there, Theodorus? For if that opinion is true to each person which he acquires through sensation, and no one man can discern another's condition better than he himself, and one man has no better right to investigate whether another's opinion is true or false than he himself, but, as we have said several times, each man is to form his own opinions by himself, and these opinions are always right and true, why in the world, my friend, was Protagoras wise, so that he could rightly be thought worthy [161e] to be the teacher of other men and to be well paid, and why were we ignorant creatures and obliged to go to school to him, if each person is the measure of his own wisdom? Must we not believe that Protagoras was "playing to the gallery" in saying this? I say nothing of the ridicule that I and my science of midwifery deserve in that case—and, I should say, the whole practice of dialectics, too. For would not the investigation of one another's fancies and opinions, and the attempt to refute them, when each man's must be right, be tedious [162a] and blatant folly, if the Truth of Protagoras is true and he was not jesting when he uttered his oracles from the shrine of his book?

Sextus comments that in the *Theaetetus* Plato criticizes Protagoras on the grounds that one cannot say that every appearance is true, meaning man cannot voluntarily assign truth (being) to every single appearance, because that would be self-refuting, as both Democritus and Plato urged against Protagoras. For if every appearance is true, it will be true also, being in accordance with the nature of appearances, that not every appearance is true, and thus it will become a falsehood that every appearance is true (Sextus Empiricus, M 7.389–90).

According to Burnyeat, as he summarizes his commentary on Sextus elsewhere, using the terms of the philosophical tradition of Plato and not those of rhetorical tradition,

> Sextus interprets Protagoras' famous proclamation "Man is the measure of all things [those that are that they are and those that are not that they are not]" as a subjectivist (thesis that every appearance whatsoever is true, and his argument is that the thesis is self-refuting because one of the things that appears (is judged) to be the case is that not every appearance is true: if, as the subjectivist holds, every appearance is true, but at the same time it appears that not every appearance is true, then it follows that not every appearance is true. The problem was to discover how this argument could be classified as *peritrope* or self-refutation. My suggestion was that in a context where it can be presupposed that subjectivism meets with disagreement, the second premise is guaranteed to hold and we can argue straightforwardly that if subjectivism is true, it is false. Such a context, I proposed, would be established by the dialectical debates toward which Greek logical reflections were typically directed, and it is this dialectical setting which provides the key for Protagoras's self-refutation.[5]

At first, Burnyeat seems to argue that Sextus's reconstruction of Plato's argument does not even look like self-refutation. Rather, it looks like an attempt to refute Protagoras by means of direct attack on his logic in which all opinions (those held by pigs and people alike) always must be true. The argument here is that not all opinions are true; hence, man cannot always measure the being of the things correctly. On that reading, Burnyeat argues, from a purely logical standpoint, the term *peritrope*, "turning around," seems to be only a metaphor, not a technical term. However, Sextus provides an interpretation from a dialectic-rhetorical standpoint in which the use of the term is correct and is indeed a technical term, rather than a metaphor. The dialectical-rhetorical, rather than purely logical approach from the example "There are no truths" helps Burnyeat to advance such an interpretation. Logically, what was the second premise in Socrates's critique of Protagoras (it appears that not all appearances are true) rhetorically and dialectically is no more than a restatement of what is obvious for both parties, according to Sextus Empiricus, that not all opinions are true.

What, then, would be the meaning of Protagoras's claim in the first place? If he means that even if some of the opinions are obviously false, they are nevertheless true in the eyes of the beholder, then such a position—Burnyeat calls it "relativist"—cannot be refuted and thus, according to Sextus, is not how Plato reads, let alone refutes, Protagoras. Rather, for Plato, Protagoras holds that man is the one who, through encountering things in the world, is the first to grant some of the things the status of nonbeing, thereby granting the status of being to other things. Man is the author of nonbeing! Men are the first and the only ones to introduce the concept of nonbeing, and as a result, also being, even if, and precisely as a result, man can also be wrong about the being or nonbeing of a particular thing. To make Protagoras's thesis self-refutable, however, Sextus had to assume that Plato interpreted Protagoras as a "subjectivist" as opposed to "relativist."

Yet with the notion that man is the author of nonbeing, who bestows nonbeing and being on things, there emerges nuance in the meaning of Burnyeat's terms "subjectivist" and "relativist." At stake here is the question: Is man simply a tool for measuring the being of things ("relativist"), or is he or she the one who genuinely bestows on things nonbeing and being ("subjectivist")? If the latter is the case, then a "subjectivist" also gains the political power of acting toward others based on an ability to bestow nonbeing on things, and as an outcome, not only to know what truly is, but also to destroy what is not. A "relativist" has no such political power, for such a man is a mere measuring rod, and like any tool, affects the outcome of the measurement in a way beyond its control. In contrast, the "subjectivist" is the subject who introduces nonbeing (and thus being) into the world. Explained in other terms, a "relativist" takes being or nonbeing as one of the properties of things, which can be measured either truly or wrongly, depending on the perspective that anyone, even a pig, can have. Yet the subjectivist (unlike the pig) bestows nonbeing on things.

The implications of Burnyeat distinction between "relativist" and "subjectivist" for understanding the political are hard to overestimate. The subjectivist bestows both being and nonbeing; the relativist assumes being and nonbeing already to be a given, so that in making ontological claims, the latter only measures the being that things somehow already have. In the subjectivist approach, in other words, things neither are nor are not until man encounters them. Being has nothing to do with things, but is only a result of the interaction between man and the world, of one's self-positing of oneself as being a man, rather than a pig. The subjectivist is therefore political—not simply because he or she claims to know what is as opposed to what seems to be, a claim that a relativist (and a pig, or a dog-faced baboon, if they knew Greek) could also make, for after all, measuring is not such a hard thing to learn, even for a pig or dog-faced baboon. But the subjectivist is political first and foremost because the subjectivist, through interaction with things, brings nonbeing into the world, thus making possible political-ontological claims about the nonbeing (or being) of any particular thing. Such an interaction of the subjectivist with the world is necessary political, for it always turns on power relationships not only between men, but also and more primordially between man and the world. It is also ontological, because that power arises not from any kind of trick along the lines of "I know and you do not," but instead comes from an initial bestowing nonbeing on things.

That of course is not to say that nonbeing and thus political ontology is the only foundation on which the political can operate. I will soon discuss a version of self-refutation that is not related to being and that provides another possible foundation of the political in relationships between people—a foundation that is interpersonal, not intersubjective.

In terms of the political ontology just adduced, however, the claim of knowing what truly is also always is a claim of power over those who may live in the world of falsity or in the world of what only seems to be, or even in a world where all depends on perspective and therefore nothing is denied being. This is why Burnyeat's seemingly merely "subjectivist" reading of Protagoras's formula makes it immediately political-ontological.

In contrast with this example, it becomes possible to explore the dimension of the political in what have seemed to be purely legal, logical, and/or ethical discussions among the characters in the Talmud. That involves an even more complex example of self-refutation, the Talmudic parallel of Sextus's *peritrope*—that is, *hilluf.* Literally the word means "exchange" or "substitution" and entails "changing around of one's argument by creating the opposite equally possible one to undermine the power of the original one."

As an example, consider Mishnah *Pesachim*, where one of the characters, Rabbi Yehoshua, emerges as a champion of the technique of self-refuting, and another, Rabbi Akiva, turns that technique against itself, or at least that is how the Mishnah's narrator presents the things to the audience. As with Burnyeat's analysis of *peritrope*, my task is to show that *hilluf* here is not a metaphor, but rather a technical term for self-refuting.

Mishna *Pesachim*, Chapter 6 Mishna 1–6,[6] reads in translation as follows:

[0] The following actions on Pesach can be done even on Shabbat: The slaughter [of the Pesach lamb]; sprinkling of its blood on the altar; removing [food remains] from the intestines; and incensing the fat. However, roasting the meat, and cleaning out the intestines cannot be done on Shabbat. Bringing the animal to the Jerusalem temple, or carrying it outside the Shabbat borders; or cutting off its imperfections is [also] not allowed for the purposes of Pesach if it's Shabbat.

[1] Rabbi Eliezer said: The latter [three] are allowed on Shabbat-Pesach. He argued as follows: if even slaughtering, which is a "[temple related] work," is forbidden on Shabbat on the authority of Torah yet is allowed [see 0] on Shabbat-Pesach, then shouldn't the latter [three] be also allowed because they are generally prohibited only under the authority of the Rabbis (to prevent one from actually transgressing the Shabbat).

[2] Rabbi Joshua answered: The case of the festive day proves [you] wrong because on the festive day the sages permitted us to do what otherwise would be forbidden on Shabbat under the authority of the Torah [namely, to do cooking for the festive meal]; yet they still forbade us doing things which are usually forbidden on Shabbat [under Rabbinic authority.]

[3] Rabbi Eliezer responded: What is it with you [today,] Yehoshua? You should not be comparing permitted with required [i.e., acts permitted on the festive day with acts required on Pesach]!

[4] Rabbi Akiva intervened [in their discussion]: The sprinkling [of water mixed with the dust of the red cow to purify a person] will prove you [Eliezer] wrong, because sprinkling is required [not "permitted"] and that comes from the Rabbis [too]; and it cannot be done on Shabbat. You, too, please don't wonder about those [bringing the animal to the Jerusalem temple, carrying it outside of the designated Shabbat area borders, and removing its imperfections] because even if they are required by Rabbinic authority only, they still are prohibited on Shabbat.

[5] Rabbi Eliezer responded: About those I will argue in the same way: if even slaughtering which is forbidden on Shabbat by the Torah is still done on Shabbat-Pesach, then why shouldn't sprinkling which is required only by the Rabbinic authority be done on Shabbat as well?

[6] [f 61] Rabbi Akiva: [I announce] flipping your argument around (*hilluf*)! If sprinkling, which would otherwise be done at the moment [of Pesach], isn't allowed on Shabbat-Pesach, then why shouldn't slaughtering—which is forbidden on a regular Shabbat by the authority of the Torah—also be forbidden on Shabbat- Pesach?!

[7] Rabbi Eliezer argued back: You have just denied that which is written in the Torah. "In the fourteenth day of this month, at dusk, ye shall keep it in its appointed season; according to all the statutes of it, and according to all the ordinances thereof, shall ye keep it" (Numbers 9:3). "In its appointed season" means no matter if it's Shabbat or a regular day!

[8] Rabbi Akiva answered: show me the "appointed season" for bringing the animal to the Jerusalem temple, or for carrying it outside of the designated Shabbos area borders, and for removing its imperfections which have the same stringency as you have it for slaughtering. Rabbi Akiva [further] said: This will be the general rule: every activity prohibited on Shabbat, if based on the Scripture and can [still] be done before Shabbat, cannot be done on Shabbat-Pesach. Slaughtering, which cannot be done before Shabbat must be done on Shabbat-Pesach.

At stake between the characters in this fragment from the third-century record of the law, or Mishnah, are conflicting obligations—the observance of the Sabbath versus the observance of Passover. The conflict arises if the latter coincides on the calendar with the former. Different names represent different positions on how to resolve it. This particular record of a law in the Mishnah is interesting not only because it is as much a record of the law as it is a record of discussion about it, but also and more important because it shows the role of refutation in how the law is recorded. In this fragment from the Mishnah, it becomes even more obvious than in others. To record a law is to refute another possible record thereof. Otherwise, the record becomes a statement of common sense, a commonplace, a locus of agreement, and is therefore not worthy of the name of a recorded law. Refutation, and in particular self-refutation, to which *hilluf* gives a name in the fragment, animates this particular record of the law.

If *hilluf* in this argument is not simply a metaphor for the move that Rabbi Akiva announces against Rabbi Eliezer at [6], but rather is a technical term and therefore a concept entailing self-refuting, then that concept is at work in this text of the Mishnah more than just once. First, in [1], Rabbi Eliezer makes the sages in [0], in the beginning and the end of the fragment of the Mishnah, sound contrary to themselves and thus self-refuting. Second, in [2], Rabbi Joshua undermines Rabbi Eliezer's thesis by a counterexample eliminating the alleged contrariety in the Mishnah (which means proving the teachings of the sages were not self-refuting). Third, in [3], Rabbi Eliezer fights back by showing how Rabbi Yehoshua's defense of the Mishnah in [2] has an internal flaw (meaning it again is self-refuting): It drew a comparison between things that cannot be compared (the permitted and the required). Fourth, in [4], Rabbi Akiva intervenes, offering a counterexample to prove there is a precedent what allegedly cannot be compared was in fact comparable, thus again protecting the sages in the Mishnah from self-refutation. Fifth, in [5], Rabbi Eliezer attacks Rabbi Akiva's counterexample in [4] in the same way in which he initially attacked the Mishnah: that it is self-refuting. Finally, in [6], as if there was not enough self-refuting going on, Akiva explicitly gives it a name, *hilluf*, and turns Rabbi Eliezer's method against Rabbi Eliezer, thus reducing to absurdity Eliezer's use of self-refutation.

In this escapade, the term *hilluf* suggests not only "turning around," but indeed flipping: Rabbi Akiva flips Rabbi Eliezer's argument, or directs it against its own purpose, in order to make Rabbi Eliezer's version of that argument self-refuting. However, and ironically, Rabbi Akiva's move still employs self-refutation as a polemical, or as Burnyeat would say, dialectical-rhetorical argument, rather than a logical claim, and indeed in even a higher degree: Rabbi Akiva does not simply practice the method of self-refuting, as Rabbi Eliezer did, but rather uses that method against that method. Rabbi Yehoshua, the champion of the technique of self-refutation, is thus outdone by Rabbi Akiva, who not only gives self-refuting a name, *hilluf*, but also turns that technique against itself, thus creating what Sextus Empiricus might have called a *peritrope* of the second degree—a *peritrope* working against itself. Needless to say, in Burnyeat's terms, a second-degree *peritrope* can only be "dialectical-rhetorical"; it can never be "logical." The argument thus is a conversation between two or more parties whose positions grow stronger as a result, not a victory of one party over another in the realm of logic, where there in principle can be only one winner. In that sense, too, the dialectical-rhetorical argument is interpersonal, as opposed to a purely logical argument, which can be intersubjective.

To begin to understand what such a use of self-refutation might mean in the dimension of the political, consider another, intellectually no less complex, but technically less sophisticated and therefore overall "simpler" example: the story of a noble Roman lady asking a rabbi for a date. The rabbi's name is telling: Rabbi Tzadok, literally "the righteous one." I will be looking into the roles of self-refutation in the story, including its immediate context in the Babylonian Talmud Tractate *Qiddushin* 39b.

> A noble [Roman] lady summoned Rabbi Tzadok [to her house.] He said to her, my flesh is weak and I did not find any food. She said to him: I have some ritually impure [meat.] He said to her: So what? One who

> does that eats this. She lit the oven and put the meat inside. He went and sat inside the oven. She said: What is that? He said: One who does this falls into that. She said, if I knew all that, I would not put pressure on you [or: would not cause you this trouble].[7]

In the story, Rabbi Tzadok first stakes out a strong position, refusing and refuting the offer ("My flesh is weak"), but then immediately gives in, saying, "I did not find any food." The lady responds playfully: "I have [or I am] impure [meat; but also connoting flesh]!" That response shows Rabbi Tzadok that his position was self-refuting. Indeed, if you look for an excuse to refuse the date, you do not ask for food. In his turn, he still listens very carefully to the ambiguity of her response, "I have/am ritually impure [meat/flesh]." Her listens "into" her words, even as the Psalm, quoted in the broader context in which this story appears in the Talmud, suggests listening "into" the words of G-d. The ambiguity he finds in her words is that, as he reckons, she already has understood that she was involving him in a transgression as far as he was concerned, even if, perhaps, in her eyes, this is a minor transgression: having the wrong meat/flesh. She perhaps just wants to see his response. Yet all he says and does afterward, including getting into the warming-up oven, is to help her understand what she had not before—how serious that "minor" transgression is for him, even if he might have indicated otherwise with "So What?"

He achieves that effect because he listens and helps her listen to the self-refuting power of both *his* and *her* words. The power of self-refuting makes both of them heroes of fulfillment through listening. Playfully, polemically and dialectically, and poetically, rather than logically or philosophically, the characters dance the dance of a series of self-refutations. First, she exposed his self-refuting, and toward the end, he exposes her self-refuting. And viewed in these terms, nothing that either says or does is absurd, as they might seem if they related to each other on purely logical, rather than dialectical grounds—which fortunately they did not, for otherwise the outcome might have been even more tragic.

Rather, their demonstrated attunement to the power of self-refuting and to the never-guaranteed mutuality of the parties in the use of that power reveals a dimension that extends beyond any merely ethical aspect of the characters' interactions. "Ethical" applies here in the sense of ethos (limited as it is to "character," in Aristotle's sense) or even in the broader anti-metaphysical but not antiphilosophical sense that Levinas developed of the subject encountering the trace of the Other—whom the subject can never encounter—in and through the face, the look, the visage of another subject that the subject does the encounter. The dimension—call it the dance of self-refutation—is not merely ethical in the Aristotelian sense, because the parties do not permanently stick to their arguments, and thus their arguments do not define their characters. Nor is it merely ethical in Levinas's sense, at the very least because what the parties encounter and self-refute is first and foremost speech and words, no matter whose speech it is or whose words they are. The effect is achieved by emphasizing the speech, rather than the faces, looks, or visages of those involved.

This is of course not to say the ethical dimension in either sense is not there in the story. Yet it is to say that the story is permeated and even controlled by something else—by a version of the political, which, however, is not logical but dialectical and rhetorical, and in that sense interpersonal. Nor is this dimension ontological or intersubjective. The version of the political in the dance that Rabbi Tzadok and the noble Roman lady perform is one in which all parties engage and no party occupies the center, that is, the subject position necessary to make any ontological claims. With no party at the center, and in fact with no center or centers in this argument at all, the intersubjective model of thinking does not apply.

Nor does the dance of the Rabbi and the lady amount to a mere use of self-refutation as a tool to manage (win over) or in Burnyeat terms "measure" the other party in terms of the bestowal of being and nonbeing. What we see here is not a technique of domination by one subject over another in an intersubjective relation based on the ontology of bestowing nonbeing on things, but rather a technique of the interpersonal development of self-refuting in which each party helps the other to self-refute, thus moving from an initial intersubjectivity, if I may temporarily borrow this modern term for describing the lady inviting the rabbi in the beginning of the story, to the interpersonality of their political relationship at the end of the story, when they have danced all the moves of the dance of self-refutations.

That dance creates and performs a space where people are surely responsible for their actions and their arguments, yet are not exactly married to them, being instead fully ready to and open for "listening into the voice of the words," in the language of the psalm for which, as I will momentarily explain, the story in the Talmud comes as an illustration. Listening to the voice of words and of other acts—of oneself and of the other—even if and precisely because these words and these acts are not exactly clearly definable in terms of what exactly they are voicing and constantly prove to be self-refuting. The dance is therefore very different from any contestation between logicians and from any relationship that intersubjectivity would entail.

An attunement to listening to the voice of the words—my own words as they reverberate in the words of another, and the other's words as I return their voice, their reverberation through my own words in self-refuting, an orientation to listening "into the voice of the words"—is the theme emphasized in the immediate context of the story of the lady and Rabbi Tzadok in the Babylonian Talmud, where it appears as a commentary on the following fragment from Psalm 103:20: "[Bless the LORD, ye angels of His] ye mighty in strength, that fulfill His word, hearkening unto the voice of His word."

The question in the context of the discussion in the Talmud is as follows: What does fulfilling one's word by listening into the voice of that word mean in the psalm? In the story fulfilling words by hearing their voice comes to mean that one can fulfill the word of G-d and even be rewarded for doing so by listening to and self-refuting one's own words and actions and those of another. Listening to the voice of all words, no matter whether they are mine or not, helps me to refrain from committing transgressions and thus betters my life. At least this is what the story of Rabbi Tzadok suggests in the context of commenting on the psalm.

What is more, the commentary suggests that listening *to* the words (paying attention to their reference and/or mimetic content) is different from listening *into* the voice of the words, to what the words self-refute, and this is precisely what the attunement to self-refutation in the story of Rabbi Tzadok and the lady helps illustrate.

In the Talmud *Qiddushin*, refuting and self-refuting are at work not only between the Rabbi and the lady, but also between other characters, named and nameless, who talk in the Talmud *ad locum*, where self-refuting works as a tool for listening into the voice of the world of the traditions of the past and facilitates remembering the Mishnah better, thereby ultimately bettering the life of the people involved in the political, rather than in ethical, economic, or individual sense of betterment.

The story of the lady and Rabbi Tzadok appears in the context of a discussion between two other rabbis. The first rabbi attempts to refute the words of the sages of the Mishnah by making an inference from these words and contrasting that inference with other words of Mishnaic sages. In the approach of the first rabbi, the sages of the Mishnah are self-refuting. In a response (defense), the second rabbi proves they are not. That is to say, the second rabbi responds by refuting the self-refutation, not only in order to restore the authority of the tradition of the Mishnah as it is remembered, but also in order to make the audience listen *into* the words of that tradition and thus remember that tradition better. The role of self-refutation and the refutation of the self-refutation can be seen by exploring each move in the rabbis' discussion. In the following quote, I will pay attention the structural organization of the text in terms of refutation and self-refutation. I add words in italics to mark the rhetorical moves of the discourse.

> [i] "One should be punished for violating commandments, and rewarded for performing them" [the Mishnah says.]
>
> [ii] *Attack:* But should one [indeed] be rewarded simply for not violating a commandment? That Mishnah seems to imply otherwise, but another tradition from the same sages of the Mishnah seems to imply that a reward can indeed be given [simply] for not violating the law, as well!

As this argument develops in the Talmud, the story of Rabbi Tzadok will illustrate a reward received for not violating the law. Because an inference from the text in [i] is that not violating a commandment is not a reason for receiving a reward and "another Mishnah" in [ii] suggests the opposite, that it can be rewarded, the question arises: Do the sages of the Mishnah as a whole self-contradict?[8] The rabbis in the Talmud begin with a claim that the sages of the Mishnah are indeed self-refuting, but end up with the story of Rabbi Tzadok (and other stories as well) that allow for the possibility that the activity of self-refutation leads to a reward simply for not violating the law.

To learn more about dialectical-rhetorical rather than (onto)logical tone of the argument of self-refutation at work, let me trace the main steps of that broader discussion in the Talmud, paying close attention to the role of refuting, self-refuting, and other technical rhetorical elements of the discussion in comparison with the role self-refuting played in the story of the lady and Rabbi Tzadok.

> [iii] *Self-refutation of the sages in the Mishnah*: Rav Tuvi Bar Rav Kisna raised [a question] in front of Rabba: It states in the Mishnah, "Whoever performs a commandment gets betterment [in life]" This implies that if one does, one gets betterment, but if one does not, one does not get betterment. But this was objected from the following [apocryphal text of the sages in the Mishnah]: "one who sits and does not commit a transgression gets rewarded, as if one has performed a commandment"!? [*By implication, the two traditions refute each other, thus rendering as self-refuting the sages as the collective authority behind the texts.*]

[iv] *Refutation of the self-refutation*: [Rabba] interrupted [the questioner]: The latter [text] pertains to a case when an "opportunity" of transgression emerges, and one gets rescued from it.

[v] *Example*: This is similar to the case of Rabbi Hanina bar Pappi. A noble Roman lady once summoned him.

[vi] *Refutation*: He said a [magic] thing, and his body got covered with boils and scabs.

[vii] *Counterrefutation*: She made a thing [potion], and he was cured.

[viii] *Admission of being self-refuted*: He ran away [in the middle of the night] and hid in a [dangerous] bathhouse in which even two people entering together, even in the light of the day, would still be harmed [by demons.]

[ix] *His self-refutation made public:* Next day [seeing he has come out from that bathhouse] our teachers asked him: Who guarded/saved you [in such a dangerous place]? Two soldiers of the Caesar watched me all night long [he replied.] They said to him, perhaps an "opportunity" to commit a sexual transgression came your way and you were saved from it, because it is taught [in the apocryphal rabbinical text] "whoever gets an "opportunity" of sexual transgression and gets saved from it, this person receives a miracle"?

[x] (Rab[ba] now allows Rav Tuvi Bar Rav Kisna to continue quoting the apocryphal text. [The latter continues:] It says in (the Psalm 103:20) "[Bless the LORD, ye angels of His] ye mighty in strength, that fulfill His word, hearkening unto the voice of His word." [*This suggests a reward for listening, not only for an act of obedience to the commandments, but also for refraining from violating them. This is now going to be supported with the story of the Lady and Rabbi Tzadok, in which their relationship is no less polemical than the one related here, but ends more peacefully.*]

[xi] *Strengthening counterrefutation*: This is similar to Rabbi Tzadok and his fellows. A noble [Roman] lady summoned Rabbi Tzadok [to her house.] He said to her, my flesh is weak and I do not find any food. She said to him: I have some ritually impure [meat/flesh] He said to her: So what? One who does that eats this. She lit the oven and put the meat inside. He went and sat inside the oven. She said—what is that? He said: One who does that falls into that. She said: if I knew all that, I would not put pressure on you [alt: would not cause you trouble].

In this larger context in which the story of Rabbi Tzadok and the lady appears, the rabbis attack and defend the Mishnah. The discussion proceeds from an attack to a defense in which process self-refuting had a systemic role: The sages of the Mishnah initially seem to be self-refuting but ultimately prove not to be. What is more, the story of the lady and Rabbi Tzadok shows self-refutation at work, showcasing how one can be rewarded even without performing a commandment, but only for not violating one.

As personalities, rather than subjectivities, the characters in the Talmud—the lady and Rabbi Tzadok, Rabbi Akiva, and the others—do not engage into dialogues to measure the being or nonbeing of things in either "subjectivist" or "relativist" ways, the terms in which Burnyeat explains the use of self-refutation in Sextus. They are completely indifferent to measuring what is and what is not. Instead, they listen to each other's words, and this entails a different kind of attitude toward themselves and toward words in which self-refutation serves the purpose of listening *into* the words.

How, then, do Schmitt's and Rancière's accounts of the subjectivity prevent from thinking like Rabbi Tzadok or like the noble lady? This question represents a moment of Talmud speaking back to philosophy, as it were. If Rabbi Tzadok were a modern political subject, the conversation between him and the noble Roman lady would have taken a radically different course and would have led to radically different outcomes. We can imagine that for Rancière, Rabbi Tzadok, if summoned by a noblewoman, would face the difficult choice of behaving either like a slave, without the subjectivity of a citizen, or as a citizen claiming his freedom and thus either willingly accepting or no less willingly rejecting the advances the woman was making to him. But Rabbi Tzadok is neither a slave nor a subject. In turn, for Schmitt, Rabbi Tzadok would be a representative of a politically persecuted group, say of a local group persecuted by imperial power. The woman would be the representative of that power, and a clash between them would have been a clash of subjectivities, as Oedipal as it could be. To imagine further along these lines, Rabbi Tzadok would consider himself as a representative of a persecuted minority and would therefore either tacitly give in or openly revolt against what for him would be inappropriate use of the mighty woman's social status to coerce him into sexual servitude. His reaction, however, might have been severely complicated by transferences of his feelings he had for his mother onto the noble Roman lady. He might have alternatively considered her desire of sexual relationships with him as the victory of a man over a woman, an even greater victory, in his eyes, because the woman is representative of the empire.

These are just some of the many possibilities both looming and lurking if the ghost of representation is unleashed in the story. But again, it is not. Instead, and simply put, the story shows a way of political action that is not predicated on subjectivity but rather on interpersonality. It is therefore beyond the horizon of what either Schmitt or Rancière can address.

This indicates a more general way by which of the story talks back to philosophy. The story and the interpersonal political it exemplifies rely on a philosophically unusual truth criterion. The truth of a claim has everything to do with what it refutes, not only with what it describes or expresses. Deprived of such understanding of truth narrows both Schmitt's and Rancière's horizon of thinking about the political to the terms of subjectivity, to the exclusion of either refutation or interpersonality.

Self-refutation is thus a helpful starting point from which to begin thinking about the interpersonal political. However, it remains to be explored whether the interpersonal as exemplified by the working of self-refutation in the Talmud might still entail Kant's "subject of reason." A more refined understanding of the personal and the interpersonal is required, differentiating the interpersonal from the intersubjective on a nonpsychological level. In the chapter that follows, comparative analysis of personhood involved in the Talmud will contribute to that refinement.

CHAPTER 4

Conceptions of the Human (Interpersonality II): The Limits of Regret

Self-refutation in the Talmud creates an interpersonal version of the political in which thinking and in particular listening *into* the voice of words from oneself and others transgress the fixed and stable identities that are the *conditio sine qua non* for modern intersubjectivity. The refutation of a refutation, that is, in the example in the previous chapter, self-refutation, exemplifies a more general element in the constitution of Talmudic refutation: Refutation translates into a certain structure of personhood and into a certain interpersonal relationship. It stages a conception of personhood that neither "subjectivist" nor "relativist" notions of the humanity of humans can neither fully grasp nor fully efface.

What is at issue in such a conception of personhood are the possibilities for a conception of humanity in general and of the human that reaches beyond notions of the human that involve bestowing nonbeing on things or measuring their being. That is to say, what is at issue are the limits of conceptions of the human not just in late antiquity, as we have explored with M. F. Burnyeat's analysis of self-refutation in Sextus Empiricus, but also conceptions of the human since Kant. A starting point for exploring those limitations is the 1929 Davos disputation between Ernst Cassirer and

Martin Heidegger over the question "What is man?"—that is, what is it to be a human being? That debate pitted Cassirer's neo-Kantian version of philosophical anthropology, in which human being is commensurable with the world, a conception that embraces an ontology in which human beings measure the world and its being, against Heidegger's then-new project of a "fundamental ontology" in which Heidegger claimed that the fundamental concern of thinking, thought oriented toward the fundamental question of being, of which the world is only a part, takes precedence over and removes limitations imposed by Cassirer's insistence on the figure of the human as the foundation of thought about the world. The task here is to identify what escapes and complicates the ontological grounds of human action, whether in Cassirer's versions of a human-centered ontology of the world or in Heidegger's ontology of being. As will become clear, such an analysis will take us back to and direct us against a version of the political articulated in modern times in Kant's aesthetics, which guided his thinking of properly intersubjective relationships in a society.

I will engage the rather complicated theoretical stakes involved here through a case study in the rhetoric of regret.[1] By a logic that will become clear in the course of analysis, this will lead to both reclaiming and reconsidering the fundamental role of the aesthetic as a discipline of thinking in relationship to thinking the political. Addressing the problem of the role of post-Kantian aesthetics in relationship to the political and ontology will provide a dimension in which to reconnect two hitherto artificially separated late ancient corpora of thought, rabbinic and "pagan,"[2] in both the late ancient and the modern context.

The modernist reception and construction of late ancient thought conventionally treats Neoplatonic thought and Talmudic reasoning as separate and unrelated phenomena. The former is typically understood as a "pagan" school of philosophy and/or magic and theurgy, while the latter is pigeonholed as a rabbinic school of rhetoric and/or sophistic. In a comparative analysis of these hitherto artificially separated corpora of thought, I undertake a heuristic analysis and critique of the partition between them by explicating the concept of "personhood" as developed by another Russian Orthodox philosopher and, one can say, political thinker, and in particular a thinker of political resistance, Alexei Losev.[3] Losev developed his notion of personhood in his eight-volume *History of Ancient Aesthetics*,[4] and I engage his thought there as a way of understanding the rhetoric of time and remembrance in the Talmud. I thus address the Talmud as a case of "Jewish rhetoric,"[5] reevaluating it in terms of and against the conventional boundaries between the Talmud and the Neoplatonic discipline of "aesthetics," in Losev's terms. By necessity, that program of critique has a modern agenda concerning the emergence of rhetoric, aesthetics, and the Talmud as intellectual disciplines in the context of the "fundamentals debate" in modernity.[6]

The Fundamentals Debate

By the first quarter of the twentieth century, scientific knowledge of both nature and society could no longer claim to understand things as they are, as if these things exist even before one comes to know or measure them. The "relativist" claim that to be human is to be the measure of being, which I addressed in the previous chapter, would no longer do. Thinkers realized the necessity of attributing any assertion of the "fact" that things exist to the ways of knowing things, rather than to the things themselves. Knowledge lost its external grounding, thus leading to a crisis. The truth of science no longer could be said to arise from the being of things, but rather, claims about the being of things became the product of science. However, science could not explain exactly how that product is made. As a result, and as one of the expressions of the crisis, science lost what used to be its most reliable claim for objectivity and truth—the reliance on what truly exists or on the initial being of what science would then simply come to know and, conversely, reliance on the nonbeing of what science understands to be false. Critical minds faced the question: If not the being of things, what else can ground the objectivity and universality of scientific knowledge of the world?

Far more complex and multifaceted than such a brief summary represents, the crisis gave rise to a debate concerning which of the disciplines of knowing can be "fundamental" in regard to all others so that knowing in all other disciplines can regain its ground or foundation, if not in the being of things, then in a "fundamental" discipline from which all other branches of knowing could safely stem. The debate reached far beyond the confines of the scientific exploration of the universe, defining the main lines of philosophical thought in various branches of the humanities as well.

Competing disciplines claimed this fundamental status. They ranged from traditional disciplines such as logic, psychology, metaphysics, or, as in the case of Alexei Losev, aesthetics, to new disciplines such as philosophical anthropology, phenomenology, or "the new rhetoric" as advanced by Chaim Perelman. Thus, in discussions of the fundamental knowledge developed from Husserl's discovery of phenomenology as a new foundation of science to Heidegger's reformulation of it as "fundamental ontology,"

Emmanuel Levinas, at the early stage of his thinking and in response to Heidegger,[7] highlighted a new project of ethics as "first philosophy," understanding ethics as both the study and the practice of infinite responsibility toward an Other who or that is never present and never absent, since, for Levinas, as consequently for Derrida, absence is limited to implying presence somewhere else. Neither present nor absent, yet traceable as informing one's relationships to small-"o" others, this not-present and not-absent Other represented for Levinas, the crucial element of the personhood or "face" of the others, who are looking at the subject, at you, yet before you can do anything about that look, and by that very look telling you, in the words of the Other, that you are not to reduce that one with the face to an object, let alone to kill and/or murder him, her, or it. For Levinas, the ethics of responsibility in view of the Other in the faces of others undermines the claim of Heidegger's ontology to be "fundamental."

Additional relevant examples of putative claims to articulate a fundamental discipline in response to the effort to propose a ground or foundation from which all other branches of knowing could safely stem would be Perelman's "new rhetoric" and Paul de Man's theory of rhetoric, or theory of the linguistic categories of metaphor and metonymy as tacitly grounding, any philosophical discourse, even if such a discourse explicitly denies the importance of language.[8] In this respect, de Man's position is comparable to as well as polemical with Derrida's "*différence*" as both a differing and a deferring that "destructures" or reveals the construction of both thinking and what thinking encounters.[9]

The variety of these examples suggests a question: Must the crisis of the foundations of knowledge be resolved in only one direction—in finding a new fundamental discipline, even if, as in case of Derrida, that discipline may insist on leaving the place of the fundamental discipline void? The question remains whether having a fundamental discipline, whether its position is vacant or not, is a necessity. In the framework of a case study of pagan and rabbinic aesthetics, I entertain this question by analyzing Losev's aesthetics and applying it to thinking about the role of aesthetics in the Talmud.[10]

Losev's position opens up a new perspective on the fundamentals debate. Like the approach of other intellectuals contributing to the fundamentals debate, Losev's turns on and turns to the analysis of ancient and in particular late ancient texts. Yet unlike other thinkers, Losev proposes aesthetics as a possible fundamental discipline. And still unlike other contributors to the fundamentals debate, he advances a view of aesthetics that undermines any possibility of there being a fundamental discipline, even if he does not undermine the idea of or the place that would be occupied by the fundamental or foundational as a ground for knowing. Losev's view of aesthetic thus enriches the fundamentals debate by opening the door for yet another late ancient text, the Talmud, and its aesthetics, so that from the periphery of the fundamentals debate, where the Talmud has kept lurking,[11] it can now advance to the center and thus to contribute more fully to the core question of the debate: Is there or can there be a fundamental discipline to ground all thinking in the sciences and humanities?

Losev's Aesthetics

It is by proposing aesthetics as a candidate for the fundamental discipline that Losev shows that nothing can ultimately function as fundamental. How that conclusion is reached can best be seen if we suspend Losev's subscription to Eastern Orthodox Christian teleology, in which the development of the "late ancient aesthetics" leads to the aesthetics of Russian Orthodox Church, and look instead at what he portrays as "pagan Neoplatonism" in its own right. As grounded in an aesthetic response to the world, his concept of personhood would indeed seem to claim for aesthetics a "fundamental" status, much the way Hume did for the passions, as opposed to reason. In the end, however, there is no "hierarchy" in the Neoplatonic threefold conception of *nous*, as articulated by Losev, and therefore, despite claims to serving the teleology of his history of philosophy, nothing, not even aesthetics, can be said to be "fundamental."

Appealing to ancient aesthetics in readings of Neoplatonist philosophers such as Iamblichus, Amelius, Porphyry, and Proclus in late antiquity, Losev abandons the post-Cartesian thinking subject and focuses instead on what he calls "personhood," discovering the fully developed form of it in Eastern Orthodox version of Christianity. Let me attend closely to his logic.

As a Russian Christian Orthodox philosopher (and secretly ordained monk),[12] Losev embarked on a lifelong project, to trace the "history of ancient aesthetics," aiming to explain the development of the unique—and, for him, tacitly politically privileged—notion of personhood in Eastern Orthodox Christianity. To that end, Losev's multivolume history of ancient aesthetics focuses on personhood as a critically important factor in understanding the history of civilization from Plato to the modern era.

Losev's use of "personhood" differs from the general English usage, in which it signifies the unique, discrete identity of an individual human being, characteristically associated with the *cogito* of Descartes—the thinking subject of classic modernity. I use the word to translate Losev's philosophically and religiously charged concept of *lichnost*, which could be glossed as an instance in which the universal and the singular intersect, bypassing both the particular and the individual to shape a "singular face," which is yet another way to translate *lichnost*. An example of *lichnost* can be found in Eastern Orthodox iconography: a "face" looking at the viewer and drawing the viewer in to help the viewer to ascend to G-d through G-d's face—the image of the other who is looking at you, rather than an image of oneself in the mirror, as subjectivity would have it. In the experience of such a look, the personal face of the viewer dissipates, and instead, the divine look radiates and absorbs me into it. "I" dissolve.[13] The locus of personhood is in the response to the look that absorbs me.[14] I have the capacity to see beauty in this look, but the result of that seeing is being drawn in, so that the ultimate person is not me, but the one who emanates the look in which I ascend. In the look, I therefore am the one looked at, rather than the one who is looking.[15] This is a conception of personhood rooted in aesthetic response, not in epistemology per se.

Losev's aesthetics of human existence as personhood, understood as *lichnost*, neither engages nor disengages from the understanding of human identity as a thinking subject. Instead, the Eastern Orthodox view, for Losev, arises from the philosophical world of late antiquity, from Neoplatonism on the one hand and from the "Jewish" tradition of a "Demiurge-G-d" as a "person," that is, as the personification of the notion of G-d in a personal name, on the other. In that framework of thinking, the aesthetics of human existence as personhood becomes, for Losev, the key for unlocking the history of "pagan" thinking leading to the "full" form of "personhood" of G-d in the icons. Losev predicates human existence on an aesthetic response that initiates an ascent to the existence of "gods" or "kinds," and he roots that ascent in the "simply being" of the Neoplatonic *nous* as a form of personhood that at once "simply is," that possesses things in thinking about them, and that notices that it "simply is" and possesses things in thinking about them.

What does this mean? Consider the claim, assessed by Losev, that "if the pine is a tree, then gods exist."

> "If the pine is a tree, then gods exist" [means that] if "tree" has "pine" as one of its kinds, then gods gave birth to the cosmos and to humans. . . . Just as a pine grows up from the seed, so, too, the cosmos and all humans are striving to become gods. Even if, due to some extraneous causes, the seed was destroyed and no tree grew up out of it, or if the tree did grow up, but was soon destroyed because of some

> causes in atmosphere or because someone cut it, such circumstances are meaningless and do not characterize the essence of the matter, but rather are only countless misfortunes that are disadvantageous for the existence of that essence. Therefore, bad theurgists or immoral uses of a cult tell nothing essential.[16]

When one sees a pine, one must have always already recognized what one sees as a pine and, at the same time, the pine as a tree, rather than, say, as an animal, so that noticing the kind "tree" is always already embedded in seeing a pine. "Kinds" thus are not generalizations derived from experience and observation, and the act of seeing the pine bypasses the observation of it and is not grounded in the observer. Instead, the "kinds" condition the seeing. In brief, in discerning the world, generalities always come before the discernment of particulars, not after. Therefore, generalities are never merely noumenal, much less merely nominal entities. Nor are they "real" in the sense of the medieval scholastic realism. Rather, they always already mingle with and condition one's experience—in this example, the experience of a pine—even if these generalities never appear as the objects of that experience. "I," "me," or "my experience" are either glaringly absent from or, if used, remain extrinsic to the process of knowing.

Likewise, one's path to knowing the existence of gods does not have to engage one's sense of an "I." Instead, it simply relies on an aesthetic given, on a "fact" or "datum," for example, about what a pine is—a tree. If, when one sees a pine, one must have always already recognized what one sees as a pine and the pine as a tree, what matters is the "always already" nature of what is recognized. That is based on the preexistence of "kinds"—of "gods"—that do not change and that are therefore timeless. The aesthetic of "always already" thus represents the ascent from the sensual to the eternal.

That means there is no true engagement with time: the "always" always takes precedence over the "already." Seeing a pine as a tree does not require seeing oneself as an individual seer. Neither is the argument about the pine pragmatically grounded in a pronouncement made by a certain person: "The pine is a tree." Both the person making the pronouncement and his or her "I" may be implied by it, but they are not implicated, because they are not essential: It does not matter who sees the pine, nor is it important who makes the pronouncement. What matter are the aesthetic "fact" and the step from that fact to the existence of kinds and of gods. This is all about observation and speaking and seeing, not about an observer or speaker or seer.

That is why bad theurgists and the abuses of magic cults provide no grounds for generalizations dismissing theurgy or magic as malpractices. The aesthetic ascent from seeing a pine to the existence of gods has both a polemical charge and a practical application: cases of evil theurgists provide no moral argument against cults, just as empirical misfortunes and circumstances, however many, are only extraneous for understanding the formative role of kinds and of gods in experience.

As Losev shows, this argument about what happens when seeing a pine belongs to Iamblichus (Syria, 245–325 C.E.) and polemically targets Porphyry (Lebanon, 234–305 C.E.), who used the negative example of villain theurgists to argue for the immorality of practical theurgy. Porphyry dismisses magic, insisting that only purely contemplative withdrawal from the world of experience, that is, for him, from the world of aesthetics, constitutes proper service to "gods" who "exist." Porphyry therefore condemns any aesthetic engagement, let alone engagement with gods. As Iamblichus counters, Porphyry simply does not know how to generalize. That is to say, he uses aesthetics wrongly. Iamblichus suggests that just as the fact that some seeds do not become a tree cannot deny the essence of seeds, which is to become trees, so, too, the fact that some theurgists malfunction does not allow generalizing against aesthetic engagement with invisible gods through cults. Evil theurgy, Iamblichus continues to argue, therefore does not render theurgy immoral, because as a matter of aesthetic principle, one cannot arrive at general notions by summarizing the data in observations.

For Losev, this polemic has a modern agenda. True aesthetics for Iamblichus cannot be a one-way street from observation to generalization, because generalizations "always already" inform observation. That critique works against the modern centering of the aesthetic on the experience of an "I" as the foundation of the modern conception of "personhood." Additionally, it is important for Losev's own program that Iamblichus cannot win in these polemics without promoting aesthetics to the center of his philosophy and thus dismissing Porphyry's appeal to pure contemplation and logic. Purified of either an "I" or empirical generalization, aesthetic ascent comes to the center of human existence among the pines and gods. That is why Losev locates aesthetic generalization at the basis of moral decisions for Iamblichus.

For Losev, the inevitably complex structure of at once being, possessing, and grasping that one is and that one possesses represents a "typical neo-Platonist triad" of *being* (ideal), *life* (becoming), and *thinking* (which takes becoming back to *being*), all of which is also included in Plotinus's concept of *nous*. For Losev, this structure is not a property possessed by an individual, because the Neoplatonic *nous* is not an individual attribute in the first place. Instead *nous* entails the three attributes in one, which makes for an "in-dividual" in neither the literal nor the conventional sense of the term.

Losev explains these three aspects as the "paradigm," as "life," and as "thinking:" "*What is* (*ontos*) or what the mind can rationally grasp is the "paradigm" for everything that exists. "Life" is a transition of the ontos into what it is not, that is, into becoming and unbecoming. Becoming and unbecoming are no longer "*what is*," but only "participate" in the latter. They are as it were, the becoming of *what is*, which thus defines them as "life." "Thinking" in turn undoes becoming, distilling the *what is* from the "life."[17] Thinking thus is creative and always already there, even if it emerges as such only as it "brings things back to existence" from "life" to the "paradigm" of being.

The pine tree argument and the polemics about theurgy that it entails illustrate Losev's more general, programmatic orientation toward aesthetics as the foundation of ethics and ultimately of the metaphysics of being. For him, moral actions are not possible without appreciating the primary role of "gods" or "kinds" in shaping human—primarily aesthetic—encounters with the world and, by the same token, human existence in the world. In that sense, even if "what is," or "life," or "thinking" cannot alone provide a sufficient "foundation" when taken separately, aesthetics, which involves their complex interplay, still grounds ethics and metaphysics and in that sense, is "fundamental."

At stake here is the relationship between personhood and embodiment. For Losev, the Neoplatonic conception of personhood that ultimately leads to the Eastern Orthodox form of aesthetics begins with Plato's impersonal, but fully embodied "dialectics of Logos" and ends with Christian personhood, in which personification and embodiment finally come together. However, in the Socratic "dialectics of Logos," as Losev defines it, there is no personhood whatsoever. Instead, Socratic dialectics are full of characters that are just bodies typifying positions in arguments and conversations. Personae such as Socrates and his interlocutors are bodies that mark thinking positions—the irony and *maieutics* of the mature Socrates versus the naiveté of his adolescent interlocutors. But in the dialectics of Logos, there are nothing but bodies in conversation. Socratic dialectics, for Losev, thus is fundamentally positional, but impersonal.

As a result, the aesthetic dimension of the dialectics of Logos is subsumed and suppressed by ontology, searching for what truly is, as opposed to what is not and as distinct from what seems to be. Contrary to that task, for the Neoplatonists, whom Losev reads critically, knowing the being of the *nous* cannot be an independent goal in itself. Knowing the being of the *nous* is impossible without and of no true value outside of aesthetic ascent to knowledge of kinds or gods or without the understanding of personhood to which that ascent leads. Ontology is thus only a part, and indeed never an independent part, of the aesthetics of personhood. With the help from Iamblichus, Amelius, and the other Neoplatonists, Losev thus departs from Socratic dialectics of Logos, as well as from privileging ontology in dialectics, replacing it with an essentially impersonal concept of personhood grounded in the aesthetics of response to the world.[18]

That concept of personhood is an especially apt way to describe what today is emerging as the best way to understand the nature and status of persons represented in the Talmud. Perhaps the most important achievement in modern Talmud scholarship has been the discovery of new characters that traditional readers of the Talmud did not see.[19] These new characters have been construed as either the literary "composers"[20] of the Talmudic discussions or as the "anonymous redactors" incorporating the sayings (dicta) of the earlier Talmudic authorities into the fabric the discussions in the Talmud.[21] These new characters were clearly distinct from any of the named and nameless rabbis and students mentioned or implied in the environments or in the acts committed in the rabbinic academies, the alleged settings of all the main plots in Talmudic texts.

The modern scholarly understanding that there are characters in the Talmud beyond these settings and beyond these acts resulted from the Cartesian model of personhood and from a reductive understanding of the rhetoric of the Talmud as dominated by the figures of refuting and counterrefuting, which of course was not foreign to Cartesian tradition, as well, even if only in a negative way. The Cartesian model of personhood implies the *ego cogito ergo sum* thesis, which the scholars of the Talmud tacitly adopted, arguing as they did that if there is evidence of thinking beyond and above what is attributable to the characters on stage in the Talmud, then so to speak, there must have existed some characters off the stage. The reduction of the rhetoric of the Talmud to refuting and counterrefuting, although that rhetoric was much older that Cartesian philosophy, still fit the modernist Cartesian view, even if it was invoked as a way of keeping both rhetoric and the Talmud distant from the central concerns of Cartesians.

As an implementation of the Cartesian model of personhood in Talmudic scholarship, however, the positing of anonymous redactors of the sayings and teachings of earlier named masters in the Talmud and of anonymous "composers of Talmudic discussions" is too quick and too simple. It comes at the expense of a subtler interpretation of a much more complex intersection of the personal and the impersonal, the embodied and disembodied, in both the genesis and the final establishment of the Talmudic discussions. Consider, as an example of a Talmudic conversation, a short text from the Babylonian Talmud Yoma76a. Let me present this text in the form of a play script.

Stage Directions:

Time and Place of Action: Undefined, presumably a rabbinical academy in late ancient Babylonia.

Narrator: Undefined, has no words.

Language of the speakers: Aramaic.

Language of quotations and paraphrases: Mishnaic Hebrew.

Characters Present on the Stage:

First Character: Unspecified, presumably a *tanna*—a student who recites by heart a fragment from the teachings of the sages of the Mishnah (a text of instructions for Rabbinic courts; Palestine, the beginning of the third century).

Second Character (or Second and Third Characters talking to each other): Unspecified, presumably a student or students in the academy talking in front of his or their peers and teachers.

Characters Absent from the Stage:

Rav, an *amora*, or a Talmudic authority

Rav Hunah, an *amora* and a former student of Rav

The text:

First Character, reciting in Mishnaic Hebrew: "One who said 'Let me sin, and I will then repent; let me sin, and I will then repent' is not getting to repent."

Second Character in Aramaic, citing in Mishnaic Hebrew: [Hmm,] why would I need to say twice "Let me sin, and I will then repent; let me sin, and I will then repent"?—The answer must be along the lines of the tradition known in the name of Rav cited by Rav Hunah. As Rav Hunah said, Rav used to say, "When a person committed a

> transgression, and then repeated that transgression, it is permitted to him [to repent for it]."
>
> Third Character (or Second Character continuing) in Aramaic, paraphrasing in Mishnaic Hebrew: Do not even dare to take "is permitted to him" to mean "permitted [to repent for it]" Rather, if done twice, [the transgression] becomes [in the eyes of the transgressor] "permitted" [and thus there remains no place for repentance].

In its own right, the dictum of Rav, "When a person committed a transgression, and then repeated that transgression, it is permitted to him" only weakly connects to the Mishnah recited by the First Character. The connection is not strong enough to contradict the verdict in the Mishnah, because "permitted" in the dictum does not have to imply "to repent for it"; it may instead imply "to expiate it" through a sacrifice or a substitution in prayer, rather than "to repent" in the sense of regretting one's actions. Nor is Rav's dictum necessarily similar to the Mishnah in its theme. The Mishnah addresses a person who has planned on sinning, hoping to repent it afterward, and is now attempting to repent. In contrast, Rav's dictum addresses transgressions repeated several times in the past, none of which was necessarily planned in advance, let alone with the hope to repent afterward. However, in the conversation that the text represents, the characters operate under the assumption that the Mishnah and the dictum match at least in theme—a repeated transgression, followed by attempted repentance. What is more, on a reading that the last-speaking character offers, the dictum matches the Mishnah in its verdict, as well: in both cases, repentance cannot succeed. Thus, by involving the dictum in the discussion of the Mishnah, the characters reframe both to match at least in theme and, on the last character's reading, also in the verdict.

However, who commits and controls that reframing? Who makes the themes match? Because such reframing converts initially unrelated pronouncements in the Mishnah and in the dictum into what initially matches in the theme, but contradicts in the verdict ("does not get to repent" versus "is permitted [to repent for it]") and ultimately even into what removes that contradiction, and because all the characters depend on at least the first step of that reframing, none of the on-stage characters can have controlled the way in which the dictum and the frame are reframed. Therefore, the perspective of modern critical scholarship on the Talmud suggests positing another character, one who is responsible for that reframing process.

Unlike the characters on the stage, that new character is absent from the discussion, but unlike Rav and Rav Hunah, it is not an identified character off the stage. Rather, the new character is elided from the world around the stage, both from the present discussion and from past discussions that it implies and thereby creates. Instead, that new character belongs to an order that neither presence nor absence can describe. If one thinks about this Talmudic conversation in terms of a theatrical performance or a movie, that character cannot be in the viewer's seat, either, because that seat is also a part of the world implied and in that sense created by the stage.

Not present in any particular place, that character is not absent from any particular place, either. Is this new character a person in the sense in which the characters and Rav with Rav Hunah are personae? On the other hand, is it possible to avoid characterizing this new character as a person, or at least to avoid personification? The seemingly easy solution, defining that new character as an "anonymous person," as some modernist theories of the Talmud have proposed, does not do, because in that case, the new character would be as present on the stage (in particular, behind the stage) as the other characters are, as nameless and therefore as anonymous as they are. A more general problem with that solution is that because this new character does not belong to the order of presence and therefore does not belong to the order of absence either, it does not belong to the order of the personal—or to the order of the impersonal, either.

One possible solution would be to differentiate the nameless and impersonal characters from the "anonymous" new character so that the latter would be impersonal, but not anonymous. What that would mean, however, is that the new character is not a person (either named, as Rav Hunah is, or nameless as some of the other characters are). If so, who or what might that enigmatic new character be?

Here is where Losev's conception of personhood as *lichnost* offers an insight that makes such a solution possible. Because "personhood" for Losev is not a property of an individual and therefore is different from the fact that an individual is a person—either in general or with specific personality traits—the new character can be construed in these terms. Losev's view of personhood as tripartite unity exemplified through the *nous* is helpful here because it both implies and exceeds the model of a person creating things and/or worlds. If a person is a creator of things and worlds, it is only as one of the three inseparable elements of the *nous* as a personhood; being, grasping, and noticing the former in the latter make creation only a part, and never an independent part, of the broader structure of the triplet.

That means personhood is always broader and always more complex than any individual or even any group of individuals participating in it.

How are we to understand a Talmudic character who is not a person and is not present in or absent from a discussion such as the one we have examined? Part of the answer lies in the elusive literary form of the conversation as it is represented there. This text leaves the characters on the stage unspecified, let alone unnamed. Even the number of these characters is not definite: Second Character may in fact be two different characters. Depending on the count, the plot and its outcome vary, as well: the discussion could be a direct defense of First Character that Second Character provides in a soliloquy consisting of a refutation ("[Hmm,] Why would I need . . .") and counterrefutation ("The answer . . . no place for repentance"). However, an alternative plot could include an indirect defense of First Character by Third Character, who undermines the attack of Second Character.

And the literary genre of this text is not clear, either. Traditional and modernist scholars of the Talmud have argued respectively that it is either a stenographic account of a "real" conversation in a rabbinic academy or a literary allusion to such a conversation. Under either approach, the main literary and intellectual form and even the genre of the conversation could be defined narrowly as refuting and counterrefuting, in the sense that the character(s) attack and defend the Mishnah initially recited by First Character. Furthermore, in a certain subset of the modernist theories on the Talmud's formation, which I will call for brevity "transformational theory,"[22] this text both hides and represents a series of transformations in the process of its genesis.

According to transformation theory, the genesis of the conversation begins with two texts that existed prior to the conversation: the Mishnah and the dictum "Rav Hunah said, Rav used to say, 'When a person committed a transgression, and then repeated that transgression, it is permitted to him,' to repent," which, as already noted, do not initially relate to each other. When the Second or Third Character is introduced, these preexisting materials emerge in a new light. The initially irrelevant dictum now becomes contradictory to the Mishnah, but is ultimately used to support it. Transformation theory ascribes that change to an agent different from the characters, a new character responsible for the transformation. However, transformation theory construes the new character as a person (individual or collective)—the "author" of the transformation.

The account of this process of transformation involves two steps, an implicit and an explicit one. The "author" first implicitly reinterprets the dictum to relate to repentance (again, as an act of regret), rather than of expiation (as an act of either sacrifice or prayer), so that the dictum can now contradict (and thus be relevant to) the Mishnah. Second, the "author" makes Second Character (or Third Character) reinterpret that dictum explicitly on the stage, thereby removing the contradiction.

Beyond the confines of transformation theory, however, there is yet another way to understand the genre of the conversation. The attacks and defenses, refutations, and counterrefutations, are not the final word about the literary form of that text, but part of a larger form. The refutation and counterrefutation can be seen as only one figure in a dance—a carnival of remembering, part of the effort to make sure that the Mishnah is remembered in the best way possible, where remembering it in the best way possible means showing as many understandings of its validity as are available. In that carnival of remembering, remembering the Mishnah is no longer and in no way a personal recollection of one's experience, individual or collective, but rather belongs to no character, at least if "character" means a person, not even to the "new character" that transformation theory proposes.[23]

In this broader view of its genre, the text represents a session in the rhetorical training of rabbis. As in other rhetorical schools, the characters practice their skills in memorization (First Character), along with techniques of refuting and defending (Second and Third Characters). However, the latter characters use refuting not for its own sake, that is, for establishing what can be said to be objectively true, but for the purpose of remembering—a new technique, not employed, to the best of my knowledge, in other rhetorical schools.

Yet this difference between rabbinical and other rhetorical schools is not as great as it may seem, because refuting serves the rabbis in connection with what other rhetorical schools knew as "memory for things," as opposed to "memory for words," that is, remembering without relating to the content of the words, a technique that First Character clearly exercises by reciting the Mishnah by heart, while Second Character criticizes that remembering for an unnecessary redundancy in the words. The memory for words, in the conversation, undergoes a test of verification in which the other character(s) refute and counterrefute that memory, arriving instead to what can still be called "memory for things"—which in this case means the memory for things that the Mishnah supposedly refuted or dealt with otherwise.

In remembering without relating to the content of the words, the characters elicit new issues, matters, or "things" to remember. For example, it transpires from the conversation that in the Mishnah, repenting for a sin committed on having previously contemplated repentance works the first time, but does not work the second time. That discovery achieves a more precise "memory for things." It also means that what looked like a mistake in "memory for words" (the repetition of "I will sin, and I will then repent") was in fact a valid memory to preserve, so that the remembering of First Character passes the test posed for it, the test of being worthy of remembrance. Furthermore, because the resulting advanced memory for things arises in the process of the discussion, a process that none of the characters can advance alone and that therefore belongs to no particular character, the characters complement each other in a process that none of them orchestrates. Nor can the memory that emerges belong to, be controlled by, or be ascribed to any "new character," as posited by transformation theory, if that character is construed, as it is in that theory, as a person. Furthermore, even if that new character is understood as neither present nor absent and thus not exactly as a person, it is neither the creator not the spectator of the process. The resulting memory is therefore not in the possession or control of any new character. Unlike the other characters, the "new character" in the conversation is neither an individual nor a person, neither present nor absent, but rather is a character representing personhood in Losev's sense as an intersection of the universal and the singular *that* that "simply is," that possesses things in thinking about them, and that notices that it "simply is" and that it possesses the things (call them attributes) in thinking about them. And as it is for Losev, the work that is done by personhood—not by any individual person—is creative. In the case of the Talmud, this is the work of remembering, which gives birth to the characters in the discussion.

Heuristically, the explication of the Talmudic conversations in terms of Losev's concept of personhood thus helps explain the creation of the Talmudic conversations without recourse to the positing of any individual person or persons as their "creator." The dance that is a Talmudic conversation "simply is" and does not exist without, and independent of, the dancers. The dance is performed through the intrinsic multiplicity of the characters. These characters are figures of changing interpretations. They do not represent stable, individual positions. What that means, however, is that the individuality or individual identity of a dancer is less significant than the arguments of refuting and counterrefuting performed in the dance. The count of characters does not have to be the same as the count of the positions and or moves in refuting and counterrefuting. There can be a several dancers or only one, a soliloquy or a dialogue; the attack and the defense can be done by one individual or by the two, three, or more; but none of the dancers owns either the arguments or the outcomes of their application. Personal identity matters less, while the conversation invariably remains an exchange between different positions and moves, of which none is reducible to another. The "simply is" of the dance is not a matter of individuals, either singular or aggregate.

What is more, neither in Losev's Neoplatonic triad nor in the Talmudic dance is there any hierarchy in what "simply is"—and consequently no position that can be said to be "fundamental." As such, at least the Neoplatonic conception of personhood and the aesthetics on which is it is based cannot be reinterpreted as in any way staking claim to grounding the objectivity and universality of scientific knowledge of the world. Yet, of course, Losev is far from simply situating aesthetics as the fundamental discipline. For him, that discipline does not indicate any single foundation, not even what "simply is." Instead, it takes us into the world of complex topologies of being, becoming, and creation. For example, Losev's privileging of the "simply is," reinterpreted in Heideggerian terms, and therefore pertaining to the fundamentals debate, might be construed as being in time—a view that embraces an always imminent possibility of nonbeing and therefore sees being as intrinsically connected to time, now understood as that possibility. But personhood, understood in Losev's terms, as we have seen, is not connected to time. The "always" always takes precedence over the "already." In addition, the plurality and unavoidable instability of the characters in the dance escapes the Heideggerian view of human existence, which is solitary and stable vis-à-vis being and nonbeing. Indeed, no concept of intersubjectivity can bridge the difference between the intrinsic plurality and the instability of characters, let alone the new character, in the dance of remembering. The two approaches to the experience of human existence are mutually exclusive. In turn, the dance that is a Talmudic conversation cannot be grasped by either a fundamental ontology or any fundamental aesthetics, leaving no room for either the aesthetically or the ontologically fundamental.

Instead, there is the nonfundamental aesthetics of Losev, which undoes the possibility of any fundamental discipline. Despite the difference in its understanding of personhood, this aesthetics follows the lines of post-Kantian transcendentalism in understanding the role of aesthetic dimension. Not totally unlike pagan aesthetics as interpreted by Losev, the aesthetics of the Talmud not only grants no fundamental discipline but also precludes the possibility of having one.

This is why the implications for Talmudic notions of being, argumentation, and aesthetics in the context of the fundamentals debate are hard to overestimate. The characters are not concerned with being in the modus of "what was" or more colloquially of "what really happened." Instead, they orient their dance toward making sure their memory of the tradition is correct in the sense of the defensibility and therefore the coherence of what is remembered, but not in the sense of its being true to any kind of historical past of any style, fantastic or realistic. Aesthetically, that means the past arrives in its proper form, as what is remembered, not in its otherwise ontologically prevalent form, as what was. That also means a change in the approach to argumentation. The goal of an argument is not to establish what is (or what is true) regarding each matter in question, but rather to probe what is remembered to determine its defensibility against attacks and refutations, thus leading to a better memory at the end of the process.

However, the "simply is" of the dance parts ways with the simple being implied in the aesthetics of the Losev's triad, let alone with any entitlement of the "fundamental" in the sense of the fundamentals debate. The dance of memory does not invoke being as a traditional correlate of thinking, not even in the sense of the being of the dancer and certainly not in the sense of aesthetics claiming to know the difference between what is, what is not, and what seems to be. The arguments of the dancers are not about what is, or what was. Instead, they are creations of memory, both in the sense that they create memory and in the sense that memory creates them.

Thus, at this point the "simply is" of the dance comes to fore. It consists in the remembering that the dance performs—not the dancers. The dancers are neither thinking subjects that produce thoughts or recollections of their own nor subject to thinking in the sense of following somebody else's line of thought. Instead, they participate in remembering. Consequently, the dancers do not grasp the thinking subject in what is subject to thinking, as the logic of Losev's tripartite *nous* would require. Rather the dance leads into an open past,[24] a past of which none of the dancers can claim ownership, either theirs, or somebody else's.

An Open Past

I have so far followed convention in using "repentance" and "repent" to render an idiom in rabbinic parlance, *teshuva*. David Lambert, however, has suggested a different translation, connecting the idiom of *teshuva* with Greek *metanoia*—"change of mind" or "regret"—thus suggesting that the term denotes regret about past actions, which are only "now" reevaluated as sins. The Talmudic discussion we have examined thus becomes an exploration of the (im)possibility of regretting one's action after having already contemplated regretting them before acting, of attempting to claim actual regret now, after having a contemplated regret in the past. In the language of the Mishnah cited by First Character, that would mean saying "I will sin, and will then regret," followed by regretting the sin after having committed it.[25]

Discussing regret rather than repentance turns on the problem of time, or more specifically of one's existence in time. Deciding whether one can successfully claim regret after having a previously contemplated regret elicits two positions entertained by the characters. Second Character initially suggests that previously contemplated regret may never be successful, disapproving of what seems to be a redundancy and thus a deficiency of memory in the Mishnah. However, as the conversation develops, Second Character justifies the redundancy to suggest that one can genuinely regret a sin that was regretted prior to committing it, but that regretting it would work only once.[26] The concern is that as contemplating regret in advance becomes habitual, the sinful act also becomes habitual and thus can no longer be understood as a sin, therefore leaving no room for regret.

Both the first and second positions of Second Character imply certain assumptions about the existence of a person in time. Time, as the Platonic tradition has it, is an image,[27] and time therefore can be as deceptive as any other image. Conceptually, the first position suggests that if you already have understood your act as sinful, you cannot commit such an act and also defer regretting it to the future. However, the second position suggests that postponing regret until after sinning still does not jeopardize true regret, even after the fact, as long as the sin is discerned as a sin. However, repeating deferred regret makes sinful acts habitual, thus no longer affording either the discernment of sin or genuine regret for that sin.

Conceptually, the core question dividing (and therefore tying together) these two positions is that of the (im)possibility of genuine change of one's thinking and feelings over time—the (im)possibility of *metanoia*. The first position restrictively assumes human identity and human views of one's act as intrinsically timeless: understanding an act as sinful (or as not sinful) would be timeless, as well, meaning it cannot genuinely change. Therefore, if you have understood an act as sinful, but still have committed it, you have left for yourself no room for regretting it, now or later. That first position assumes no radical difference between the past and the future, because both belong to one and the same dimension of human existence: time.

The second position, in contrast, takes the past and the future to be two different dimensions of human existence, therefore no longer implying that time is one universal dimension. On that view, there is a significant difference between discerning an act as sinful before committing it and interpreting the act as a sin after the fact. The divide thus concerns the question of whether the terms "past" and "future" express time as *the* dimension of human existence (a position supported by a long tradition from Augustine to Heidegger)[28] or, alternatively, whether "past" and "future" amount to two different dimensions of human existence, thus making time a derivative of one of these dimensions, a derivation of the future, as Hermann Cohen and Heidegger had it.

Even if the first position equates the past with the future and the second highlights the difference in these two dimensions of human existence, in both positions, regretting always concerns past actions, retrospectively reevaluated as sins. Regretting also may intimate something about one's future, even if, and indeed precisely because, regret is neither a promise nor an implicit, let alone explicit obligation not to repeat the sin. Instead, according to the second position, regret has a much greater power—the transformative power of changing the nature of past actions, that is, their initially being without sin, and creating a new past in which the actions now were sinful, thus breaking free from a past, something that the first position does not allow.

This transformation implies that the past is open. This is possible only if the past is understood precisely as a "power" that may or may not have a hold over one in the present, rather than as the mere content of "what was." Seen as content, the past remains open for interpreting it anew. However, seen as a power, the past remains independent of any specific interpretation. Even if any particular interpretation of the past may claim to grasp the content of the past in its ultimate truth, the power of the past exceeds all particulars of interpreting "what was," thereby granting a person the possibility to break free not only from the old past by reinterpreting it—here, by reinterpreting it as a sin—but also from the new past, because the new past is likewise revealed to be as relative as the old.

Personhood between Aesthetics, Rhetoric, and (the) Talmud

What, then, are the implications of Losev's aesthetics and the Talmudic aesthetics of personhood for a "new" thinking sought by Heidegger, Levinas, and other participants in the fundamentals debate? The preceding analysis of Talmudic and pagan aesthetics as never fundamental, undoing the possibility and canceling the vacancy of any fundamental discipline, complicates the broader discussion of the relationships between the disciplines of philosophy, rhetoric, and aesthetics. In the fundamentals debate, Kant's and post-Kantian aesthetics already were an intrinsic part of those disciplines, as well as modern scholarship on the Talmud (if only implicitly), and (this time explicitly) in Losev's analysis of pagan aesthetics. To address these disciplines in the entirety of their respective scopes and interactions, I both follow and depart from John Poulakos's map of the relationship between philosophy, aesthetics, rhetoric, and, as his map importantly highlights, poetry, in order to isolate the way in which that map is changed by the personhood-based aesthetics that emerges both in Losev's analysis of pagan aesthetics and in the renegotiation of his analysis in application to the relationships between rhetoric and aesthetics in the Talmud.[29]

Poulakos's interpretation of rhetoric as the "depth" from which Kant's aesthetics originates provides a point of view from which we can discern how competing notions of personhood complicate the more general map of the relationship between rhetoric and aesthetics.[30] In play are the three aesthetics of personhood: Kant's notion of the individual as the subject of reason; Losev's notion of personhood (*lichnost*), which neither centers on nor begins with an individual; and the Talmud's notion of personhood as a different way of an individual's participation in thinking.

The key element on Poulakos's map is poetry. For him, aesthetics emerges from and changes the relationships between rhetoric, poetry, and philosophy. His map is initially framed by the figure of Alexander Baumgarten as the recognized father of modern aesthetics. For Baumgarten, the difference between poetry and rhetoric is one of degree, but between the latter two and philosophy is one of quality. The role of philosophy is to guide poetry in how to discern and describe concepts in an area that philosophers traditionally had neglected, the area of sensations. The problem that Baumgarten helps solve by means of this thesis is how to describe in a rational, philosophical way those areas of sensation in which concepts are not simply hidden or blurred in their habitual uses, but are also evasive and even subverted, due to the alleged irrational and/or "singular" nature of sensational experience in individuals.

For example, how is one to describe in rationalistic, philosophical terms the undeniable sense of color, which is not reducible to numbers, wavelengths of light, or coefficients of refraction? For Poulakos, poetry is the answer, because it is best suited to describe that aspect of sense, is not completely foreign to the language of rhetoric, and a philosopher, even if traditionally despising rhetoric, understands the language of rhetoric and so via rhetoric can understand poetic language as the language of sensation. Thus, rhetoric serves as a lingua franca in which a philosopher can talk to a poet, helping the latter to discern and describe concepts in the midst and mist of sensations. In this example, the poet thus needs the guidance of the philosopher, and rhetoric provides tools for making that happen, thus also making philosophical guidance of poetry feasible in the form of aesthetics. For Baumgarten, a radically new discipline of aesthetics becomes possible: as both a theory of sensation and a theory of the beautiful (the "perfect," in Baumgarten's terms), uniquely positioning it to become a theory of the sensation of the beautiful and thus provide a way for rationalist philosophy to police the irrational nature of sensation as experienced by individuals.

That prepares for the emergence of Kant's aesthetics. With the arrival of Kant's *Critique of Judgment*, the map undergoes a drastic change. Kant "rescue[d] aesthetics from the tenets of rationalism,"[31] Poulakos writes: "'The feeling of the subject' could now claim independence from the tenets of traditional [that is, "rationalist"] philosophy and logic."[32] There is of course more to that change, and for the purposes of my argument, a further explication is necessary. While for Baumgarten, rhetoric was simply a convenient instrument by which, theorizing sensation in aesthetics, a philosopher could teach concepts to a poet and thus impose rational discipline on the unruly sensations, for Kant, beauty, and thus aesthetics, become the core of transcendental philosophy.

The transcendental dimension of experience, the dimension not given in sensation itself, guarantees the independence of the feelings and sensations of the subject of reason, so that the subject's free moral judgment is not the result of the imposition of one individual's opinion on another. Kant's transcendental philosophy becomes impossible without accounting for aesthetics, and in particular without the "subjective universal" as a "symbol," as opposed to a "schema," in Kant's terms.

A schema is "a concept that the understanding has formed, and the intuition corresponding to it is given a priori," as in the concept "dog" as Kant treats it in the *Critique of Pure Reason*: "The concept 'dog' signifies a rule according to which my imagination can delineate the figure of a four-footed animal in a general manner, without limitation to any single determinant figure such as experience or any possible image that I can represent *in concreto*, actually presents."[33] Once again: We call a dog anything that appears to be a dog. It is a concept of the understanding, not a judgment in the realm of pure reason. By contrast, as Kant explains it in the *Critique of*

Judgment, a symbol is "a concept which only reason can think and to which no sensible intuition can be adequate." A symbol "is supplied with an intuition that judgment treats in a way merely analogous to the procedure it follows in schematizing." It does so "in terms of the form of the reflection rather than its content." Words such as "*foundation* (support, basis) . . . express concepts not by means of a direct intuition but only according to an analogy with one." In these terms, "the beautiful is the symbol of the morally good." Unlike a claim such as "I like this," which is no more than an assertion that something appears to me to be likeable, the judgment "This is beautiful" stakes a claim for universal assent, just as the claim that something is morally good stakes such a claim.[34] The claim "This is beautiful" thus serves, for Kant, as a template ("symbol") for the "subjective universal," that is, for the independent moral judgment of the subject of reason, At stake here, as in Chapter 1, is no less than the contrast between free moral judgment and the imposition of "positive" moral and/or religious values, which is one of the central stakes in Kant's philosophy.

The claim "This is beautiful" is far more than an expression of a feeling or affect. As a universal rational statement, a subjective universal, it is an invitation that the claimant sends to others in the hope that it can be universally accepted by virtue of rational judgment. This is in no way an imposition by force of affect,[35] let alone by force of authority. In the same way, in order to avoid the "positive" imposition of a rule or judgment from without, a free moral judgment must follow the symbolic structure of the subjective universal in the aesthetic claim of beauty. This is why Kant's aesthetics becomes one of the central elements of his transcendental philosophy. Unlike the claim "This is beautiful," the claim "I like it" leaves anyone to whom it is addressed with only three possibilities: to share the feeling of liking, to refuse that feeling, or to maintain tolerance, masking, as it often does, mere indifference to the feelings of others. Exclusively controlled by the affect of liking, these choices leave no room for a genuinely free rational judgment. Of course, in poetry, the sense of beauty must come via the allegedly genuine production of an allegedly independent individual, rather than result from a manipulation a skillful rhetorician exerted on feelings and affects of the audience. Certainly, in a traditional philosophical allegation that Kant might still share, rhetoric imposes and manipulates feelings, and therefore, along with the "Jewish Law" would be criticized by Kant as "positive." However, only genuine poetry can witness or even produce an authentic, that is, a nonmanipulative sense of the beautiful not imposed on the subject by another, and only that kind of beauty can adequately symbolize a genuinely free moral judgment, leading to a genuine moral action. This is why poetry in the form of the aesthetic claim of beauty lies at the formal core of Kant's transcendentalist philosophy.

In this new, transcendentalist dimension of aesthetics, aesthetics cannot be traced back to its origins in the tradition of rhetoric. Yet the centrality of aesthetics in Kant's transcendental philosophy does not mean a full departure of aesthetics from rhetoric. As Poulakos shows, even if Kant, like other philosophers, "dismisses rhetoric arbitrarily,"[36] he still affords rhetoric a conditional acceptance. Rhetoric, for Kant, must be "disinterested," to use Poulakos's term. In other words, it can be accepted into philosophy to serve the needs of aesthetics, as long as the use of rhetoric is not motivated by "one's own purpose." A good use of rhetoric that combines "force and elegance" is therefore to be included in aesthetics. "Force" would thus mean the force of delivery that the subjective universal requires, and "elegance" would thus mean producing the sense of beauty.

Yet is it indeed merely because rhetoric can be "disinterested," or is it rather, and more precisely, because, if motivated by any external "purpose," rhetoric defeats the authentic purpose of Kant's categorical imperative to act so that the maxim of one's will can be a foundation of general legislation? That formal, symbolic element remains underemphasized in Poulakos's otherwise correct reconstruction of Kant's aesthetics in its connection to rhetoric. Kant clearly endorses rhetoric that does not manipulate, deceive, or otherwise rob an individual's emotional and intellectual freedom and that therefore is a "manifestation of artistic expression, the result of mental clarity, linguistic dexterity, imaginative resourcefulness, and ethical standing."[37] Is this, however, merely a matter of "disinterest"? It would seem, on the contrary, that "disinterested" rhetoric for Kant serves a particular kind of interest: maintaining the social bond between subjects of reason who freely arrive at universally shared judgments of value.

In Poulakos's reconstruction, "disinterestedness" has to do with the *topos* of common sense in the classical rhetorical tradition. That includes the common sense about what is or is not beautiful, according to him. For Kant, the rhetorical *topos* of common sense "sustain[s] the social character of human beings and enhance[s] their communicative faculties."[38] As the result, we can "estimate whatever enables us to communicate even our *feelings* to everyone else."[39] One might say that in this formulation, "us" means "we humans." But more precisely, it means subjects of reason, in Kant's sense, which can include nonhumans, as well, but which can also exclude those humans who do not subject themselves to the limitations of reason and rational knowing, those in thrall to "positive" impositions of judgments of value from without.

The difference between the subjects of reason and those who only appear to be human, but do not act as subjects of reason, is one of the ways in which the other others are excluded from the world controlled by representation and thus by beauty. By the logic of the exclusive inclusion of the subjects of reason, appearing human or even being recognized as having a face (to whatever extent, as a human, as a dog, or even as a snake) does not protect the other others from being excluded from society on the grounds of the subjectivity of reason and its aesthetics.

If to employ common sense in the judgment of beauty is to "sustain the social character of human beings," then to make a judgment of beauty is to be a member of a society, rather than simply to be among a crowd of people feeling or sensing the things "commonly" or along the lines of their common affect and/or common sense. This is because claiming "It is beautiful" involves the possibility of sharing or not sharing that judgment. By contrast, claiming "I like it" either involves nothing and nobody else in particular or else invites another to share or not share the affect of "liking," leaving no room for judgment and no room for a genuine social life, except in the sense of an emotional bond.[40] Such a bond lacks the formal transcendental and free intersubjective judgments of value that characterize subjects of reason at large.

To illustrate that point in even more technical and therefore more concrete terms, as Poulakos notes, "for Aristotle, all rhetorical appeals, including the appeal to one's sense of beauty, are grounded in the commonly held beliefs (*ta endoxa*) of the audience"[41]—that is, they are grounded in some kind of preexisting commonality of sense, literally, the "common sense" of what is beautiful and more generally of what is. That is the basis for the possibility of an allegedly "disinterested" rhetoric. However, for Kant, the beautiful as a symbol of moral judgment cannot be based on the shared *ta endoxa* of the audience, but rather only on the formal act of inviting others to accept the universal judgment "This is beautiful," freely arrived at by every subject of reason. The opposite, for Kant, would once again be the claim "I like it," which, at best, invites sharing an emotion, yet offers no subjective universal judgment. Offering no judgment, "I like it" therefore must appeal only to *ta endoxa*, which is not the case with Kant.[42]

What would then be its place?

Unlike Kant's aesthetics, as other research on the relationships between rhetoric and the Talmud has shown,[43] the aesthetics of the Talmud does not exactly come from the same "depths of rhetoric" as Kant's.[44] The similarities and differences between Kant's and Losev's aesthetics helps shed light on those depths in the Talmud. Charting those depths requires us to redraw the map of the relationships between rhetoric, poetry, philosophy, and aesthetics.

What Losev's construction of ancient aesthetics and Kant's transcendentalism share is the tradition that both ancient aesthetics and ancient rhetoric deal with the possible, as distinct from the impossible and the necessary, not just with persuasion and the manipulation of sense and affect alone. Indeed, Kant's transcendental aesthetics informs Losev's inquiry into the philosophical aesthetics of the ancient world. Conversely, it can be argued that Kant's transcendental aesthetics follows the same lines of the possible as Aristotelian rhetoric. In judging both the universal and the beautiful, Kant is concerned with the possibility (and not the necessity, let alone the impossibility) of an individual willing to become the foundation of universal judgments of value. If instead the individual were to insist on the necessity of either a moral or an aesthetic judgment, it would require imposing the individual's opinion on another by force of persuasion alone. Even if that traditionally was a philosophical misconstruction of rhetoric, Kant's turn to the possible in both aesthetic and moral judgment directs him away from that tradition. In this Kant is congruent with both the Aristotelian and the Talmudic versions of rhetoric, and thus with Talmudic aesthetics as well.

However, the centrality of the aesthetic for the subject of reason in Kant illuminates the point at which Losev's pagan aesthetics, though post-Kantian in its origins, parts ways with Kant's view of aesthetics. That parting of the ways concerns the notion of personhood. Kant's subject of reason always stands at the center of the possible, in the middle of the process of rational thinking, while inviting other subjects of reason to share that position by the logic, or rather by the rhetoric of the possible. In contrast, the personhood of the Losev's *lichnost* not only never stands at the center of the possible, but it also does not entail the existence of any center or any fundamental position whatsoever, even in the "pagan" version of reason, which, in Losev, emerges in the name of the tripartite *nous* of Iamblichus.

The Talmud shows yet another configuration of personhood: an individual participating in the memory of the open past, in which no person stands at the center, either in the space of remembering or on the sites of thinking that are remembered in the process. As I argued earlier, the aesthetics of the Talmud thus advances a conception of personhood that differs significantly from both Kant's transcendentalist subjectivity and also from Losev's pagan Neoplatonic ideal of personhood. That difference charts an important aspect of the changing relationships between aesthetics, rhetoric, poetry, and philosophy. For Kant, as Poulakos highlights, "rhetoric is the art of transacting a serious business of the understanding as if it were a free play of imagination; poetry that of conducting a free play of imagination as if were a serious business of understanding."[45] By contrast, the Talmud displays the art of transacting the serious business of remembering the past as if it was the free play of imagination in understanding the refutation of another understanding. That emphasis on the free play of imagination transforms the rhetorical operation of refutation into what now can be understood as a genuinely poetic form, a form of which the Talmud is an example. Unlike Kant, but not unlike Losev's aesthetics of "pagan" Neoplatonism, in the Talmud, the configuration of rhetoric, aesthetics, poetry, and the rational discourse of a dynamic personhood operating in the form and for the purposes of memory and remembering leaves no room for any fundamental discipline as a way to think[46] or rethink[47] either human being or any other subject of reason.

The Talmud thus also emerges as an example of the political performed along the lines of personhood and interpersonality, rather than of the subject and intersubjectivity. In the next chapter, I explore how the interpersonal political exemplified in Talmudic and Neoplatonic thought makes its way into medieval commentary on the Talmud, despite the commitment of the tradition of medieval Talmud commentary to the philosophy of Aristotelianism interpreted, at the time, along the lines of the thinking subject and subjectivity at the expense of personhood and interpersonality. A seemingly marginal case of apodictic irony, which next chapter introduces and addresses, will help illustrate how the interpersonal political performed though rhetorics and aesthetics of the refutation of a refutation develops in and despite an environment of the predominantly logical-philosophical conception of subjectivity. In this context, the question of certainty comes to the fore as soon as one notices traces and thus the effacement of the interpersonal political in the domains of logic, ontology, or aesthetics.

While in logic, ontology, rhetoric, and aesthetics, the subject positions (indeed, centers) herself in the coordinates of the possible, the impossible, and the necessary (what is necessary and impossible for logic and/or ontology and what is possible for rhetoric and/or aesthetics), in (the) Talmud, personae, rather than subjects, pose and dispose themselves eccentrically and/or ecstatically by replacing the possible by the refutable and counterrefutable, the necessary by the irrefutable, and the impossible by the fully refutable. Through an analysis of a fourteenth-century case of Talmud's interpretation, the next chapter will allow us to begin to understand this (inter)personal disposition of personae in the late-ancient Talmud as the site of the vanishing and appearing of the other others, those who have no representation, but still resist the ongoing process of their effacement. That is, it will allow us to understand better the interpersonal as an element of the political in the Talmud.

CHAPTER 5

Apodictic Irony and the Production of Well-Structured Uncertainty: *Tosafot Gornish* and the Talmud as the Political after Kant

This chapter embarks on the difficult task of capturing a moment—one instantiation—of the effacement of the intrinsically interpersonal character of the thinking process displayed in the Talmud's late ancient text—the effacement of the interpersonal by the (inter)subjective. As the analysis in Chapters 3 and 4 helped us to see, the interactions between the characters in the Babylonian Talmud are interpersonal, rather than intersubjective. They involve refutations and counterrefutations in which either single or multiple personae participate, but no individual subjectivity stands at the center of any given movement of refuting or counterrefuting. By the same token, these interactions do not allow for the intersubjective universality of either subjective or objective judgment, such as respectively, the subjective universal judgment "This is beautiful" or the objective judgment "Two plus two equals four."

Talmudic Irony

One way to capture a moment of the effacement of the intrinsically interpersonal in the Talmud, a moment in which the interpersonal character of the encounters in the Talmud simultaneously both emerges and disappears, that is, becomes noticeable at the moment of its disappearance, is to examine an instance in which the interpersonal is effaced by both the intersubjective and the ironical. We have already addressed the issue of subjectivity and intersubjectivity in relation to the Talmud. Here, we address the rhetorical issue of irony.

Scholars of the Talmud have so far conceptualized the interpersonal conversations there as dialectical. In its most precise form,[1] such a conceptualization means that these conversations are ironic rather than intersubjective. In other words, they do not perform a "dialectical" exchange between the two subjects who at the end come to share either an answer to a question or an understanding of why that answer cannot be reached (an aporia). Instead, dialectics here leads to Socratic irony. In reference to the interpersonal exchanges in the Talmud, "dialectical" does not mean that a subject (say Socrates) wins the argument against another subject (say Phaedrus). Instead, it implies a political engagement (in Rancière's terms) in which Socrates assumes that Phaedrus is pregnant with a truth and then "helps" Phaedrus to deliver it. Ironically, however, the typical outcome is either that Socrates delivers no final truth, no healthy baby, or, if the delivery is successful, the baby does not belong to Socrates. Thus, Socrates represents (in Schmitt's terms) a position with no content, an ethical and political position in which the truth is that he still does not know the truth. He merely invites others to offer truths for him to consider. Unlike what Kant would envision, Socrates does not invite others to share knowledge and/or judgments with their interlocutor; rather, he remains in the position of wanting to commit but ultimately not committing to any particular truth or judgment whatsoever. What that means, however, is that despite the seeming open-mindedness of Socratic dialectics, the outcome of his interaction with his interlocutors is established in advance: The interlocutors lose, which sometimes also means opening up the position of the latter to give way to a truth, that is, to the content of some particular final truth-claim or judgment, but these are things to which Socrates still will not commit, because this is not his political role in either Schmitt's or Rancière's sense. The outcome of Socratic dialectic is established in advance, but ironically, what is determined is not any particular truth or judgment. Applied to the Talmud, that very general portrayal of dialectical irony means that despite the seeming open-mindedness of all discussions in the Talmud vis-à-vis any statements in the Mishnah suggesting a diversity and even a contrariety of opinions and/or rulings, as Daniel Boyarin argues, the outcome of the Babylonian Talmudic dialectics is established in advance: The Mishnah and all opinions therein must win, just as Socrates always does. But ironically, the onstage characters in the Babylonian Talmud, do not commit to any of the claims they advance in the course of refuting and counterrefuting the reports of the Mishnah. What is more, they even openly smile at themselves and at their ways of initially attacking but ultimately defending the Mishnah. They offer multiple ways of counterrefuting the same refutation, thereby acknowledging that no counterrefutation is serious enough to be seen as fully sufficient. This openness shows "a smiling face,"[2] and this smile is not always ironic. Looking at this smiling face, one can hear loud laughter; more often than not, that laughter transgresses the limits of irony and reaches what I will soon, following Lieberman and Boyarin, address as satire.

In broader strokes, while Socratic irony begins from the hope to arrive at certainty about what is the case in each case, as opposed to what seems to be the case in each case, and even if it also always ends up maintaining a distance from any particular result achieved, the onstage characters in the Talmud work very hard to begin precisely where there is no longer any hope for ontological, let alone commonsense closure. They start or aim to start where such hope no longer possible. It is at this point of no hope for any ontological and/or commonsense closure that they show the Mishnah to be a valid and authoritative intervention. This is also precisely the point at which irony borders satire: The onstage characters maintain an ironical distance from any result, and indeed from any turn of the argument in their refuting and counterrefuting of the Mishnah, but they also position themselves beyond irony—precisely because they strive to envision the Mishnah as a just action where there is no initial hope for certainty—a political position that is therefore beyond irony.

The ways in which Talmudic irony is like Socratic irony require further articulation. Socratic irony is ironic because while seeming open-ended, the outcome is determined in advance, for Socrates always wins, but what is determined is not any particular truth claim or judgment, because what Socrates does is interrogate truth claims and judgments, not endorse any of them. Similarly, for the onstage characters in the Babylonian Talmud, the Mishnah always "wins" or at least is supposed to do so, since for them, the Mishnah must be proven to be authoritative, and any refutation of it must be met with a counterrefutation. Socrates and the Mishnah always win; in this comparison, the question then is: What is the parallel in the Talmud with the Socratic refusal to endorse any particular truth or judgment arrived at dialectically? This parallel has two aspects.

First, in the Talmud, the onstage characters' main modus operandi is refutation and counterrefutation, which by definition implies no endorsement of any particular statement except for the purposes of refuting and counterrefuting. There is no commitment to the referential aspects of any case, only to refutation and counterrefutation. Second, and most interesting, just as Socrates's irony is a formal political act, not an endorsement of any content, so too, based on how they approach the Mishnah, for the characters in the Talmud, the Mishnah is a formal political act, albeit in a radically new sense that neither political theology nor political ontology can fully grasp and that therefore does not lead to Socratic irony. Instead, it leads to satire.

This political act is an intervention in response to and a creation of a break in the commonsensical and/or the ontological discourse of justice. More specifically, and as the readings in this chapter help illustrate, these characters approach the Mishnah's instructions as interventions made where and when common sense no longer suffices to resolve an issue, a conflict of interests, or the competing claims of litigants in a just manner or with a reasonable certainty.

As I will explain, that political act creates a distance from any argument or any conclusion the characters in the Talmud propose or react to or arrive at in regard to the Mishnah. When common sense proves not enough to arrive at justice, Socrates would offer a dialectics of hope as ironical as it proves to be—to distinguish what is the case in each case as opposed to what seems to be the case in each case. The characters in the Talmud, instead and in parallel, see the Mishnah's instructions as pertaining precisely where there neither is a way to distinguish what is the case in each case as opposed to what seems to be the case in each case, nor any other way for the judges to rely on the hope for arriving at such a distinction or for the certainty it would promise. Instead, the characters direct their efforts of refuting and counterrefuting to prove that the Mishnah's instructions are political interventions, interruptions of common sense or of the ontological order of the world. The Mishnah intervenes both to create and to remedy such an interruption. What that means, however, is that the duality of creation and healing the interruption is already a step beyond irony and toward satire.

Yet there is more. One and the same instruction in the Mishnah can be construed as such a political intervention in the ontological order of justice in more than one way. None of these multiple ways becomes final, let alone immune to being either refuted in the next move or counterrefuted in the move after that. Not only do the characters do not own their arguments and therefore to do not endorse them, not only do the characters posit no intrinsic end to the chain of refutations and counterrefutations through which they proceed, but they also keep their distance from any particular way in which the dance of refuting and counterrefuting advances.

It is therefore both necessary and insufficient to say at this point that just as all the characters participating in Socratic dialectics work hard to discover the truth, all characters the Mishnah work hard to prove that it can be defended against any thinkable refutations of its contents and that in that way, Talmudic dialectics resembles Socratic dialectics in that both are ironic. Rather, it is not just that in straightforward irony, what appears to be an open-ended process is not, but that Socrates maintains an ironic distance from the particular truths or judgments arrived at by the dialectic that he initiates and shapes, and irony is quintessentially the trope of distance—of surface meaning versus the depth of what's meant. So too, in Talmudic dialectics, it is not only about refutation and counterrefutation of the Mishnah's content, but is also about ironical distance the characters in the Talmud create between the content and the authoritative power of the Mishnah. They strive to prove the latter with as much variation in the former as has been identified so far or could be claimed in the future. That power is in the Mishnah's formal status of an intervention where common sense does not suffice, not in how specifically that intervention occurs. The characters find such an intervention authoritative there and only there where they find common sense insufficient to resolve a particular issue, a conflict, or confrontation of litigants. It is thus not only about remembering, but also and first of all about establishing the Mishnah as a formal political action, the intervention where common sense fails, which is at the same time the creation of such a failure, a failure that the characters in the Talmud commit in potentially infinite number of ways without committing to any of those ways.

Neither political theology nor political ontology can fully account for the Mishnah as a political intervention beyond either common sense or the dialectical irony of justice as its extension. Such an intervention responds to and creates points at which common sense proves insufficient or at which uncertainty about its application becomes unavoidable. In other words, for the characters in the Talmud, the Mishnah instructs (or if you wish, strikes) precisely where ontology-grounded dialectical discourse of justice fails. What creates ironical distance, however, is not just in identifying such an intervention but also in maintaining that the same instruction in the Mishnah can entail several such interventions, to none of which any particular character in the Talmud will commit.

Thus, just as all the characters participating in Socratic dialectics work hard to discover the truth, all characters in the Mishnah work hard to prove that the Mishnah can be defended against any thinkable refutations, and in that way establish the Mishnah as a political intervention, and the act of justice there where certainty can no longer be gained. The result is programmatic distancing from any particular truth-claim, and or argument. In that sense of a distance, Talmudic dialectics resemble Socratic dialectics. Yet, as Boyarin further argues, there is a radical difference between Socrates and the rabbis. For the former, irony is a "serious" political-philosophical position. For the latter, what underlies irony is something much less "serious": satire. As the anecdote with Rabinovitch illustrates in the modern context, satire in the ancient context is of course no less of a formal political power than irony. Yet satire does not draw on the solid positions that "seriousness" implies. Rather, in satire, there is no solid ground on which, say, Schmitt's idea of representation or Rancière's idea of "disagreement" relies. Nor is there a strong commitment of a person to any position that such a person advances. The only strong element in play is refuting the position of the other person by thinking along the lines of that person's argumentation.

The interpersonal political in the Talmud does not resemble either the intersubjectivity of post-Kantian philosophy or Socratic dialectics/irony, because as Bakhtin, from whom Boyarin draws his notion, argues, satire explodes the subject and subjectivity, or at the very least, involves a distancing from and liquidation of the solidity of any serious commitment to any particular claim or judgment, lest the claim or judgment becomes either a dogma or a manifesto of relativism. What is there to explode or liquidate if, in the interpersonal encounters in the Talmud, a subject is not involved in the first place? Satire does presume the seriousness of a steadily established political subject—a subject to be attacked. Yet what if, in the interpersonal, there is none to begin with?

What follows in this chapter is a case study of both appearance and disappearance of that interpersonal ironical-satirical move in the Talmud at the moment of a logical-mathematical interpretation of the Talmud's irony by *Tosafot Gornish* in the fourteenth century—an appearance and disappearance that becomes noticeable only with the advent of universal (inter) subjectivity after Kant. We will see how satire vanishes from the horizon completely and irony becomes dressed in the iron cladding of universalist logical thinking.

Apodictic Irony: Tosafot Gornish

The site of the effacement of the interpersonal by the intersubjective to which I attend here is called *Tosafot Gornish*, a fourteenth-century logical commentary on the thirteenth-century commentary on the commentary of the Talmud. I read that document as a program of apodictic irony. Its program is apodictic, because it seeks to explain each choice of a particular way to conduct a rhetorical argument in the Talmud in terms of the logical necessity of that choice. It involves irony, because it seeks to read the arguments in the Talmud as ways to move one's interlocutor from what seems to be true opinion to a logically correct standpoint, as Socrates typically does and as philosophy has does since Plato. The program's main highlight is the notion of a well-structured uncertainty, which the commentary helps to discern as the logical ideal of interactions between the characters—judges and witnesses in the Mishnah that the personae in the Talmud discuss. Well-structured uncertainty emerges as a way to avoid either the dogmatism of complete certainty or the complete uncertainty of relativism.

In reading the Talmud as a case of apodictic irony that leads to a well-structured uncertainty, the rhetorical-interpersonal in the late ancient texts of the Talmud becomes reduced to irony, and the logical-apodictic becomes as a way to explain the logical perfection of each of the moves in dialectical/ironical arguments that make what is uncertain well-structured. In that way, the logical (and by implication intersubjective) is promoted as the ultimate virtue of any given move in an argument between personae in the Talmud. Thus, the *Tosafot Gornish*'s logical reading of Talmudic arguments both constricts their interpersonal rhetoric to the logic (and irony) of intersubjective necessity and reveals the otherwise unnoticeable logical irreducibility of that rhetoric to any philosophical account of relationships between logic and rhetoric in the Aristotelian tradition.

In the *Tosafot Gornish*, logic deals with the necessary and the impossible by eliminating it, letting rhetoric deal with the possible. At the same time and by the same token, that move modifies the distinction between the necessary and impossible, on the one hand, and the possible on the other, when it comes to interpersonal encounters in the Talmud. The impossible is replaced by fully refutable, the necessary by irrefutable, and the possible—the traditional domain of Aristotelian rhetoric—by the never-stable balance of the refutable but defensible, thus simultaneously opening up and shutting down a glimpse of the interpersonal in the Talmud's rhetoric, which had disappeared already in the medieval commentaries on the Talmud and again both reappears and vanishes in *Tosafot Gornish.*

The trajectory of that double move is the effacement of interpersonal rhetorical encounters between personae in the Talmud behind the intersubjective reading of these encounters under the rubric of apodictic irony. The outcome is a view of the interpersonal discussions in the Talmud as aiming at what, from a logical standpoint, is as a well-structured uncertainty, a balance of refutations and counterrefutations, with each being logically the best and thus necessary way to do what it does, to the exclusion of what is logically certain or apodictic.

The Effacement of the Effaced

Chronologically, the effacement of the interpersonal in the intersubjective, of satire in irony, and of the ecstatic dance of the interpersonal in well-structured that is to be found in the *Gornish* occurs in what according to scholarship on the history of Talmud and its interpretation immediately precedes and informs the theory of disagreement as a goal of discussion advanced in *The Ways of the Talmud* by Rabbi Isaac Canpanton (d. 1463) in the fifteenth century, which thus can be seen as the effacement of an effacement. If *Tosafot Gornish* shows the effacement of Talmudic satire by logical irony, that effacement in turn becomes effaced by how *Tosafot Gornish* was seen in light of its later reception: as a marginal predecessor of what later became central, Canpanton's normative view of how to read the late ancient Talmud and commentary.

In Canpanton's view, disagreement becomes the goal of discussion and the truth criterion of what the late ancient Talmud is. His view also provides a normative and thus stabilizing sense of what it means to study ("learn") the Talmud "appropriately," or in his own terms, how to scrutinize (lit., "contemplate") arguments therein, a technique that generations of Talmud scholars thereafter assumed. However, this stable and stabilizing normative view emerges at the moment and at the price of effacing another, no less precision-oriented approach and/or style of commentary on the Talmud and the Talmud's interpreters, which the *Gornish* displays. Canpanton's reading of the Talmud promotes creativity and innovation on the side of the reader, which he then hopes to ascribe to the Talmud itself, the *Gornish* limits their task to describing analytically each move in the Talmud's arguments, validating no creative impulse. The approach of the *Gornish* consists in logical commentary on every rhetorical move of the argument in the Talmud and its interpretation; more generally, it is an attempt to measure the rhetoric of the Talmud by Aristotelian logic, which as I will argue, becomes tacitly modified when applied to commenting in the Talmud, if not on the Talmud's interpreters. Unlike how it has been evaluated in the little scholarship it received so far, I will discern that approach in its own right, rather than as a mere predecessor of Canpanton's normative and stable view of the Talmud's learning.

The goal of this "pre-Canpanton" logical commentary on rhetorical argumentation was not simply to measure but also to justify rhetoric by logic. Here it means justifying rhetorical arguments as logically necessary, or apodictic. In particular, that means proving apodictic necessity in choosing to conduct a given rhetorical argument in this and only this way at the exclusion of any other possible way. It is an attempt to discover logical necessity, rather than rhetorical arbitrariness, behind every rhetorical argument in the Talmud and in its interpreters.

That also means a complete lack of interest in developing any new rhetorical arguments or in deriving any further conclusions from the arguments in the Talmud. Devoted so strongly to the logical necessity of every rhetorical move in the Talmud and its interpreters, the practitioners of that approach are at all not interested in deriving any further conclusions from the already existing rhetorical arguments in the Talmud or commentary and even less so in deriving any new rhetorical implications for these rhetorical arguments. To draw a rough comparison with the language of geometry, one might say that the *Gornish* is an attempt to analyze each move in the proof of a theorem without ever attempting to prove any new theorem. It is an attempt to take up what is naively obvious, to prove that it is not obvious at all, and to end up by showing that it is indeed "obvious," that is, provable and logically necessary—apodictic. In sum, it is a logical commentary on the Talmud, an attempt to justify rhetorical argumentation as strictly logical rather than "merely" rhetorical.[3]

The Talmud after Kant

The *Gornish* thus is a site of effacement that in turn becomes effaced in Canpanton's appropriation of it. Yet, as I have noted, each single effacement is by necessity a bidirectional move in which what appears as new is clearly discernible only in light of what is effaced.

More broadly, reading the *Gornish* in terms of this bidirectional movement thus must proceed from modern problems to ancient texts and from ancient intellectual disciplines and practices to modern problems. Enacting such a bidirectional move leads to two questions: how classical rabbinical texts resist and escape the political theology exemplified by the work of Carl Schmitt and the political ontology developed by Jacques Rancière in modern political thought, and how the lens of modern political thought helps discern that power of resistance in late ancient rabbinical texts.

Following the logic of this bidirectional move, this chapter presents a case study or, to borrow a term from the New Criticism, a "close reading" of the *Tosafot Gornish*, which, according to its genre and chronological time, is a logical commentary on the late medieval rabbinic commentary on the Talmud, the *Tosafot*.[4] This case study will show one of the initial instances of the effacement of the interpersonal political by the intersubjective, an effacement observable in the way in which logic or apodictic thinking becomes conjoined with a rhetorical trope in many ways opposed to logic: irony. Logical apodictic thinking demands, in the same way in which Kant's judgment of beauty does, all others to share in it, leading to an ultimately attainable logical (apodictic) certainty and on that basis establishing the intersubjectivity of subjects controlled by logic. In this way, differences between thinking subjects can become overcome by shared and logically (again, apodictically) controlled thinking. On the other hand, irony absolutely requires that the many do not become one, even if, as it will turn out in this particular case study, logical apodictic thinking would still attempt to control the differences involved and even if it attempts to do so programmatically, without any legal or other practically applicable results.

The commentary of the *Tosafot Gornish* provides a marginal and therefore telling case in which these two apparently different positions intertwine, resulting in the peculiar combination that I term "apodictic irony." However, because, as already explained, I can make the case for this characterization only by negotiating modern and ancient contexts, my argument has both a modern and a late ancient component. In its modern counterpart, Kant's transcendentalism and subsequent modern notions of intersubjectivity to which it led—including the political thought of Schmitt and Rancière—can be understood as a response to the dilemma of dogmatism versus skepticism,[5] or, in the theological terms that Kant used, between anthropomorphism and deism.[6] If so, and if the latter two are versions of what Kant criticized as "positive" religion[7] and "Jewish" influence, then the commentary of the *Tosafot Gornish* represents another way of out of the dilemma of dogmatism versus skepticism: apodictic irony, which, unlike Kant's transcendentalism, does not involve and is not involved in the logic of supersession.

What is more, apodictic irony and the well-structured uncertainty that it creates belong to and modify what, by the logic of effacement, appears as an older and broader line in rabbinic tradition of irony as distinct from satire[8] as different ways to understand the political. To continue with the example with Socrates and to juxtapose it to the Talmud, Socratic irony is a political action, according to Rancière, because it is a discussion about common good. The characters in the Talmud, however, as Daniel Boyarin has argued,[9] might still be ironical in the "dialectical" parts of Talmudic discussions, but are satirical in the "narrative" parts. The "dialectical" parts are "ironical" because despite the seeming open-endedness of the dialectical arguments, their end is presupposed: Ironically, the Mishnah and all possible divergences and disagreements therein are in fact to be proven defensible, one way or another. The narrative parts are "satirical," revealing the lack of any seriousness about the dialectical arguments, which their "ironical" tone still presumes—they laugh out loud. The commentary, however, looks for logical apodictic grounds in the ironical parts, thus remaining completely blind or deaf to the satirical component in the "dialectical" parts of the Talmud.

The seriousness of the apodictic thinking in the commentary of *Tosafot Gornish* completely occludes the satirical element of the Talmud. And yet, however hard the *Gornish* works to take irony seriously and thus reduce it to logic, the *Gornish* commentary does not achieve such a reduction. Instead, the commentary both recognizes the demand for logical irreducibility in the position and arguments of one person vis-à-vis another and looks for the logical necessity by which each person has chosen his or her way of arguing as compared with other logically possible ways. Thus, the apodictic and the ironic contravene one another, but without any full-fledged conflict or contradiction, because, after all, dialectical irony, in its classical form, does presume interlocution and the irreducibility of the interlocutor's positions and/or standpoints.

The result is that apodictic irony in the *Tosafot Gornish* is a political form that is different from the medieval political-theological forms that Schmitt described. The peculiar political form of apodictic irony in the *Gornish* commentary is an opening through which it becomes possible to discern the effacement of the interpersonal political on the way from the Middle Ages to the early modern period and the modern form of the political as grounded in the intersubjective. The *Gornish* interprets the Talmud logically by first construing the Talmud as irony, for logic can attempt to measure irony, but cannot attempt to measure satire as "apodictic." In sum, highlighting the effacement of the interpersonal and the resulting image of the effaced as ironical-dialectical provides a viable alternative to Kant's transcendentalist solution to dogmatism-skepticism dilemma.

It thereby yields a new insight into the nature and history of political thought.[10]

The late ancient and early modern component of my argument is that apodictic irony emerges in the *Tosafot Gornish* against the broader backdrop of how irony and satire were used in late ancient rabbinical thought. Apodictic irony first emerges as a marginal case as compared with what can be found in other Talmudic commentaries of the late medieval and early modern periods between the tenth and fourteenth centuries. These commentaries are too serious to be ironical, let alone satirical in their tone. However, the marginal position of the *Tosafot Gornish* among classical Talmudic commentaries makes possible what otherwise might not have come into being, the study of the Talmud through a process of *contemplation* or עיון. However distinct from the apodictic irony of *Tosafot Gornish*, its subsequent appropriation led to the formulation of what I would briefly define as Aristotelian Talmudic rationalism, a position in studying and interpreting the Talmudic text that—as many researchers of the Talmud and its interpretation agree—became one of the cornerstones of many subsequent and of all dominant schools of Talmudic interpretation and that therefore was often taken for granted and not widely studied.[11] The times and places of appropriation of that new approach to the Talmud and its study ranged from the fourteenth to the nineteenth century in the European and West Asian countries in which the Talmud was studied in rabbinic communities to the study of the Talmud in universities during the most recent two centuries. In sum, in the late ancient and early modern component of my argument, I examine what first emerged as a marginal line of study and then became one of the taken-for-granted and thus forgotten cornerstones of subsequent Talmud interpretation.

Capturing the elusive moment of the effacement of the interpersonal political by intersubjective in the *Tosafot Gornish* commentary will help articulate an alternative to the political theology of Carl Schmitt and the political ontology of Jacques Rancière. For Schmitt, the particular disagreements or divergences of positions or claims in everyday political life lie outside of and are secondary to what he understands as the political. For Rancière, disagreement in the sense of *mésentente*—dissent and discord—both permeates and grounds economic, social, and other orders and dimensions of life, and disagreement and the uncertainty it entails remain disturbances impossible either to tolerate or too eliminate. As I read the *Tosafot Gornish* commentary, a different view of political form will emerge in which disagreement (in this case in relation to apodictic certainty) combines with a broader view of irony, which the logic of certainty attempts to explain, as well as with a view of the satire in the interpersonal encounters in the Talmud, which the logic of that logic occludes.

Dogmatism versus Skepticism after Kant

Schmitt and Rancière think in a context defined by subsequent versions of Kant's transcendentalism as a response to the dilemma posed by the alternatives of dogmatism and versus skepticism.[12] In response to a skeptic's criticism of dogmatism's promotion of obedience to absolute statements and principles, the dogmatic argues that denying anything the status of an absolute is an absolute statement and thus self-refuting. Kant addressed this traditional dilemma in a radically new way. In transcendentalism, he found a way to address what is immanent in experience, but nevertheless independent of experience and in that sense absolute and unchangeable. He thus proposes transcendentalism as capable of justifying both scientific knowledge of the world and one's ethical behavior vis-à-vis other rational and moral beings, who are also subjects of reason in Kant's sense of the term.[13]

The notions of political form articulated by both Schmitt and Rancière can ground the political only if they are understood as transcendental forms, permeating all economic, state-institutional, or other spheres of life in a society yet without being located in a sphere separate from these.[14] They are immanent in the world of everyday political life, but not grounded in any sphere beyond it.

Although Kant's transcendentalism provides a way out of the dogmatism-skepticism dilemma, what in everyday life is regarded as morality, religion and law are dogmatic, not transcendentally grounded. They are "positively revealed law," and, by extension, positively formulated moral rules or religious norms of behavior. Anthropomorphism and deism, for Kant, exemplify two extremes of such "positivity" thinking of G-d.[15] Their "positivity" consists the use of images and the faculty of imagination to produce "schemata" for ethical and religious behaviors, actions, and judgments. As Kant puts it in the *Critique of Pure Reason*, "schemata" "serve only to subordinate appearances to universal rules of synthesis, and thus to fit them for thoroughgoing connection in one experience."[16] Thus, "The concept 'dog' signifies a rule according to which my imagination can delineate the figure of a four-footed animal in a general manner, without limitation to any single determinant figure such as experience or any possible image that I can represent *in concreto*, actually presents."[17] Schemata thus deal with appearances, not with absolutes, that is, with judgments regarding being or nonbeing. They do not rise to the level of the universal judgments of reason. By the same token, both the possibility of deciding on an exception from the legal order in view of an emergency, for Schmitt, and the unavoidability of disagreement, for Rancière, are efforts to liberate the legal order from that "positivity." The schematic application of concepts to intuitions leaves no room for genuine disagreement, to speak of Rancière; and, as for Schmitt, it is only by going beyond the schematic understanding of the law as "positive" that one creates room for the decision on the state of exception, rather than following the schematic rules of positive law, for schemata allow no decisions, only the correct or incorrect applications of rules.

For Kant, if in the matters of morality and religion one thinks in schemata, that is to say in direct applications of concepts to intuitions, one becomes either a dogmatic or a relativist, and in application to thinking G-d, either a deist or an anthropomorphist. Jewish religion in its entirety and some of Christianity fall into this category for Kant. In their place, he proposes "religion within the limits of reason alone," a religion that is good for all subjects of reason, human or not, with the very important exclusion of those humans (or others) whose religion and morality involve schemas, not symbols—those whose understanding of the good and the beautiful is determined by rules, not the freely arrived at judgments of reason. That move in Kant follows the theologem of supersession in which the New Testament supersedes the Old Testament and Christians as Israelites in spirit supersede Jews as Israelites in the flesh: the Old Testament and Israel in the flesh become stepping-stones for the New Testament and for Israel in spirit. In that theologem, the New Testament must both reject and retain the Old Testament, and Christians must do the same to the Jews. Similarly, a certain group of others (human or not) must be a stepping-stone for the advent of genuine subjects of reason (again, human or not). Those who appear to be human, but are not subjects or reason must be both rejected and retained, so that the subjects of reason can include those who do not appear to be human. This is very similar to how Christian theology treats "Jews" as an irremovable stepping-stone toward Christian identity.

To situate the case study at hand in the modern context, this particular implementation of the logic of supersession through schemas versus symbols in Kant demands more detailed interpretation. In Kant's first *Critique*, "schemas" are images through which concepts fuse with intuitions,[18] resulting in partitioning the experience into distinct participants and distinct matters with which these participants interact. "Symbols" work differently—by analogical association. As I noted in Chapter 4, for Kant, there can be symbols not only for concepts but also for judgments. Because symbols are concerned with form, not content, the structure of one judgment can be a symbol for the structure of another. That is why the judgment that something is beautiful can serve a symbol for the moral judgment that something is morally good.[19]

Once again, the distinction between schemas and symbols in Kant already implies the dismissal of "Jewish law," either Mosaic or rabbinic, as "positive."[20] If universal legal, moral, or political concepts cannot be attained in schemas, but only in symbols, the Mosaic Law, including its rabbinic extension, the Talmud, as well as the dogmatisms or formalisms of positive Christianity (for example, rituals) are, for Kant, confusions resulting from mistaking a schema for a symbol, for example, mistaking the descriptions of G-d in the Bible, however carefully interpreted, for G-d. Deism and anthropomorphism are Kant's examples of such a mistake. Kant's solution of the dilemma of dogmatism versus skepticism thus requires the denial of Jewish Law as "positive" as opposed to transcendental.

However, the rabbinic tradition can be read in a way that yields a solution to the dilemma of dogmatism versus skepticism without entailing the opposition between positive and transcendental law. An elided alternative to that opposition consists in resisting understanding rabbinic tradition in either of the senses of "law," positive or transcendental. What then are the conditions of possibility of reaching beyond the dogmatic versus the skeptical and the positive versus the transcendental? As the case study that follows will suggest, the answer involves a version of rabbinic irony, the apodictic irony in the *Tosafot Gornish* commentary.

Rabbinic Irony, Satire, and "What Might Have Always Happened"

Irony emerges in Plato as a way of attempting and failing to move from what seems to be to what is. As I have noted, Daniel Boyarin has argued that if Socratic irony drives the dialectical-technical parts in the Talmud, the narrative parts are satirical, and that satire reveals the hidden side of what otherwise looks as only ironic: the satiric foundation of Talmudic irony as distinct from ironic foundation of Socratic dialectics.[21] In the view on the Talmud that the *Tosafot Gornish* helps illuminate, irony (albeit not satire) in the Talmud differs from Socratic irony. In the rabbinic exegetical tradition, irony serves to maintain a well-structured uncertainty as the foundation of moral action—a position that defies the philosophical denigration of sophistics as immoral relativism, but at the same time that escapes the dogmatic commitment to certainty.[22] Boyarin interprets Talmudic irony thematically as satire and programmatically as using sophism for the sake of morality as distinct from its immoral use for any purpose whatsoever and from the philosophical ideal of certainty guaranteed by what is.

Irony (and satire, which it occludes) in combination with well-structured uncertainty, however, are only one aspect of the ways in which the rabbinic exegetical tradition points to an exit from the dilemma of skepticism versus dogmatism that does not involve Kantian transcendentalism. Despite all differences between dogmatism, skepticism, and transcendentalism, all three treat memory and remembering within the scope of the question of what is (or was) versus what seems to be (or seems to have been). The alternative entails treating memory beyond the ontology of what is.

In this perspective, memory can be seen as a third way where Aristotle saw only two, only poetry and history. There can be a third option—call it, for now, ironical memory. For Aristotle, history is an account of what happened, and poetry of what can always happen. Accordingly, he privileges the latter as both more pertinent and more precise. In contrast, memory, understood in light of irony, would be an account of "what might have always happened." In application to the reading of the Mishnah in the Talmud, that means "what the Mishnah might have always been addressing, and in particular refuting." That would be a poetic—and, in particular, an ironic—reading of history.

In the late ancient texts of the Talmud, the path for ironic memory is paved by the chains and branches of heuristic refutations and counterrefutations of the Mishnah or other records of the rabbinic tradition. However, both medieval commentary of the *Tosafot* (a running commentary on a commentary on the Talmud) and the *Tosafot Gornish* commentary on it do not quite follow that path. Unlike the characters in the Talmud, for these commentators, both the Mishnah and the Talmud are axiomatically authoritative—and thus very serious—givens to be understood, but in no way questioned in terms of their authority, not even provisionally. That leaves no room for irony, let alone satire, in these commentaries. Instead of questioning authority, the *Tosafot* engages refuting and counterrefuting of the Talmudic arguments across the corpus in order to maintain intellectual coherence of all potentially relevant arguments in the Talmud, now assumed to be a finished product—a codex, a book.

The Case of the Tosafot Gornish

The *Gornish* is concerned with providing mathematical or logical apodictic grounds for the *Tosafot* commentary on the Talmud. The Tosafists, in their analysis of the Talmud, attack and defend the coherence of the characters in the Talmud and their dialectical-ironical arguments across the corpus. In turn, the *Gornish* commentary addresses the apodictic foundations of each refutation and counterrefutation that the Tosafists advance in their commentary on that dialectics. The analysis or justification of the refutations and counterrefutations of the Tosafists often means attempting to provide logical apodictic grounding for the dialectical refutations in the Talmud, as well. But unlike the *Tosafot* commentary on the Talmud, the *Gornish* commentary is not concerned with counterrefuting all refutations—a concern specific to discussions in the Talmud, although not so comprehensively as in the *Tosafot.* Nor is there in the *Gornish* any concern with the rhetorical closure of the commentary for the sake of the "coherence" of all arguments in the Talmud, which is the concern in the *Tosafot* commentary. Instead, the *Gornish* commentary microscopically, mathematically investigates each move in the *Tosafot* commentary and the pertaining moves in the Talmud by focusing on the logical-mathematical or apodictic foundations of each of these moves. The *Gornish* thus makes no new progress in the legal discussions that are being conducted in the other texts, but the progress already made is now mathematically dissected, thereby making progress in comprehending the progress already made.

In the *Gornish* commentary's approach to both the *Tosafot* commentary on the Talmud and to the dialectical-ironical (and, in its narrative, satirical) dance of memory in the Talmud, the apodictic certainty of mathematical thinking helps to attain and ground a well-structured uncertainty as a foundation for just action on the part of judges.

Due to the complexity of the case, I first present the *Gornish* argument in a form of libretto, and then proceed with a close reading.

Gornish: A Play in Four Prologues and Five Acts

Libretto

Stage direction: Place: a courtroom. Chronological Time: undefined.

Personae: Judges; Witness 1; Witness 2; Defendant; Rabbi Meir and Rabbi Yehuda in part *in absentia.* All are characters in the Mishnah.

Rabba and Abaye, authorities in the Talmud; a *tanna* or a reciter of the Mishnah in the Talmud.

Tosafists, the medieval commentators on the Talmud.

Gornish, an early modern commentator.

Implied Analytically Minded Reader of the Mishnah, Talmud, Tosafot, and *Tosafot Gornish.*

Modern Post-Kantian Critical Reader.

Prologue in the Third Century

The judges confront a pair of witnesses whose testimony shows discrepancies in terms of days of the month or hours of the day when the purported crime occurred. The judges wonder if they must consider the witnesses' testimony to be refuted, based on that discrepancy in their words, and thus to dismiss them, or whether they must ask further questions to see if the discrepancy in dates and times was the result of a mistake that people commonly make.[23] With neither common sense nor any ontological consideration yielding a certain and just solution, the judges turn to the Mishnah for instruction. The Mishnah instructs them about different types of discrepancies and respective actions. On one particular discrepancy in dates—the third versus the fifth of the month—the Mishnah records that Rabbi Yehudah instructs differently from Rabbi Meir. That discrepancy both displays and emphasizes that no common sense and no universal judgment are capable of resolving the issue, or so must be the working assumption in the Mishnah.

Prologue in the Fifth or Sixth Century

In the Talmud, Abaye attempts to reconstruct Rabbi Yehuda's and Rabbi Meir's competing assumptions about the margin of what can be considered a common mistake. Rabba criticizes Abaye's reconstruction and (perhaps mockingly, that is more than ironically) offers his own, instead. He does so by grotesquely, that is satirically, enlarging the margin so that there remains almost no practical relevance in the difference between the correction of a common mistake and letting the witnesses change their testimony by answering further questions.

Prologue in the Seventh Century

Students in a rabbinic academy reconstruct Abaye and Rabba's argument as these students discuss whether the *tanna*, the reciter, reported the Mishnah correctly. The implied reader is presented with two reconstructions of Abaye's position and with one of Rabba's. The characters, including the implied reader, get the feeling that the recitation of the Mishnah is defensible, after all. The irony in this argument undermines Abaye's reconstruction of the difference between Rabbi Meir and Rabbi Yehudah in the Mishnah by attempting to follow that strategy to its grotesque end. Yet despite, and precisely due to that satirical tone, the students, and the implied reader, however, get the feeling that the polemic between Abaye and Rabba makes the *tanna*'s witness of the Mishnah reliable. The Mishnah is shown to be reliable precisely because common sense or ontological reasoning leaves the characters with nothing but the satirical cancellation of any hope for certainty. That makes Mishnah's intervention necessary and its memory justified.

Prologue in the Thirteenth Century

The Tosafists, for whom all of the above takes the form of a book or codex, which they call "The Talmud," study each page to establish the correctness of each relevant argument across the whole of the text. They come across the events described in the "Prologue in the Seventh Century" and discover a logical incoherence between the argument that is made there against allowing correcting common mistakes and another place in the Talmud where the very same statement of the *tanna* is used to allow for common mistakes and reaching the opposite conclusion from the same premises. (There is no longer any ironical let alone satirical undertone at this point.) In order to make sure that the argument in the "Prologue in the Seventh Century" is possible, the Tosafists also employ a certain reading of the Mishnah in which there is a logical inconsistency between the situation addressed in the Mishnah and the ruling that the Mishnah offers: The ruling in the logically applies to a different situation, not to the one being addressed at that point in the Mishnah.

The Tosafists defend the Mishnah and the Talmud against these attacks. To that end, they suggest distinctions between a nominal mistake, common as it might be, which, if a witness (directly or indirectly) corrects it by answering the next question, entails no effective change in the claims the witness makes and a mistake whose correction the judges cannot classify with certainty as merely correcting a nominal mistake, so that by answering further questions, the witnesses actually might be changing their testimony without the judges being able to tell if that is happening. The inability to do so leads the judges to dismiss the witness, because the judges cannot allow for a witness to in effect change his or her testimony, even if that is only as a possibility, without potentially favoring the witness against the defendant.

The Tosafists solve the problem proposing that in the second instance, the judges must dismiss the witness, but in the first, they may continue interrogating the witness, as is concluded in the other place in the Talmud. The formal distinction between the ability and inability of the judges to tell the difference between a correction of a commonly made mistake and effective change in the claims of a witness results in preserving the harmony and coherence across the two remote pages of the book, the Talmud.

Act 1. Gornish Studies the Tosafot *Commentary on the Talmud*

It is the fourteenth century. On stage is an unknown human entity, the composer of the *Gornish* commentary. Gornish—let it be her name—thinks mathematically or logically. The objects of her thinking, however, are rhetorical refutations and counterrefutations performed on the previous stages, as seen in the prologues. (The ironical, let alone satirical, component of these refutations has totally vanished from her view.) Gornish seeks apodictic logical grounds for each rhetorical move of refuting and counterrefuting. One way to do that is to prove each move to be justifiable against any other logically possible way of committing a move with a similar rhetorical function in a given context. Gornish attempts to explain the selection of a given choice as compared with other possible ways, which she thereby considers to be logically deselected.

Step by step in the acts that follow, Gornish prepares her implied reader to approach the *Tosafot* in such apodictic mode of thinking by giving apodictic scrutiny to the logical (de)selections of the language in the Mishnah. To that end, Gornish proves that the cases that the Mishnah omits (deselects) are omitted on logically conceivable, or apodictic, grounds. It is what that process produces that is important—what I have been calling "well-structured uncertainty" about both the Mishnah and its application to the case in hand.

Act 2. Why One Counterattacks as Opposed Another?

Gornish wonders why, in the last prologue, the other Tosafists (whom she peculiarly calls "Talmud") responded to the attack of the Tosafist Rabbi Yehudah ben Eliezer on the Talmud the way they did, as opposed to another logically possible way. She is curious about this (de)selection.

Act 3. A Twilight Attack on the Tosafot

In the previous act, Gornish wondered why the Tosafists selected one way of attacking the Mishnah and its analysis in the Talmud as opposed to another logically possible way. As opposed to the deselected one, the selected way was an attack based on equal possibility that the witnesses understand or do not understand the intricacies of transiting to a new month, when courts, not calendars, regulate the transition—that is, when a new month is proclaimed in court versus when it actually begins, based on that proclamation. The deselected alternative was an equally possible attack based on the naturally conceivable mistake of not knowing which day it was at twilight, between the sunset and the appearance of first stars on the sky, a time when the old day is ending and a new one begins.

Act 4. Apodictic Reformulations

Gornish returns to the beginning of the *Tosafot* commentary to justify—logically—what for the implied reader might sound like an extremely unusual attempt of the *Tosafot* commentary to attack the wording of the case in the Mishnah, in the first prologue, the "Prologue in the Third Century," bypassing any attacks on it in the Talmud itself, as if the Tosafists acted like rabbis in the Talmud. That attack claimed the ruling in the Mishnah did not match the case that the Mishnah addressed. what is unusual, indeed, outrageous for the implied reader, is the *Tosafot*'s reformulation of the actual language of the Mishnah, even if only for the purposes of an attack. This, in the eyes of such reader, is beyond the authority of the Tosafists. Gornish solves that problem by proving that despite the tactical rhetorical use the *Tosafot* gives to the scandalous reformulation, logically, the original and the reformulated wording remain the same. What rhetorically looks like an outrageous violation of the lines of authority logically represents a mere repetition of the same thing in different words. The authority of the *Tosafot* is thereby saved in the eyes of the implied reader.

Act 5. All Stages Fade to Black

A contemporary, post-Kantian reader remains alone.

The end.

There emerge pertinent lessons that the post-Kant audience can derive from the play, even if able to watch closely only a selection of it. To navigate these lessons, in the pages below, I provide an analytical exposition, a closer examination of the penultimate act of the full play, Act 4.

Given the complexity of the original text, I undertake an analytical exposition of the text, rather than interpreting the original text in translation, because at least in this case the conventional format of translation would hide the interpretation behind the illusion of an approximated original. Instead, I take inspiration from how Picasso interprets but does not translate *Las Meninas*. He moves through a series of analytical expositions rather than offer a single copy of the original. What follows is to be taken as one such exposition, even if the full series is not present. I present an analytical exposition of Act 4 of the *Gornish* commentary as a point of view from which to look at all other stages, because in navigating the Act 4, the implied reader goes through the stages attuning that attune such a reader to the analytical, apodictic mode of thinking.

Gornish first attunes the audience to an analytical-apodictic mode by way of a simple, indeed artificial exercise: reading a line in the Mishnah. The Mishnah says, "One [witness] says [I saw it] on the second [day of the month] etc." Before proceeding with the words of the Mishnah, Gornish asks about this simple case of logical (de)selections. Why does the Mishnah list this day but not that day, or more broadly, select this but not that date as an example? The characters in the Talmud commonly ask similar questions about the Mishnah. Yet these characters no less commonly respond by undermining the question's power rather than by offering a direct answer. In contrast, the *Gornish* commentary takes up the question directly and provides ("exacts") an elaborate, full-fledged answer by revealing the apodictic justifications for each example in terms of why it was selected and why another logically possible example was deselected. That way, each selection, and in particular, each omission becomes a logical deselection and thus receives a logical explanation, which justifies if not the logical necessity. then at least the logical viability of any given (de)selection. Thus, Gornish argues,

> "One says [I saw it] on the second [day of the month] etc." That sounds a little bit strange, for why did not it start from the first of

> the month?—Seemingly this is because of the presumption that people do not usually mistake the date right in the beginning of the new month. For the same reason, we can explain why the Mishnah started from the second and third hour, too. And when done with the third, it went to the position of Rabbi Yehudah on [the discrepancy between] the third and fifth [among the witnesses;] and when having finished with the fifth, it went, similarly, to the fifth and seventh. That [explanation] survives even if, as the Tosafot say later on in regard to the witness, one never doubts there might be a confusion (of hours) when the sun stands in the middle of the sky; AND THIS NEEDS FURTHER EXACTION.

Through this artificial exercise in what was not a real problem but only an "a little bit strange" set of selections, Gornish helps the implied reader to expect that there must be a logical, apodictic ground behind any explicit selection, including any implicit (de)selection of an example (a particular date or hour) that the Mishnah addressed. More broadly, this simple exercise of Gornish is to signify for her implied reader that there is apodictic logical dimension of (de)selections behind what otherwise would be only an empirical set of word choices.

The reader is now prepared for more serious tasks of logical analysis, but not yet for approaching the direct target of the *Gornish*, the *Tosafot*. Instead, by way of further preparation, the *Gornish* reveals other apodictic elements in play. These elements are the logical impossibility or logical necessity behind any seemingly questionable choice of strategy on the side of any given refuter in the Talmud, if the latter attacks the Mishnah in one way, but, could have conducted the same attack in a seemingly even more effective way. In other words, the focus is now on the logical impossibilities or necessities of deselections in each attack and defense in the Talmud. The apodictic justification of a deselection now switches from (de)selecting examples to deselecting ways of refuting that the characters in the Talmud employ. Gornish addresses the analytical reader to this effect. To understand this address, however, we first need to gloss involves some legal idioms.

In the address there are two technical terms, *ibbur* and *hazzamah*. *Ibbur* can refer either to the legal process of transitioning to the new month on the decision of court on seeing new moon or to the old month being a "full" month of thirty days, as opposed to a "short" month of twenty-nine days, again on the basis of a court decision. It is the task of the analytical reader to decide which of these meanings applies. The term *hazzamah* refers to refuting a witness by claiming that the witness was not at the scene of the crime at the time when the witness says the crime happened. Thus, Gornish further says,

> [PROBLEM:] The justification in the Mishnah of why if one says [it happened] on the second and another on the third of the month is not [considered] a prohibitive discrepancy between the witnesses is that "This one knew of the *ibbur*[24] of the month. . . ." Such a justification is refutable. It is because just as below when the Talmud refutes "how can we then find *hazzamah*[25] in hours" the refuter here, too, could have used the same argument in application to "on which date of the month"—to argue that the witness, too, can say "I have just made a mistake in the *ibbur* [thus becoming no longer vulnerable to *hazzamah*]."
>
> [SOLUTION:] It seems to me that it was better for the Talmud to attack the case of [the discrepancy in] the hours [between the two witnesses in the Mishnah] by using the argument of losing [the witnesses'] vulnerability to *hazzamah* even when there is an [unwanted] possibility of retroactive correction of [the allegedly real] mistake. However, in the case of dates of the month, if one [of the witnesses] said [it was on] the second and another on the third [of the month,] then if the witnesses have consequently [i.e., after more questions] indicated the same date, there is no longer an (unwanted) possibility of retroactive correction [of the witness by one of the witnesses] and thus [unlike the deselected target, the discussion of hours in the Mishnah] the breakage [of the witness, that is, the necessity of dismissing this pair of witnesses] due to [their] invulnerability to *hazzamah* [is not an issue.]

Gornish claims that the refuter in the Talmud must have logically selected the more difficult target, the case of the discrepancy in hours, and deselected the easier target, the case of days, thereby covering both. This is why the refuter selected the example of dates of the month rather than hours of the day.

Gornish then continues and concludes with yet another possible logical reason for deselecting the discrepancies in dates and selection of hours:

> Additionally, perhaps, the refuter thought that because vulnerability to *hazzamah* is necessary from the fifth hour or from the sixth hour [when sun is high and a mistake in hours is easy to make] it is the same as vulnerability to *hazzamah* of the day [that is, there is no room for the unwanted retrospective correction]. AND THIS NEEDS FURTHER EXACTION.

This last move affords Gornish the explanation that the refuter in the Talmud deselected dates in favor of hours because these would be logically "the same" in maintaining the witness's vulnerability to the allegation of having been absent in order to maintain the witness's credibility. That means there indeed was no deselection, for logically, both the selected and the deselected were "the same." Whether by the first or the "additional" way of explaining, the result to which Gornish leads the implied reader is that there indeed was a logical basis, a logical necessity, by which the character in the Talmud, the "refuter," selected one approach to attack or refutation over the other.

Gornish has just posed the problem of the deselection of a refutation and solved it in two ways, thereby preparing the implied analytical reader for the next, considerably more dramatic step, which occurs when a similar problem of (de)selection has no solution. The context in which the problem arises is the following. The Mishnah explains why, despite the discrepancy in testimony by the witnesses between whether it was the second or the third of the month when events occurred, they still allowed to testify. The Mishnah says that it is plausible "that this one knew of the *ibbur* [and this one did not]." On that, Gornish says the following.

> [PROBLEM:] And [what] if one will object, Why do I need this particular reason [in the Mishnah] if even when both of them knew of the *ibbur*, their witness would still to be sustained [in court]—because perhaps the [alleged] crime fell out [between sunset and first stars] when the second day was ending and the third beginning, in which case there is no way [for the judges] to say [to themselves] people do not make common mistakes of confusing the day and the night. In any case, let us say the event fell out in the twilight, and one witness thought it was still the day [the second in the month] and another that it was already the evening of [the third].

The first part of the problem is why the Mishnah deselected the seemingly more plausible option—that both witnesses had the same level of knowledge about new month, but one witness was just confused by it being twilight.

> Similarly, [one may object] why, Rabbi Meir [in the Mishnah] according to Abaye [in the Talmud] cancels the witness if one says [the alleged crime was] on the third and another on the fifth? Indeed, perhaps the one who said on the third referred to the very end of the third, and the one who said on the fifth referred to the very beginning

of the fifth, so the discrepancy between them is due to a mistake of one day [only, which would thus still be within the margin of common mistake] and if we defend that by arguing "this one knew of the *ibbur* and the other did not," then there is no way to say they both were indicating the same date [and thus there is no danger of unwanted retroactive correction of the witness, so their testimony is to be sustained in court, not dismissed or "cancelled" as it is in Rabbi Meir in the Mishnah]. What is more, this, too, could be called a confusion between day and night, for one thought it was still day and another that it already was night [of the new day]?

[SOLUTION:] [None is provided]

In the first part of the problem, Gornish attacked the deselection of the more viable logical explanation in the Mishnah. In the second, she attacked Abaye's explanation of Rabbi Meir's dismissal of the witnesses on the grounds of the discrepancy between the two witnesses of the third versus fifth of the month. At stake is the same issue of the unwanted retroactive correction of a witness. The problem is that on Abaye's interpretation of Rabbi Meir, this problem does not pertain, thus making the interpretation invalid, if one allows for the concern with retroactive correction of the witness that the commentary of the Tosafists has advanced. The other part of the second problem is almost verbatim similar to the first problem: Why assume what the Mishnah assumes if another, better selection is available? Despite the provisional solutions considered, they are dismissed, and Gornish leaves the implied reader to contemplate the full glory of a logical problem with no solution.

The implied reader will have learned by now that positing a problem, even if without solution, is of value for understanding logical (de)selections that the characters in the Talmud have made. That helps prepare the implied reader for the next, even more important step. Understanding the stand-alone logical value of the problem of (de)selection prepares the implied reader to go where Gornish was leading in the first place: to an apodictic reading and in particular for a direct apodictic attack on the Tosafot commentary on the Talmud. Having trained her reader in the logical analysis of (de)selections, Gornish now approaches her main target, the role of (de)selections in how the Tosafists conduct their own attacks on the Talmud.

The *Gornish* will now attack the attack that the Tosafists selected to approach the Mishnah. Ultimately, as will momentarily become clear, the

Tosafists attack the ways in which the Talmud approaches the Mishnah as the Talmud draws conclusions from it. Gornish says here:

> [PROBLEM the Tosafists posited: A *rule* does not fit the *justification*] [On the *rule* in the Mishnah "This one says on the second day and this one on the third. If so their witness is still sustainable," and on the *justification* of it in the Mishnah, "because perhaps one knew about the *ibbur* (meaning either transitioning to the new month from the full thirty days of the old, one as opposed to twenty-eight or twenty-nine) and another did not."]. The Tosafot wrote: "such would be the rule, if the Mishnah said this one knew about the shortness of the month [and this one did not know the month was short]."

The problem here is that the Mishnah's rule that the judges are not to dismiss the pair of witnesses if one said the crime was on the second and the other on the third of the month does not fit the justification that the Mishnah provides for it: that "one knew of the *ibbur* of the month and another did not." An effective justification would use *kizzur* (shortness) of the month, not *ibbur*, which in this context must mean the "fullness" of the old one, not "transition" to the new. As already mentioned, the implied reader, if accustomed to Tosafot commentary, would be shocked to see the Tosafists offering an emendation to the Mishnah, even if only tactically. This is the traditional prerogative of the characters in the Talmud. Perhaps this is why what Gornish presents as an attack on the problem is her way of alleviating the surprise by suggesting that there might be a logical justification for it. As she will show, there is.

> [ATTACK ON THE PROBLEM] You should wonder what the Tosafot invent thereby. [ELABORATION ON THE PROBLEM] It looks like they found it hard to explain why the Mishnah [later on in its discourse] ruled to dismiss the witnesses, when one says on the third day of the month and another on the fifth. For why would not the judges [in the Mishnah] assume each witness made a mistake in one [day of the] month only. For example, if one [month] was full and another short; and one witness thought both were full, and another that both were short.[26] And this is *the question* the Tosafot were responding to by saying "if *the situation was* of that sort, their witness would have been true [and, contrary to the Mishnah, sustainable, rather than cancellable.]" Yet matters would not be of "that sort" at all, (and the problem would not arise) if [as the Tosafot propose the Mishnah should have had it] one witness knew of the shortness of the month and the other

did not know the month fell out short. [Such is the concern of the Tosafot.]

[SOLUTION] It seems to me that the opinion of the Tosafot is as follows:

[ELABORATION on how the Mishnah's *rule* would fit its *justification* in the Mishnah, according to the Tosafot commentary] Such would be the *rule* in the Mishnah if and only if the *justification* said, "this one knew of the shortness of the month [and the other did not know the month fell out short,]" meaning that the reason the Mishnah did not say so was [simply] because one [logically] depends on the other: for the witness who knows of the *ibbur* [meaning "the announcement of the transition to"] the new month must also know the month fell out short, because it is logically impossible that a witness got the *ibbur* (in the sense of announced transition) but did not [also] get that the [old] month fell out short.

[SOLUTION] On these grounds, one can never make such a mistake [of assuming the month was full when it was not.] And without such a mistake being [logically] possible, there is no way to assume dependence on such a mistake either, for the argument of the Tosafot was [precisely] not to assume the dependence on each witness having made a mistake, as per how the Tosafot built a defense below according to Rabba. AND THIS NEEDS FURTHER EXACTION.

The necessary and the impossible are heavily in play here. What the *Tosafot* presented as a reformulation of a *justification* in the Mishnah (from "it may be that one witness knew the month was *full* and another did not" to "it may be that one witness knew the month was *short*, and another did not" was, as Gornish tells her implied readers, the introduction of two logically, apodictically identical statements. The effect of introducing a deselected logical equivalent was to disambiguate the term *ibbur.* When readers of the Mishnah juxtapose *ibbur* to *kizzur* (full versus short month), the Mishnah loses the connection between the rule and the justification of it. Under such a mistaken reading, there are two opposing formulations of the Mishnah. Yet if reader understands *ibbur* as "transition," the second reading (with *kizzur,* or short month) is logically identical with the actual one with *ibbur,* because they by logically *necessity* come together, and are logically *impossible* to separate. And this is precisely the "invention" that Gornish shows her readers: *ibbur* here means "transition," thereby also by logical necessity meaning *kizzur* as well.

What the implied reader learns from this passage is not only that behind every logical analysis of the (de)selection of the formulation of the Mishnah by the Tosafists there must be an invention ("what . . . invent thereby?"), but also that this invention might mean the discovery of two logically identical selections, the originally selected formulation in the Mishnah and advancement of logically identical (de)selection of it by the Tosafists. The deselected option is what the Tosafists retrieve ("invent"—that is, both create and rediscover), for the (de)selected wording of the rule better suits the purpose of the Tosafists' commentary—to prepare the attack on the Talmud in the name of one of the Tosafists' masters, Rabbi Yehudah ben Eliezer.

At this point, Gornish sends the implied reader back to shed the new light of the apodictic analysis of (de)selections on the attack on the Talmud in the *Tosafot* as represented in the second prologue, the "Prologue in the Fifth or Sixth Century." The attack comes in two moves. First, as Gornish has already shown to her implied readers, the empirically given formulation of the Mishnah did not make sense, whereas an alternative formulation does. That will serve as a good preparation for the next step, where her readers will learn how to explain apodictically, that is, in terms of logical necessity and impossibility, the refutation of the Mishnah that Rabbi Yehudah ben Eliezer, an authority among the Tosafists, offers based on two seemingly mutually exclusive uses of the Mishnah in the Talmud. Her reader will further learn how to provide a counterrefutation against what seemed to be logically impossible by a disambiguation of the cases to which two seemingly contradictory derivations from the same Mishnah were applied in the Talmud. This, for Gornish and her implied readers, will logically defend the rhetorical defense that the Tosafist provided in advocating the intellectual coherence of the Talmudic usages of the Mishnah, despite their seeming discrepancy. The implied reader will be sent even further back to follow the light of the apodictic analysis of (de) selections in the midst of the empirical flow of the attacks and defenses in the Tosafot that second prologue represents. In her turn, the modern critical reader who has followed the implied reader is now left all alone, where all stages fade to black.

The simplest and the least precise impression about this drama of the logical defense of rhetoric the modern reader may be left with is a wonder how and why the Tosafists could have reformulated the Mishnah without the authority to do so. In a bit more complex and precise way, the wonder would be: If such a reformulation were a heuristic device for the Tosafists in order to ask a question about or raise a problem with the actual formulation in the Mishnah, as expressed in Rabbi Yehuda ben Eliezer, then why and how did the *Tosafot* empirically depart from, and, as Gornish argues, implicitly logically return to the original formulation of the Mishnah? What is more, why and how does the departure from the original formulation return the implied reader back to that formulation? The reading loop that the *Gornish* commentary builds, away from the original language and back to it, moves from a hypothetical reformulation of the Mishnah, to the cause justifying it, to an explanation of why that hypothetical reformulation is theoretically (that is, with apodictically certainty and thus logically necessity) identical with the actual one, if the implied reader reads the latter correctly, and finally to an empirical confirmation of that theoretical result.

Even with as many apodictic reformulations of deselections as it engages and performs, this trajectory is still animated by the logic of refutation as the foundation of meaning that which we find both in the Talmud and in the Tosafists. Paradoxically, the logical elucidation of the process of refuting ultimately follows the path of refuting. The new element that Gornish brings in is the "theory" of apodictic identity of empirically different languages, an attempt to create a logic of (de)selection behind each move of refuting and counterrefuting. She addresses deselections of language in the composers of the Mishnah, in the works of refuters in the Talmud, and in the commentators in the *Tosafot*, even if the deselected possibilities are no less and no more than discoveries and/or inventions of her commentary, possibilities at which she arrives along the path of refuting. The harmony of rule and justification, of refutation and counterrefutation in the Talmud now emerges as a result of other, logically apodictically retrieved options that the *Gornish* commentary reconstructs, also deploying the techniques of refuting and counterrefuting as the ground of this analytical thinking.[27]

Decision in the Talmud

The apodictic precision that Gornish performs in the play just described and analyzed helps us see the discussion between the characters in the Talmud as a "political form" comparable with and distinguishable, from Schmitt's conception of political form.

What is at stake here is the formal basis on which decisions are made with regard to the law, and what is enacted here is a form of decision that is not based on what Schmitt would call "techno-economical rationality," or what for Kant are merely "positive" rules or protocols. Nor is it based on any ontological or theological claim such as is found in Schmitt's concept of the representation of representation. Instead, it is designed to produce decisions on the basis of a well-structured uncertainty.

The point of view established in the *Gornish* commentary on the Mishnah, on which the characters in the Talmud comment, is no more than a preparation for the *Gornish*'s analysis of the *Tosafot*. From that point of view, the adjudication process in the Mishnah is not rooted in ontological concerns of establishing what happened. Rather, the judges, the implied characters, and in particular implied addressees of the Mishnah, have no ontological concerns about what happened or how to characterize what happened, that is to say about "what *was*" in terms the law.

Instead, they focus on establishing the refutability of a witness's testimony and thereby the creditability of the witness. In an effort to avoid either protecting a witness at the expense of the defendant or dismissing trustworthy witnesses at the expense of justice, what they seek is a well-structured uncertainty about the witness and his or her testimony. To that end, the judges, in this particular case, deal with a formal question of whether they are to dismiss a pair of witnesses who have given contradictory testimony or, alternatively, to continue interrogating the pair, thus trying to eliminate the discrepancy through additional questions.

The general principle at work with the judges, as the *Gornish* commentary helps show, is parallel to the rhetorical emphasis on the possible, as opposed to the impossible or the necessary.[28] Just as the art of rhetoric deals specifically with the possible only by identifying and the excluding the impossible and the necessary, the judges here develop formal procedures enabling them to sort out both those witnesses whose testimony is absolutely refutable (impossible) or absolutely irrefutable (necessary) in order to focus on those remaining, whose testimony may be both refutable and defensible (possible). The formality of the procedure is designed to guarantee that sorting out.

This is a formal concern with where to stop with the questions rather than an ontological or legal concern with what happened and how to characterize that in light of the rules. This formalism entails a way out of dogmatism-skepticism dilemma via an ongoing consideration of the reliability of the procedure of inquiry itself—that is, via a formal emphasis on the nature and quality of decisions. That focus on identifying the possible stands in contrast to any focus on ontology-bound truth-claims about being based on certainty, claims that dogmatism, skepticism, and transcendentalism alike entail. In short, such an approach reveals a political form not predicated on political ontology.

Instead, the political form performed in the Talmud is based on what can be called apodictic precision in the face of radical uncertainty, which becomes the condition on which the judges can decide on the refutability of the testimony of the witnesses, rather than applying rules and statutes. This allows judges to decide responsibly, accounting for the effect of their intervention, rather than mechanically, as if the application of a rule to a case were only a matter of following a protocol. For example, in light of the *Gornish* commentary, the judges do not merely make determinations guided by rules. They do not use the Mishnah as a direct instruction for a mechanically driven action. Instead, they turn to the Mishnah only when they need to make a genuine decision—and, most important, to measure their own responsibility for that decision. The main point of deciding is not about the state of exception from the otherwise regularly applicability of the law, but in making sure the judges do not favor the witnesses over the defendants and vice versa, a requirement that cannot be answered by the obedient performance of a proscribed procedure.

At the center of the decision is the responsibility of the judges in the face of the conflict brought forth in the court, and this responsibility cannot be alleviated by obediently mechanically relying on the Mishnah as a source of direct instruction. The judges in the Mishnah are no more and no less than idealized recipients of its teachings who do not receive a univocal set of instructions. Instead, the decision process about the instruction of the Mishnah is performed in interpersonal relationships between the characters in the Talmud, as well as by the Tosafists, who scrutinize the latter, and to that extent attack the Mishnah, as well. The law as articulated in the Mishnah is a matter of rhetorical elaboration the judges are supposed to master at precisely those points—what may or may not be possible, as opposed to what is necessarily true or impossible—when common sense or, speaking in modern terms, the subjectivity of reason does not suffice to determine a course of just action. In such political form, the characters simultaneously have to validate or invalidate the witness of the tradition in which the law is transmitted and to apply the same process to the witness in the courtroom. The main formal element in the process of deciding is not the voluntary act of proclaiming a decision (comparable to what Schmitt would call declaring the state of legal exception), but the process of discovering if there is anything irrefutable or anything easily refutable in both the testimony and the legal tradition itself with the understanding that either must give way to what is both refutable and defensible.

The resulting decision is a course of action that by excluding the absolutely refutable and the absolutely irrefutable, that is based on a well-structured uncertainty. The judges aim to attain that, because for them, unquestionable certainty about one's action is a guarantee of injustice. The judges, and the political form they perform, thus decide on the creditability of a witness only, not on the case in ontological terms of what was or the positive application of law would to it.

The judges thus perform an interpersonal rather than either a subjective or intersubjective act of decision. This well-structured uncertainty is attained, as Gornish attempts to show, with the limited help of the apodictic analysis that which the *Gornish* commentary commits. The analysis helps not only and not primarily to sort out the absolutely refutable from the absolutely irrefutable, but also, and most important for Gornish, to explain the (de)selection involved in every step of deciding on the law, tradition, and witness testimony. In other words, Gornish discovers the apodictic certainty behind what initially seems, for the implied reader, to be only a rhetorical, probabilistic dance of refuting and defending for the sake of attaining the better memory of the Mishnah.[29] Certainty in their analysis serves only to produce well-structured uncertainty but does not perform it.

The political form exemplified in the *Gornish* commentary implies no grounding of political power in striving for an agreement on the basis claims about being versus seeming. Nor is it an attempt to embrace the unavoidability of disagreement about being, as Rancière argues. Rather, the form of the political based on well-structured uncertainty combines the situational rootedness of a rhetorical discussion of the possible with the attempt to distinguish apodictally the impossible and the necessary from any discussion of the given situation and thus to translate what is possible, impossible, and necessary into what is (respectively) refutable but defensible, ultimately refutable, and ultimately irrefutable.

The form of the political revealed here thus is inherently dialectical-ironic (even and precisely at the expense of occluding any satirical interpersonal foundation therein). It is based on the production of apodictic certainty about what is uncertain, and as a discursive form, the production of well-structured uncertainty can also be ironic.[30] For example, one of the apodictic rules the *Gornish* commentary implies about the Mishnah is the rule that the potential vulnerability of a witness's testimony to refutation actually (that is to say, dialectically-ironically) increases the witness's credibility. The resulting precision about what is uncertain—the production of a well-structured uncertainty, which Gornish sees and promotes as what the Tosafists saw in the Talmud—thus entails what I call "apodictic irony."[31] Unlike Cartesian doubt or transcendentalism's notions of subjectivity and intersubjectivity, which include a hoped for-homogeneity of all subjects of reason through shared (onto)logical certainty, apodictic irony always involves more than one active subject, and for that matter, no collective, let alone homogeneous, subjectivity can be anticipated, demanded, or hoped for. Instead, irony entails a dance of participation, in which and each participant can play any role and any part of any role, while the structure of the dance is not rooted in any rigid distributions of heterogeneous roles of refutation and counterrefutation between individual participants. Even if Talmudic ironical soliloquies already intrinsically require several subject positions, either one or many individuals can perform these positions interchangeably. There is multiplicity of the positions, but no individuality of the positions.

If the political form in the *Tosafot Gornish* commentary fits fully neither to the political understood in terms the representation of representation in Schmitt nor to the political as the art of the possible, but rather advances a view of the political as what mathematics/logic can describe in the irony-dialectics of the refutable and counterrefutable to the exclusion of the irrefutable as necessary and the fully refutable as impossible, then where does it leave the interpersonal political that takes shape in late ancient texts of the Talmud and both appears and disappears in the *Gornish*'s political form?

If the interpersonal political deals with the ironic dialectics of the refutable and defensible as the way to approach interpersonal existence and, thus, to reach the political, and if this is clearly distinct from both the political ontology of the possible in contradistinction from either the impossible or the necessary and from the political theology of primary representation before mimesis, then what does the interpersonal political—including its occluded root in an nonintersubjective satire—mean for rethinking the scope of the modern human and the modern Jew as intersubjective *types*. In the next chapters, I explore this question by looking into the effacement of the interpersonal in modern, post-Kantian constructions and appropriations of the medieval and late ancient Talmud, first (in Chapter 6) within the confines of the traditional study of the Talmud and then (in Chapter 7), in modernist responses to it.

PART III

The Political for Other Others

CHAPTER 6

Formally Human (Jewish Responses to Kant I)

The previous chapter addressed an early modern instantiation of the effacement of the interpersonal political in the Talmud by conceptions of universal (inter)subjectivity and logical-apodictic reasoning. This process first tacitly erased the interpersonal political in the late ancient Talmud by reducing it to dialectical irony. In a second step, the erasure advanced from irony, a Platonic concept, to logical-apodictic reading of it in the Aristotelian tradition. Only when viewed through a post-Kantian lens could it become clear that this was not merely a Platonic interpretation of the late ancient Talmud in early modernity, followed by an Aristotelian interpretation, but rather a complex and multistep process of the effacement of the interpersonal. Through this lens, one can witness how the interpersonal in the late ancient Talmud emerged through the long process of its vanishing—in other words, how it was effaced.

The story of that effacement does not stop with the arrival of Kant's philosophy. The slow, centuries-long process of the effacement of the interpersonal by the (inter)subjective not only becomes noticeable as a result of Kant's philosophy but continues after Kant, too. It continues after Kant in a variety of ways. In the first two chapters of this book, I have already highlighted how such post-Kantian thinkers of the political as Carl Schmitt and Jacque Rancière participated in that effacement and how the linked notions of the human being and the Jew contributed to that process. This chapters and the next tell another, closely related part of the story of the continuation (and further complication) of the effacement of the interpersonal after Kant. That part of the story has to do with the anti-Jewish element embedded in Kant's concept of (inter)subjectivity, the polemic against any positive law and any positive view of the human (including a natural view of the human), a view that Kant's transcendentalism had to oppose.

Modern Impasses: Allegiant Resistance to Kant

These two chapters examine how Jewish thinkers after Kant, both tradition-oriented and modernism-oriented thinkers, attempted to defend Rabbinic traditions and/or Jewish existence either by proving their full commensurability with the demands of the (inter)subjectivity of reason or by revealing internal problems in post-Kantian (inter)subjectivity while still remaining faithful to its larger framework. Either move aimed to afford a due place for rabbinic tradition or for Jewish existence within the paradigm of the subject of reason after Kant.

However, far from describing a "decline" of the interpersonal political in the thought of modern Jewish religious (the present chapter) and secular (Chapter 7) interpreters of the Talmud after Kant, these chapters reveal a radically new "construction" of the origin—here, the origin of the Talmud—as a disappearing and thereby newly appearing "object." Doing so opens up a new stage of the effacement of the interpersonal political in the Talmud as either an object of "denial" by religious modernists (the present chapter) or as a model for a tacit "reappropriation," which effectively also means a denial, by secular modernists (Chapter 7). In the overall structure of the book, the two chapters close the loop of narration by coming back to where the book started—to the modern site and sight of the effacement of the political in political ontology and political theology, this time in the reception and reappropriation of the Talmud by post-Kantian Jewish thinkers.

The story that this and the next chapter tell also is another side of the emergence of both the political theology of Schmitt and the political ontology of Rancière from philosophical thinking after Kant. These parts are closely interconnected and even mirror one another. They either respond to or build on the same component of Kant's transcendentalism—its embedded supersession of both "positive law" and, as a result, adherents to it by Kant's transcendentalism. Political theology and political ontology build on that supersession, as do Jewish responses to Kant—both those oriented toward tradition and those with a modernist orientation. They either attempt to prove the rabbinic tradition to be transcendental rather than positive or rethink this tradition in various modernist (post-Kantian) frameworks to criticize and advance them both.

All these lines of thought—political ontology, political theology, and traditionalist and modernist responses to Kant—thus build on the intrinsic anti-Jewish component of Kant's transcendentalism, the component of the positive law. Jewish respondents to Kant attempted to defend Jewish tradition as in no way positive, but at the price of having the interpersonal in the Talmud radically effaced from the horizon of their thinking. As we will see in the next chapter, not only the defense of the existing tradition but also rethinking it critically produced the same result: the effacement of the interpersonal in the Talmud from the horizon of thought. The story that these two chapters tell is thus the story of a paradox: the allegiant resistance to Kant. The two chapters expose attempts to think Rabbinic tradition, including its biblical component and its modernist translations, as a way to escape Kant's critique of positive law and of his concomitant notions of what constitutes the humanity of the human. The two chapters thus aim to articulate the limits and the impasses into which the allegiant resistance to Kant leads any attempts to think the political, as long as the interpersonal continues to be banished from that thinking. Such attempts and the impasses they reveal inevitably repeat the logic of the effacement of the interpersonal political in the Talmud from the horizon of political thought after Kant as the main and the most tacit move of that thought.

Formally Human

As Jewish neo-Kantians attempted to rescue Rabbinic tradition from Kant's allegation of its being positive law and Rabbinic Jews from his allegations of their being stigmatized as adherents to such a law, they developed the notion of the "formally human," or, closer to their vocabulary, the "formal man." It is therefore only through post-Kantian discussions of the (inter)subjective universal, with the underlying notion of the (again universal) "formally human" that the erasure of the interpersonal after Kant can be accounted for in its proper scope.

The formally human or "formal man" is radically different from those whom Kant excludes from the subjects of reason. By advancing that notion,

Jewish philosophers after Kant attempted to repair the embedded anti-Jewish element of Kant's universalism. While Kant criticized both adherents of positive law and natural man as not necessarily belonging to authentic subjects of reason, the Jewish thinkers argued for a formal concept of the human, for the man who by definition acts within the limits of reason alone. This chapter will show how these thinkers found and interpreted such a man in the depth of the Rabbinic tradition.[1]

The story here more specifically concerns a series of attempts to defend Rabbinic tradition by reformulating it in post-Kantian terms. That meant remaining allegiant to how Kant criticized both the positive law (for which Jewish Law would be a model) and to how Kant criticized the adherents to positive law, those who might look human, but do not act as subjects of reason. It also meant arguing that neither Rabbinic tradition or Jewish existence entail adherence to positive law, but instead fully comply with and even exceed the demands of the (inter)subjectivity of reason after Kant.

The argument in this chapter follows one line of the effacement of the Talmud after Kant, a line developed by traditionally oriented modern readers of the Talmud. It focuses on the work of Hermann Cohen, Rabbi Chayim Soloveitchik, and Rabbi Joseph Soloveitchik. At the center of attention in this chapter is the process whereby a particular form of intersubjectivity, the formal notion of "man" and/or the "human being" (in Kant's sense of the formal and in the universal sense of the "human") comes to the fore in the chapter as Cohen, Soloveitchik, and Soloveitchik attempt to rescue the universalist intersubjective notion of the human being from the critique of the universality of human being that arises from Kant's notion of "the subject of reason." At work here (and, as we will see, in the modernist allegiant resistance to Kant's subjective universalism) is a certain construction of what Talmud is, a construction that advances the erasure and effacement of the interpersonal by the intersubjective, now through the notions of the human condition of the intersubjective humanity of humans.

The Formal Man: The Construction of "the Talmud" from the Brisker Rav to the Mishneh Torah

After Kant, the effacement of the interpersonal by the intersubjective not only continued, but also assumed a new form, that of construction. Construction is effacement that implies a subjectivity and that therefore is much more static, but in no way less complex, than the forms of effacement of the interpersonal by intersubjective that we have seen so far. Construction is a modern form of effacement, implying the subject and in particular its withdrawal.

The construction of the medieval in Talmud scholarship modernity both implies and sheds light on the construction of the ancient in the Middle Ages. Together, these actions shed further light on the nature of the shifting subject position from which such seemingly objective historical epochs are constructed. Of course, the notion that many things—identities, genders, and epochs, among them—are "constructed" is a postmodern truism, but what does this construction entail?

The concept of "construction" often is simplistically understood as the opposite of and corrective for the positivist notion that things just naturally "are." What exactly makes a constructed object "objective" or "natural" is no trivial matter. Attributing the process of construction to an agent, say to "society," as in the clichéd term "a social construct," makes "society" the agent in this process, which is no less naturalistic than the "naturalistic" position it purports to oppose.

Although construction implies an agent, construction is not a matter of pure fabulation, of making things up from scratch. Rather, it implies extracting objects from their "natural" positions and assembling them into a new unity. Construction is in effect the inverse of the Romantic conception of expression, in which the subject, typified by the artist, openly puts his or her thoughts and emotions on display and even stresses them, in part at the expense of objectivity or "realism" in the representation of objects. By contrast to both naturalism and expressionism, the construction of "objective" phenomena is attained by the *withdrawal* of the subject from the representation, as if, even though constructed, the representation is still objective. The act of construction thus always implies a certain kind of subject position—the withdrawal of the subject from the resulting representation of the object.[2] And how that object is constructed in turn illuminates the nature of the subject position involved.

The ordinary logic of the representation of "'objective' objective" entities suggests that what is represented precedes the representation in time. Contrary to that logic, the constructed object does not precede its representation, but rather emerges concurrently with the withdrawal of those subjects whose construct it is. This makes the withdrawal itself a purely structural matter, an essential part of the logic of construction, rather than a specific event in terms of time or chronology.

The construction of antiquity and the Middle Ages in the history of the Talmud and its interpretation is no exception to this process. Modern interpreters construct Maimonides by reenacting, in a new way, how

Maimonides constructs the "ancient" Talmud as a merely rhetorical form of thinking, as opposed to a rational, philosophical mode of thought, and he thus redeems the content of the Talmud in a new, more philosophical-rationalist form, that of a legal code. In the works of Maimonides's modern interpreters, Maimonides then becomes a figure of transition from the "medieval" subject position to the "modern" subject position of the post-Kantian transcendental philosopher. In this process, the effacement of the interpersonal can be traced as Maimonides privileged philosophy and dismissed the Talmud's form as merely rhetorical, critically withdrawing from the supposedly rhetorical form of the Talmud to a purely philosophical subject position from which he translated the Talmud into a philosophically rational code of law.

What is involved in the construction of antiquity and the Middle Ages in the history of the Talmud and its interpretation is a double withdrawal in which, first, the supposedly "ancient" nature of the Talmud is constructed from a subject position, typified by Maimonides and his contemporaries, in which philosophical modes of thinking and the rhetorical modes of thinking that we have previously explored in the Talmud are positioned as opposing each other. In regarding philosophy and rhetoric as opposed to each other, Maimonides was in agreement with other medieval Talmudists, the Tosafists, although they privileged the practices of rhetoric in what was seen as ancient, whereas Maimonides privileged philosophy.

Then, in a second act of construction and critique, modern commentators have redeemed Maimonides from this now supposedly "medieval" context and have reinvented him as a modern philosopher-Talmudist, seen now from the subject position of neo-Kantian transcendental philosophy. Both withdrawals construct and deny the "ancient" view of the Talmud as a narrowly "rhetorical" (that is, antiphilosophical) form of thinking and with it the personal and the interpersonal, as opposed to the subjective and intersubjective, as the implying and implicated in the political. However, modern Talmudic critics have withdrawn from the subject position based on the opposition between philosophy and rhetoric to a position that putatively transcends that position.[3] This final position is typified by the work of the Brisker Rav in the nineteenth century and by that of his grandson, R. Joseph Soloveitchik, who, following the work of the greatest of the Jewish neo-Kantians, Hermann Cohen, overcame the "ancient" opposition of philosophy and rhetoric as far as the Talmud is concerned, interpreting it as neither one nor the other, but instead as "pure thought," a position that modern Talmudists would find "already" in Maimonides, thus reshaping him into a modern thinker. All this, however, does nothing and can do nothing to shake the initial construction and critique of the "ancient" form of the Talmud in philosophical terms as "rhetorical," because this construction has created a fantastic "ancient" and consequently a fantastic "medieval" as epochs against which critical thinking can operate.

This process of double construction and denial is a new and even more advanced form of the effacement of the interpersonal. The first act of constructing and denying the late ancient Talmud as the rhetorical exchange of refutations and counterrefutations tacitly implies that these acts are committed by thinking subjects and in intersubjective settings. A subject attempting to refute another subject with the obviously "unsatisfactory" arrives at "no definitive conclusion" in the Talmud, and that explains the need to "replace" the rhetoric of the Talmud with the "Roman" splendor of a systematic outline of the "law" (as if the Talmud was one), done in a systematic way, that is, beyond refutations and counterrefutations. The assumed refutations between thinking subjects justifies the dismissal of refutation as practiced in the Talmud in favor of a philosophical system of law in which there is with no role for disputes. The interpersonal disappears precisely as the philosophical thinking subject emerges where the late ancient Talmud had been.

Constructing the "Old": The Talmud as Refutations

Maimonides constructs the Talmud as an object of criticism in his comprehensive legal code of Jewish law, the *Mishneh Torah* (MT). His self-declared intent seems to be to remove all debates and to organize and present the final rulings so that all of the Oral Law is accessible to everyone without the need for anything else. However, because the subject position in constructing the Talmud is structural, rather than temporal, it is neither bound to the intellectual program of any particular thinker nor confined by the historical circumstances of any thinker's work. Therefore, while understanding the process by which Maimonides constructed the Talmud and the way in which he did so must begin with Maimonides's own historical period, it must not be limited to it, much less to his self-declared intent in writing the code of the MT. In fact, exploring the self-declared intent of Maimonides does not advance our understanding of the process of construction. As Moshe Halbertal has argued, the ambivalence in that intent is irresolvable: it remains impossible to determine whether Maimonides was proposing the final and therefore obligatory formulation of the law or only a more systematic and therefore more convenient rendition thereof.[4] The irresolvable ambivalence of Maimonides's self-declared intent thus prompts us to analyze not the thinking of Maimonides as an individual, but rather the subject position from which Maimonides's interpretation of the Talmud stems. While the intent in Maimonides's MT might have been ambivalent, his construction of the Talmud is not. The Talmud emerged, or rather, was constructed in his work, as a certain form, approximated as a "debate," which the thinker transformed into a new form, that of the Code of Law.[5]

Maimonides's construction of the Talmud is one of a number of landmarks of medieval innovation found in the context of broader culture, such as the invention of zero in mathematics, of the vanishing point in painting, of paper money in economics, of the problem of creation *ex nihilo* in theology, and of the virtual agent in moral philosophy. A common denominator of all these innovations is that all represent the virtual, rather than simply the experientially accessible elements of reality. You cannot touch zero, but you can use it; the vanishing point is the point at which vision appears to cease; the value of paper money is not real, but effective; *nihilo*, nothing, is definitely not Plato's *meon*, "a specific thing, which is not," but rather an amorphous, but still effective material of creation; and finally, the virtual agent of free will, although not a part of the physical world, in which everything is physically determined, still produces effects in human actions, thereby making humans both free and responsible. Yet another example of such a virtual entity is the idea of the composer of the Talmud, for which the figures of Ravina and Rav Ashi serve as genealogical equivalents. At least such is their role in the text of Maimonides's "Introduction" to his Code of the *Mishneh Torah*.

Both Maimonides and modern academic Talmud criticism of the last century depend on the notion of a virtual composer. From "the exact science of the Talmud" in J. N. Epstein's programmatic formulation to the theories of anonymous redactors in/of the Talmud of Ch. Albeck, to D. W. Halivni and their followers, modern academic scholars of the Talmud not only criticized the "old" view of Ravina and Rav Ashi as the Talmud's redactors but also tacitly have depended on it. They did so because critique depends on how its object is constructed, even before the work of critique can begin. In other words, a critical reading of a text must rest upon an "old," precritical way of reading of that text, which the "new," critical reading comes to replace. The theory of anonymous redactors thus presumes a traditional view of the Talmud, which it then denies. The "new" depends on the "old" as its stepping-stone and therefore presupposes a certain understanding of what that "old" is. Because of that dependence, the "old" continues to inform the "new." The dialectics of "old" and "new" is a significant part of the construction process: Construction is precisely rethinking what was before as the "old" so that it could be replaced by the "new."

A particularity of the effacement of the interpersonal in this construction is that even if the withdrawn subject does not have to be a universal human, the addressee of the resulting construction does. As will become clear in the reading of Rabbi Chayim Soloveitchik and in the consequent reading of Rabbi Joseph Soloveitchik, the code of MT is to either replace or reformulate the "law of the Talmud" by addressing that law to (and purporting to regulate the actions of) a subject who is formally human, rather than just someone who looks or acts like a human. If there remains any sense of the interpersonal in how Maimonides understands refutations and counterrefutations in the Talmud, it is erased as he explicitly proposes to replace it with such a philosophically universal codification of the law.

In the case of Maimonides, the "old" is defined as the rhetorical form of the Talmud, its ongoing refutations and counterrefutations, which he already understands as taking place between thinking subjects, not as structures of personhood and of interpersonality, an understanding in which the interpersonal becomes effaced by the thinking subject, and the "new" is the systematic form of the code, the MT. Because attaining the "new" is not possible without constructing the "old," in the his "Introduction," which served as the raison d'être for codifying the Oral Torah, Maimonides describes the Talmud in a way that coins the view of the "old" Talmud to be shared by post-Maimonidean tradition, including the modern Talmud criticism, as well. Multiple traces of the process of construction can be discerned in the following extract from the "Introduction":

> Ravina and Rav Ashi stand at the end of the generations of the masters of the Talmud; and Rav Ashi is the one who composed the Babylonian Talmud in the land of Shinar, approximately a hundred years after Rabbi Yochanan composed the Jerusalem Talmud. The matter of the two Talmuds is interpreting the words of the Mishnah and clarifying its depths, as well as inventions of every rabbinical court from the days of Our Holy Rabbi [who composed the Mishnah] until the end of the composition of the Talmud. From the two Talmuds, as well as from [the parallel versions of the Mishnah in] *Tosefta*, from the [midrashim] of *Sifra* and *Sifri* [on Leviticus and Deuteronomy, respectively] and from additions [to them] from all of them, it becomes clear what is forbidden and what is permitted, pure and impure, obligatory and

> exempt, kosher or unusable, as the authorities were copying each other from the mouth of Moses on Mount Sinai. [In the Talmud,] it also becomes clarified which of the above rules were enacted by the sages, or prophets in each generation, for the sake of building "protective walls around the Torah," as they have explicitly heard from Moses "Therefore shall ye keep My charge" (Lev. 18:30) which suggests "you should protect my commandments." Similarly [in the Talmud] it becomes clarified which of the above are customs and legal adjustments enacted or customarily performed in a certain generation, as a rabbinical court of that generation saw fit; because it is forbidden to deviate from them [too], as it says, "thou shalt not turn aside from the sentence which they shall declare unto thee, to the right hand, nor to the left" (Deut. 17:1). And [it] also [becomes clarified regarding] the criminal laws and rulings, which were not received from Moses, but the Great Assembly of that generation decided on them using [analogical] rules by which Scripture can be expounded, and which were consequently approved by the elders, who passed down a tradition that the ruling is such and such. Rav Ashi composed all of it in the Talmud, [covering the period] from the days of Moses till his own days.[6]

That description carefully constructs "the old," the Talmud, in order to justify replacing it by "the new" form, the MT. Maimonides talks about the "depths of the Mishnah" that the Talmud "clarifies." Presenting the Talmud that way sets the stage for replacing one clarification with another, the Talmud's clarification of the Oral Law with that of the MT. That second "clarification" both brings forth and denies—and thus, through these two moves together—effaces the Talmud's form of refutations, placing the form of the thinking subject in its stead.

Understanding the dialectics of the "old" and the "new" requires an interpretation of "depth." What exactly is that "depth"? And what does "clarification" entail? To "clarify" means to isolate an idea and to ascribe it to an authority in a way in which one is not possible without the other. Indeed, without genealogical rooting, the "depth" of a text has no authority to support it, and without that "depth," the authorities devolve to empty placeholders on the "surface" of the immediate or explicit meanings of texts. What that means, however, is that "clarification" is not the linear process of retrieving an idea from the past to the "here and now" of the interpreter. Instead, "clarification" is the purely intellectual work of an interpreter who moves from the present (understanding an idea) to the past (placing it in the rank of authorities). "Depth" is thus reached neither by purely logical analysis of the text nor by a historical reconstruction of the ideas in it, because "depth" implies an initial "obscurity" or "opaqueness" of the text in terms of both ideas expressed and the authority to which these ideas must be ascribed. Eliminating that implied opaqueness or obscurity in the Mishnah is exactly the task of "clarification," which is the work of the interpreter, who both describes ideas and ascribes them to an authority of a certain rank. Such "clarification" leaves the question of the historical genesis of these ideas outside of the realm of "clarification," thus opening up the space for speculative invention.[7] The resulting view is that the "old," the Talmud, is an apologetic project of the "clarification" of either the Mishnah or the post-Mishnaic rulings of the sages, which is neither an empirical reconstruction of the history of Jewish law nor a logical-theoretical contemplation of legal ideas, but rather is precisely what the intellectual idiom of "clarification" reflects—reading texts to produce ideas and to rank them by ascribing them to different authorities in the past.

The central element in Maimonides's construction of the "old" is the rhetorical element of refuting and defending in the Talmud. As Maimonides has it, discussions in the Talmud are driven by what he calls *kashiah* and *peruk* (that is, by refutations and counterrefutations, or, more literally, "mounting a refutation and then putting it off"). The reference is to a rhetorical process of heuristically refuting either a text of the Mishnah or of what "was invented" in rabbinical courts after the Mishnah, but before the completion of the Babylonian Talmud (in chronological terms, between the third and fifth centuries C.E.), followed by deflecting that refutation. Maimonides finds refuting and defending in the Talmud to be "unbearable" and proposes to dismiss that process altogether. To this effect he writes:

> Relying on the help of the Rock blessed be He, I intently studied all these books, for I saw fit to write what can be sorted out from all of these works in regard to what is forbidden and permitted, and unclean and clean, and the other rules of the Torah: Everything in clear language and terse style, so that the whole Oral Law would become thoroughly known to all; without refutations and defenses or diverging arguments, but rather clear, convincing, and correct statements, in accordance with the legal rules drawn from all of these works and commentaries that have appeared from the time of Our Holy Teacher to the present.[8]

Maimonides's project both negates the form of the Talmud ("refutations, defenses, diverging arguments") and translates its legalistic content into a new, philosophically rational form ("clear language and terse style").

What the Talmud "clarifies" rhetorically, which it must imply "irrationally," Maimonides comes to "sort out" philosophically or "rationally."[9] His task is thus to "sort out" what was "clarified" in the Talmud about what is forbidden and permitted and so on. It goes without saying that in his new project, Maimonides proposes to replace the complex and "obscure" rhetorical analysis in the Talmud by "sorting out" the laws in a more "clear" outline of the Oral Law in the style of philosophical rationalism, that is, "with neither refuting nor defending," but rather by formulating the law in the rational and universally accessible form of a logically graspable code.

It is worth paying more attention to what is negated here, not only because what is negated is the basis of what is asserted but also because Maimonides's view of the Talmud is located precisely in what he negates and replaces. That process is even more radical because not only the negation but also the negated is already the effacement of the interpersonal dimension of the refutation process in the late ancient Talmud. The negated form of the Talmud is portrayed as *kashiah ve' peruk*, heuristic refuting and ultimate defending as a tool that serves the main goal of the Talmud: "clarification" as defined earlier. As a result, the second feature of his view of the "old," the Talmud, that is, its rhetorical format of refuting and defending, stands at the service of its first feature, which is the hermeneutical task of the "clarification of the depth" of the law. Maimonides thus takes up the task of "clarification," but replaces the "old" means thereof, "debate," with "new" means, the systematic analysis of the law. This version of the "old," however, is already an effacement of the interpersonal character of refuting and counterrefuting in the Talmud.

Both critical academic scholars and traditional interpreters of the Talmud after Maimonides shared these elements of the view of the Talmud, inheriting that view from Maimonides. In their view, the Talmud was also primarily a series of refutations (*kashiah*) and counterrefutations (*peruk*); secondarily, it also included a separate, albeit, legalistically less important part—homiletic or *haggadic* texts. Additionally, that view ascribed refutations to the named characters in the Talmud (*amoraim*), and in particular to the most recent among them, Ravina and Rav Ashi. Traditional interpreters after Maimonides thus continued to interpret the text of the Talmud using that constructed view of the "old," without changing it, while modern critical scholars of the Talmud analyzed the genesis of the text in a "new" way while still drawing that analysis on the "old" understanding of the Talmud as primarily a series of refutations. For both groups, the view of the "old" continued to serve as the foundation for transforming the "old"

Talmud into the "new" code, that of MT (for Maimonides), or for refining the understanding of the refutations (for example, for the medieval commentaries of the Tosafists), or for criticizing the "old" view as "illusory" (for modern critical scholars).[10] In either of these versions, the reduction of the primary form of the Talmud to refutations and counterrefutations creates yet another act of effacement, the partition of the late ancient corpus of the Talmud into "the law" and the "narrative" (*halakhah* and *haggadah*, respectively). That effaces the interpersonal element, which permeates the corpus of the Talmud across the division between the law and narrative. The insufficiency of such a characterization has to do with an additional complexity of the process of effacement. Seeing the Talmud as primarily refutations and counterrefutations does two things at once: It loses sight of the intrinsically interpersonal rather than intersubjective component of refuting, and it partitions the corpus into the law and the narrative.

There are more elements of construction of the Talmud by Maimonides that are characteristic for these scholars and interpreters of the Talmud. One is a suggestion that the "here and now" of the Talmud is fifth-century Babylon and the Talmudic schools of the *amoraim* Ravina and Rav Ashi, who are the latest among most recently listed authorities mentioned in the Talmud by name. Modern critical scholars of the Talmud have used that understanding of the "here and now" of the Talmud both as the main target of critique and as a model for a replacement. That is to say, they reconsidered the "when" of that "here and now" but left untouched the idea that there is a historically accurate here and now of both the Talmudic discussions and of their production, not only in literature, but also in history. According to another element in that view of the "old," the genealogical order of the generations of the named masters in the Talmud, the *amoraim*, coincides with the chronological order of their lives, as well as with the descending ranks of authority of the teachings ascribed to each master. This triple coincidence of genealogy, chronology, and authority is then a component of the view of the "old" Talmud.[11] When genealogy, chronology, and authority coincide, the chronologically and genealogically most recent automatically becomes not only less authoritative but also emerges as nameless or anonymous. Yet anonymity by definition lacks personality, allows for no personhood, and therefore does not suffice to account for the interpersonal character of the corpus, which thus entails yet another aspect of the effacement of the interpersonal nature of relationships between the characters in the Talmud, both across the generations and in any synchronic moment in diegesis, if there is one.

Embracing all the elements—refutation as the main intellectual paradigm of the Talmud, the literary and historically real "here and now" of Talmudic discussions, and the coincidence of genealogy, chronology, and ranks of authority—the "old" approach is both defined and dismissed in Maimonides's own project of the Oral Law, which he presents anew, now "without refutations and counterrefutations"—*le'lo kashiah ve'le'lo peruk*—in a form that is free from refutation-defense pattern. Dismissing the Talmudic form of refutation and defense in favor of the philosophical form of systematic reasoning, Maimonides leaves his heirs and rivals with only two options: to follow him in rejecting the form of refutation and defense or to object to him by proving the rational-philosophical validity of refutations, as Rabbi Izhak I. Canpanton did in one way and Chaim Luzzatto and the Rabbi Chaim Soloveitchik did in another. That choice, however, entailed the using refutations and defenses to elide the larger programmatic element of Talmudic discussion, its fundamentally interpersonal character, which comes before and is effaced by any partitioning of the Talmud either chronologically or genealogically or into a "narrative" versus "legal" segments.

For the purposes of illustration, I mention one alternative way to construe the broader scope of where the Talmudic refutations intellectually belong: in terms of memory as the main orientation in thinking, as opposed to using both memory and thinking as only instruments of knowing.[12] If, in contrast to what Maimonides emphasizes, the refutation-defense pattern in the Talmud serves a specific kind of memory—approximated by what the rhetorical schools describe as "memory for things" ("things" includes general ideas, thoughts, arguments, and of course, the "things" that perception and/or imagination can grasp), as opposed to "memory for words"—then memory is not only purely rhetorical but also an intrinsically philosophical concept, implying a certain performance that, contrary to Maimonides, cannot be done without refutations and defenses, *le' lo kashiah ule ve'le'lo peruk*. The memory performed thereby is not a recollection of either an individual or a collective. Rather, it is an intrinsically interpersonal act, which becomes erased when stripped from *kashiah* and *peruk*.

Along the way to that broader context of refuting in the Talmud, the problem to address is how Maimonides comes both to envision and to dismiss the form of refutation as the main form of the Talmud. This problem involves the duality of envisioning and dismissing, constructing and denying, which together entail the "logic," or rather the paradox, of the process of effacement. If Maimonides constructs and denies the Talmud as an intellectual form of refuting and thereby effaces the interpersonal

Talmud, what are the grounds on which he both erects and denies that construction? A "modern" answer to that question will have to do with the "new" subject position that Maimonides assumes in the process of construction. As the next two sections will show, that position promotes, as the Brisker Rav (Rabbi Chayim Soloveitchik) will help us to see, "modern" (post-Kantian) formal and a priori thinking about the humanity of the human being and about issues in the law and demotes both "medieval" universalist metaphysical thinking about these issues and "ancient" rhetorical thinking about situational argumentation, thus taking the effacement of the interpersonal in the Talmud yet another step further.

Do Two Lives Weigh the Same? The Subject Position in Construction

As I have argued, Maimonides constructed—and thereby effaced—the Talmud as a form of "clarification of the depth" of Mishnaic law, in which refutations, ascribed to *amoraim*, are to be replaced with the new form of a systematic code of law. This means that Maimonides, as he constructs the "old" form by withdrawing from it, also withdraws from the discipline of rhetoric, positioning himself in the discipline of rational systematic thinking. In other words, he withdraws from the discipline of rhetoric and positions himself as a philosopher. The question then is: What is the role of philosophy in constructing the Talmud in that way?

As I argued earlier, Maimonides's self-declared intent is not sufficient to answer this question. At stake in it is what the nature of philosophical thought itself might be conceived to be, and it is precisely the reconceptualization of the nature of philosophical thought that is one of the central aspects of the construction of "the medieval" as opposed to the modern. At stake in the question of the role of philosophy in constructing the Talmud, in other words, is a second withdrawal in which Maimonides's subject position becomes reinvented as that of a post-Kantian transcendental philosopher-Talmudist. Because the Brisker Rav both clarifies and reinvents the subject position from which Maimonides undertook the construction of the Talmud as "ancient," the Brisker Rav's *Novellae (Hidushim)*, an apologetic commentary focusing on Maimonides's interpretation of the Talmud in the MT, is helpful for discerning the withdrawal of Maimonides into a new, "modern" subject position, due to and precisely despite of the Brisker Rav's intention to show the continuity between Maimonides as a philosopher and Maimonides as a reader of the Talmud. As the following example will soon help us to see, in this modern subject position, the notion of a formal and universal human being comes to fore, reaching a point at which the interpersonal fully disappears from the site of thinking about the humanity of the human.

Uninterested in highlighting any rupture or any formal change between the Talmud and the MT, the Brisker Rav nevertheless occupies the same subject position in constructing the Talmud that he attributes to Maimonides. Structurally, his position remains as antirhetorical as that of Maimonides, even if the Brisker Rav merely offers to read the Talmud philosophically rather than also dismissing it as rhetorical. In that sense, the similarity in their subject positions is apparent. But the Brisker Rav performed in a different philosophical context, that of the neo-Kantian philosophy of his time, rather than in the context of Aristotelian and Platonic philosophies still regnant in the time of Maimonides. As we will see, that is a difference that literally makes a difference.

As the Brisker Rav reads Maimonides,[13] for example, he transforms the Talmudic rhetorical-situational approach to the topic of weighing the value of human lives one against another into a universalist-philosophical (metaphysical) approach to human life. In the latter approach, life is understood as a substance equally imparted to all human beings, as opposed to a transcendentalist approach in which it is a formal value equally granted to each individual.

The topic of weighing the value of human lives occurs in the Talmud when it discusses how the law is to be applied in the case of a Jew publicly coerced by the difficult choice of being ordered to murder someone or be murdered himself, and this case and the resulting discussion serves as a master case for discussing the seemingly related situation of a recently engaged Jewish girl who is faced with the publicly coerced choice between committing adultery or dying. The master case is reported in the Talmud as follows:

> [O]ne [of the people of Israel] who came before Rabba and said to him, "The governor of my town has ordered me, 'Go and kill so and so; if not, I will slay thee.' He answered him, 'Let him rather slay you than that you should commit murder; who knows that your blood is redder? Perhaps his blood is redder.'" (TB Sanh. 74a; Soncino translation, emended)

The Jew appeals to the authority of Rabba to see if it is permissible to take the life of another person to save his own. The response comes as a question: How do you know that your blood is redder (by implication, in the eyes of your Creator) than the life of another person?—suggesting one cannot preserve one's own life at the expense of another. In the case of murder, if there is no way to escape, according to all medieval authorities cited by the Brisker Rav,[14] one should allow oneself to be killed rather than murder another person. But does the same rule apply in the derivative case of the girl? After all, when facing the choice between death and adultery, at stake is only *her* life—no other person is in danger. Perhaps she should preserve her life at all costs. However, Maimonides, in the MT radically allows only one legitimate option in either case: do not commit adultery, and do not murder, but rather, die as a martyr.

In his commentary on the MT, the Brisker Rav asks why, in the case of public coercion to commit adultery or die, Maimonides does not allow the engaged girl to protect her own life by "sitting and doing nothing," provided she does not actively engage in adultery but is used only passively, as an object. The Brisker Rav notices that when commenting on the preceding Talmudic discussion, other medieval commentators, the Tosafists, introduced what seems to be a valid alternative for the girl's behavior, which Maimonides—quite stunningly—fails not only to approve, but even to mention. The Tosafists approach her case based on the master case of public coercion—that of a Jew publicly presented with the choice "murder or die." They turn to the Talmudic text in discussion. Using an inference from an enthymeme (*svara*) of Rabba cited earlier, which is found in the respective *sugya* in the Babylonian Talmud ("How do you know your blood is redder [in the eyes of your Creator] than the blood of your fellow?"), the Tosafists propose that a Jew in such a situation might have just done nothing by arguing "precisely because I do not know whose blood is redder, I am to sit and do nothing." Both the man coerced to murder and the girl coerced to commit adultery, when confronting doing something or dying, could allow their bodies but not their actions to be used as an instrument of murdering. The Jew would then only passively participate in the murder—as an instrument, an object, rather than as an agent or subject. The argument is that if the governor uses the Jew as a tool for killing—say he throws the Jew as a projectile on a child, and the child dies—this is the governor's responsibility only.

In their allowance of passive (rather than active) involvement in murder, the Tosafists drew on a certain understanding of the example of Esther discussed in the Talmud *ad locum* in which Esther must have participated in adultery with King Achashverosh passively, or as the Talmud has it, as *karka olam*, that is, without any active role at all. That precedent allowed the Tosafists to help the engaged girl to survive the adultery by behaving as they thought Esther did. Assuming Esther was engaged to

Mordechai, when publicly coerced to commit adultery, she did not accept martyrdom, but instead behaved as *karka olam*, thereby preserving her life. Based on that reading of the biblical story of Esther in the Talmud, the Tosafists allowed the engaged girl to escape martyrdom if she does not actively participate in adultery. Maimonides, however, shows no such leniency. Strangely—indeed, radically—he, without any stipulation, prescribes that the girl should die rather than commit adultery, even if she is involved in the adultery only as an object, that is, passively, not actively.

The Brisker Rav explains the difference between Maimonides and the Tosafists as the difference between a rhetorical-situational (or in the terms of the larger argument in this book, the interpersonal) approach to thinking, a "medieval" philosophical-universalistic approach (contemplated and rejected by the Tosafists), and a "modern" formal a priori approach, which he ascribes to Maimonides. He submits:

> This question [of Maimonides's radicalism] requires contemplation [instead of searching excuses as others have done]: Behold, the Tosafists proved [she could sit and do nothing without accepting martyrdom] by inference from the [master] case of "murder or die," where if there is a place for "sitting and doing nothing," he [the Jew] does not have to devote himself [to martyrdom]. [If so,] then why did Maimonides establish that in either kind [either active or passive involvement in adultery] she is rather to be killed than to transgress?
>
> There is to say that in the [master] case of "murder or die," the distinction between (*hilluk*) "sit and do nothing" and "active involvement" is [justified] (by Maimonides)] not because an active murdering is more severe than a passive one is, but only because two souls weigh the same. This is why [the Jew] is to sit and do nothing, and the law to apply to him is the law of two murders, of which neither takes precedence, in which case the law is that he is to sit and do nothing. Therefore (*hilluk*) the classification of the case of passive involvement "sit and do nothing" as a new [i.e. derivative] category does not apply to adultery, because if we [dare] say protection of one's own life (*pikuah nafsho*) weighs the same as adultery, [the answer to that would be that] because we learn that from the [master] case about "murder or die," and because in that master case [the consideration of] protecting one's own soul was not a factor, therefore obviously in the derivative case [about the girl to "commit adultery or die"], active and passive participation is the same, and in both scenarios she is rather to be killed than to transgress.[15]

The Brisker Rav thus answers that in the master case of "murder or die," the passive involvement (sit and do nothing) was allowable only because "two souls are weighed one against the other." This is why the same conclusion does not apply in the derivative case of "commit adultery or die," where it is only the girl's life that is at stake. One might think that because there is only one life in danger, the principle of "protecting one's life," which generally allows violating the requirements of rituals, would apply. However, as the Brisker Rav explains, since protecting one's life did not apply in the master case, it does not apply in the derivative case of the girl, either. In short, because the case of the girl is derivative from the master case of "murder or die," neither saving one's life nor the rule of two lives weighing the same apply to the girl: the former is not used in the master case at all, and the latter, even if found in the master case, does not apply to the derivative case.

In the Brisker Rav's interpretation, Maimonides agrees in part with the Tosafists. Like the latter, he follows the Talmudic stratification of cases into a master case and derivative cases and makes inferences from the master case to the derivative. The only difference between him and the Tosafists is the principle that "two lives are weighed one against the other," which, according to the Brisker Rav, Maimonides adopts and they do not. This principle thus plays the key role in the Brisker Rav's explanation of Maimonides's radicalism, in which Maimonides applies it the master case but not to the derivative case of the girl, where there is one life at stake.

The question, therefore, is how the Brisker Rav understands "two lives are weighed one against the other." The answer has everything to do with positive and formal notions of human being. Since this is an interpretation of the Talmudic "How do you know that your blood is redder than the blood of your fellow?" does Maimonides, according to the Brisker Rav, see that principle as a universal ontological equation, "all lives are equal in value"—that is, as a formal rule invariably applicable to both active and passive involvement in murder? Alternatively, does Maimonides interpret the principle like the Tosafists, as an expression of the rhetorical enthymeme of not being sure whose life is more precious, which, when used differently in situations of active as opposed to passive involvement in murder, makes it impossible to refrain from martyrdom in either case?

The continuation of the Brisker Rav's discussion of the Tosafists, who, on his reading, apply the Talmudic enthymeme about blood situationally, rather than uniformly, suggests that for him, not only Maimonides, but also the Tosafists read the Talmud's enthymeme as a declaration of an ontological universal principle of equality of life. The basis for that conclusion is the Brisker Rav's argument in which he proves that not only Maimonides but also the Tosafists should have followed "two lives are weighed one against the other" as a universal rule of bioequality. In particular, in the context of his discussion of the Tosafists, he asks: Why should being merely a physical tool for a murder imply involvement in a murder in the first place?

> Indeed it is yet to be explained how the Talmud's enthymeme (*svara*) "How do you know your blood is redder than the blood of your fellow, perhaps the blood of your fellow is redder" is applicable to both active and passive scenarios of involvement in murder: because we can either read it as suggesting that "since two lives are weighed one against the other, the Jew is to try and sit and do nothing first," or we can read that enthymeme in the Talmud as suggesting that "since two lives are equal, protecting one's life is not a factor in 'murder or die' situations."[16]

In either interpretation, "two lives are weighed one against the other" is an ontological claim of bioequality that underlies a legal decision, not a rhetorical counterbalancing of two enthymemes in a situation of passive, as opposed to active involvement in murder.

Yet Maimonides is still different from the Tosafists in the way in which he uses the ontological principle of bioequality. For the Tosafists, life is a physical entity, equally imparted to all living beings. As a natural-philosophical principle, this could still be applied variably, depending of on whether it is a situation of active or passive involvement in murder. However, for Maimonides, according to the Brisker Rav's interpretation, life is not a physical substance, and bioequality is not a physically presumable factor that could or could not be applied depending on situation. Rather, bioequality is a formal, a priori principle, the formal principle of humanity that therefore must apply invariably. This allows the Brisker Rav to explain Maimonides's radicalism in the case of the engaged girl as a result of Maimonides's abstract philosophical notion—a formal and a priori principle of bioequality (the equality of all lives), as opposed to the Tosafists' concrete, rhetorical-situational, and/or natural-philosophical understanding of the Talmud's enthymemes, as if the latter allowed for differentiating between passive and active involvement, theoretically in murder and practically in adultery. This all presents Maimonides as a thinker who thinks like the Tosafists, or, rather, it claims that the Tosafists think like Maimonides, yet it also presents him as someone who operates on the basis of a philosophically universal formal and a priori understanding of life and bioequality, rather than on a naturalistic-ontological and therefore still situational-specific understanding of the Talmudic enthymeme about two lives.

It is here that the Brisker Rav creates an opening for the withdrawal of Maimonides and his way of thinking from the "medieval" world in which philosophy and rhetoric were seen in opposition to each other into a modern, post-Kantian subject position in which that opposition is overcome. The Brisker Rav's move undermines the simple opposition between the Talmud and philosophy that reigned among those who criticized Maimonides for his alleged dismissal of the former in favor of the latter. The new, more refined line of distinction that the Brisker Rav draws is not between Talmud and philosophy, but rather between the natural philosophy of the Tosafists, of which a rhetorical-situational approach can also be a part, and what is now characterized as the transcendental-formal philosophy of Maimonides. In the latter, as the Brisker Rav has interpreted in his commentary, the concept of the universal human being is what makes it possible to assign the two individuals, or the two lives, equal value. It is not longer about applying the same rhetorical argument in the opposite way in two different situations, but about being unable to act precisely because two lives weigh exactly the same. The foundation of biopolitics is no longer in an interpersonal encounter, but rather in a subjective universalist formal principle of humanity: All human lives weigh the same, and therefore everyone who looks human is human, too. What is more, the Brisker Rav's position in reading both the Talmud and Maimonides's code can also be characterized as transcendental in method. He does not ask *why* the authorities in the Talmud say what they say, but rather *what* they say in conceptual terms, that is, in terms of what makes their saying possible in a conceptual way. If the *why* question is answerable in a natural-philosophical way, answering the *what* question requires use of the transcendental method, in which one ascends from givens to the conditions of their possibility, which, however, are far from the same as natural causes bringing the givens into existence. The Brisker Rav, in this light, is a conceptual analyst isolating the a priori "what" of what the Talmud and/or Maimonides says. In this particular case study, it is the bioequality principle. Seen in that way, the result of his analysis is independent of how Maimonides historically approached reading the Talmud or of how pronouncements in the Talmud historically developed. The Brisker Rav here thinks completely along the lines of Kant's subjective universality, and that becomes, for him, possible only by denying the Tosafist's approach. However much the latter might already be an effacement of the interpersonal in the dialectical, this is not enough for the Brisker Rav. As a transcendentalist thinker, the Brisker Rav must do away completely with any refutation as a foundation of bioaction. History realizes only what is possible, and by using a transcendental approach, the Brisker Rav is asking *what* exactly is conceptually possible and how.[17] In that sense, the Brisker Rav uses an a priori method to read Maimonides as a philosopher, which of course does not yet make the historical Maimonides a transcendentalist, but definitely helps answer the question of how the philosophical agenda of Maimonides informs his construction of the Talmud.[18]

In his analysis of Maimonides the Talmudist, the Brisker Rav introduces Maimonides the modern philosopher,[19] and he does so without any connection to the *Guide of the Perplexed*.[20] Even more important, showing a formal, a priori aspect in Maimonides's thinking helps us to understand the subject position that Maimonides occupies. He both constructs the Talmud as a form of rhetorical refutation and dismisses it in favor of a systematic outline of the law in the MT, which, as we now understand, originates from a formal, a priori point of view—the point of view of "formal man," a formal concept of the human, the man who acts within the limits of reason alone.

The transcendentalist formal position that the Brisker Rav discerns in and ascribes to Maimonides thus becomes possible not merely as the effacement of the interpersonal in the Talmud, but also and fundamentally as the effacement of that effacement. To the fore comes the formal transcendental notion of the human being as subjective universalist, so that even the effacement of the interpersonal is being effaced. However, and once again, that effacement of an effacement is never complete. Under the seemingly stable structure of the formal human, there is at work a dynamic and never-ending process, the effacement of the interpersonal in all the complexity and multiplicity of that process.

The process of effacement we have observed so far is complex enough to grant a summary before we proceed to its final stage of the effacement of the interpersonal in pure thought. To that end I will provide an example of an account of how the interpretation of "How do you know your than the blood of your fellow?" changes in the different phases of the effacement of the interpersonal.

The first step concerns the intersubjectivity of self-refuting. The rabbi in the Talmud sees a questioner approaching him for advice about how to justify his *conatus* of self-preservation at the expense of the life of another person. The rabbi does not give any positive advice to the questioner, he only self-refutes his *conatus*-driven position from within by a move that Chapter 3 discussed in detail. No assumptions about natural value of human life are at work in this interpersonal exchange, in which one self-refutes the other, no more and no less.

The second step involves the transformation of refutation into a rule to apply differently in different contexts (active versus passive involvement in murder). Things thus change for the Tosafists. The Tosafists presume varying natural values of human life, however unknown. For them, the argument does become "naively naturalist" or "psychologist." The rabbi's answer also changes from a refutation to a rule to be applied differently, depending on whether the person is involved in murdering another in any active way or only as a passive instrument and/or a tool.

The third step institutes a formal universal rule of natural bioequality. In his turn, Maimonides, on the Brisker Rav's reading, posits a formal principle of bioequality that all lives are equal. The rule created in the second stage of effacement is now applied as a formal universal principle of bioequality. Maimonides therefore applies it invariably, whether there is an active or only passive involvement in murder, the Brisker Rav argues. To highlight and to anticipate the next step in effacement: this bioequality is not only formal, but also "naïvely naturalist:" it presumes the natural equality of all lives, a naturalist view to be overcome in Rabbi Joseph Soloveitchik's reading and more specifically in his perspective on Maimonides from the point of view of the pure thought, which the next section will address.

As we will now see, the fourth step involves pure formal thought at work, without any residue of naturalism, and hence a radical conception of the formal man, the human who acts solely on the basis of reason. On Rabbi Joseph Soloveitchik's reading, inspired by his reading of Hermann Cohen, the question of bioequality becomes a question that pure reason posits, with "a known unknown"—Soloveitchik calls it a "relative nothing"—that the question implies instead of an answer. As I will explain in the next section, thought is no longer natural-formal, but purely formal, or simply "pure." Practically, however, it entails the same universalism as in the case of the Brisker Rav: Because there is no answer to whether or not all lives have the same value, one cannot practically (or if you prefer, ethically) differentiate between active and passive involvement in murder.

Pure Thought: Transcendental over Rhetorical? Philosophical over "Talmudic"?

Formal, a priori argumentation is thus what characterizes Maimonides's subject position, from which he both constructs and dismisses the Talmud and its rhetorical, rather than philosophical trappings of antiquity. That also means pushing beyond the horizon of thinking about the Talmud in Maimonides the role that refutation plays in intrinsically interpersonal ways of thought and action. Yet, why would Maimonides prefer transcendental thinking about Talmudic law to the natural-philosophical and/or rhetorical thinking of the Tosafists? What makes formal and a priori analysis preferable to situational and a posteriori analysis? Maimonides's allegiance to Aristotelian philosophy does not explain that preference. After all, both philosophically and forensically, he is more dismissive of the use of rhetoric than was Aristotle.

Rabbi Joseph Soloveitchik's interpretation of the philosophy of Hermann Cohen helps to address these aspects of the construction of the Talmud in and after Maimonides by both grounding and reenvisioning the subject position that Maimonides assumed in his construction of the Talmud. In light of Soloveitchik's reading of Hermann Cohen, we can see that Maimonides dismissed the Talmud not as a natural philosopher would dismiss rhetoric, but rather as a transcendentalist would dismiss both natural philosophy and rhetoric as its branch. It is no longer a natural human being, however much natural or even formal transcendental bioequality that notion can entail, but rather a purely transcendentalist principle, in which both subjectivity and intersubjectivity threaten to disappear, taking with them any remainder of any stable human identity, either formal or natural. That means when thinking correctly about the thinking subject, one is to opt for complete purity of thought, even at the expense of the subject, subjects, intersubjectivity, and as a result, of bioequality. In the case of Joseph Soloveitchik, it means not only that interpersonality disappears as soon as intersubjectivity claims its right, but that subjectivity, let alone intersubjectivity, must fade when it comes to the formal purity of what it "really" takes if one is to think. However, that purity of thinking must not be confused with what one might construe as the purity of rhetorical thinking, in which instead, bioequality comes a rhetorical argument that the value of the life of a person is unknown in comparison with the life of another person, which therefore is to be applied differently, depending on either the passive or active engagement of the subject whose life is at stake in the action. Instead, pure thinking for Soloveitchik takes a different path.

Soloveitchik insists along with Cohen that thinking needs to be pure, and, in particular, absolutely independent from the givens of the senses or of situations. What is more, however, thinking also has to be independent from the transcendental givens of reason, in Kant's sense of the term. The latter refers to reason's ability to discover that there are things in themselves that thinking can grasp only as ungraspable, that is, graspable only as the limits of reason, and therefore thinking, cannot grasp them in any detail. For Kant, this readily explains both the objectivity and the necessity of thinking. Cohen, however, instead of relying on the transcendent things in themselves as limits or reason, seeks to justify necessity and objectivity in thinking by means of the "origin" of thinking *in* thinking, not in anything beyond it. That origin is immanent in thinking, just as pure thinking is immanent in its origin. Cohen's and Soloveitchik's program thus consists precisely in looking for that inner "origin" of thinking. If attained, such and only such an origin can make thinking "pure." This gnomic and apparently tautological claim concerning the origin of thinking in thinking requires an extended explanation, and for Cohen, four facets of the notion of the origin help to explain it. First of all, thinking has an origin, but not a beginning: All the "elements" or steps of thinking connect in an endless chain, and each element can be deduced logically, if only retroactively, from the preceding one as from its origin. This, however, does not introduce a spurious infinity of 1+1+1 and so on, for the rules of connection between the elements are intrinsic to each pair of elements, rather than imposed on them. The rule of connection is derived from the fact of connection by Kant's method of transcendental deduction: the rule is what makes the connection possible de facto, but not necessarily what causes it initially.

Thinking understood in this sense unfolds in a lawful way because every move of thinking stems from a question.[21] Questions, in turn, mold problems that thinking consequently addresses. Problems by definition indicate "a known unknown" or "relative nothing," that is, what thinking cannot define before a solution to a problem is found, but what is nevertheless already implied in the problem. From a question, thinking proceeds to molding a problem with a "relative nothing" in it and then goes on to a new question, which arises from the previous one. Thinking thus goes from one element of the chain to another, and questions make for the origin of that movement and explain its lawful nature.

Questions thus make thinking move and make that movement lawful. In Soloveitchik's words, "Knowing unfolds from questions in which a relative nothing, that is, a problem, is constituted."[22] Still, the origin of all thinking in questions explains only the lawful nature of thinking while leaving unexplained why thinking is also unified and objective. This leads to the third facet of the notion of origin.

The transcendental method is the answer to the question of unity and objectivity in thinking. In Kant, Soloveitchik argues, the transcendental method consists of analyzing regularities in the givens of experience or in their understandings in science in order to discover conditions making these regularities possible. In the more technical terms of Kant's philosophy, which are borrowed from the legal terminology of his time, that means "deducing" (from "deducing a case under a law," establishing under what law a case is to be tried, as occurs in European legal systems), that is, not moving logically from premise to conclusion but rather moving the other way, from the givens of either experience or rational analysis to the conditions of their possibility.[23] The transcendental method generally helps to explain the objectivity of the data of experience by thus deducing them under their "transcendental" conditions, which contrasts with the "transcendent" means immanent to the experience, but not depending on it. Examples include space and time, as well as the forms of understanding.

Yet Cohen, in Soloveitchik's interpretation, goes further than Kant or the other interpreters of his philosophy in the neo-Kantian Marburg School. For Cohen, the objectivity of thinking has to do with what Soloveitchik highlights as Cohen's particular interpretation of the transcendental method. In this interpretation, Cohen both builds on and differs from the work of other scholars in Marburg. These scholars make an important innovation: The unity of thinking is not guaranteed by a thinking subject. Instead, the unity of thinking is due only to the pattern of moving from a question to a problem, and so on. However, they left an open question: If not for the subject, what makes this pattern apply uniformly in all thinking? For Soloveitchik, Cohen goes beyond other representatives of the Marburg school, not only asking whether can we ascribe the force and origin of thinking to a person, together with other Marburg philosophers he answers: certainly not in a psychological sense—but also answering that question in a positive way with his notion of origin as both a starting and continuing force in thinking.

This leads to the fourth facet of Cohen's notion of origin. This is the notion of identity in thinking. Soloveitchik calls it "the deepest aspect of Cohen's notion of origin," which gives "a clue about the general character of the pure thinking in Cohen."[24] Thinking is not only infinite or only a movement from question to question. It is not only coherent (has unity and objectivity), but it also stems from an identity. In Cohen's words, "Thinking is thinking of the origin, and [only] through this is it thinking of knowledge."[25] In light of Soloveitchik's interpretation, this means that its origin not only moves, unites, and regulates thinking, but it also makes for what the thinking is always "thinking of." In sum, a moving, unifying, and regulating principle of thinking within thinking, its origin, is also what thinking is "of." Driven by the origin, thinking also thinks of the origin, but reaches instead an object grasped in logical terms.

We can now understand this development as yet another step in the effacement of the interpersonal after Kant. In Cohen's terms, Maimonides emerges as a thinker who occupies the subject position of pure thought, a thought that depends neither on the external givens of a situation nor on the subject who thinks. That helps explain why Maimonides prefers the invariable, formal, and a priori applicability of the notion and value of life (the bioequality principle) in all cases of forced murder or adultery to a situational, a posteriori, and therefore variable application. If Maimonides strives for pure thinking in law, it explains not only how Maimonides differs from the Tosafists, but also why, for the Brisker Rav, formal and a priori thinking in law is preferable to the putatively a posteriori legal thinking of the Tosafists. The answer is that Maimonides adheres to the purity of thought in the law in the Cohenian sense—that is, without any external factor involved, even without a subject who thinks. What is more, adherence to the purity of thought also explains how Maimonides comes to see the Talmud in terms of "legal" as opposed to "homiletic" thinking and to dismiss the legal-rhetorical form of thinking as either natural-philosophical or rhetorical.[26]

The Brisker Rav's interpretation of Maimonides with the help of Soloveitchik's reading of Hermann Cohen creates an obviously complex perspective that affords what simpler points of view do not: a view in which modern thinkers invent and interpret medieval thinkers while taking for granted how the medieval thinkers construct the ancient, in this case, the Talmud, as an "old" form of thought to criticize and/or to replace. This more complex perspective shows how radical the effacement of the interpersonal had become. It is much more radical than locating thinking in the thinking subject at the expense of the erasure of the role of refutation, let alone of the interpersonality of which refutation is an intrinsic part. It extends beyond the thinking subject to the pure thinking of the origin. As we have seen, because this origin cannot be thematized, it becomes available only as a problem along with its correlative, the "relative nothing" that the problem brings forth. What is more, that move toward a never-thematized origin even embraces what otherwise would belong to refutation: the necessity of problems posited for pure thinking to be what it is, pure. It is this purity, rather than the thinking subject, that guarantees the "objectivity" of the thinking. What that means, however—and this is where the dual dynamics of the effacement is heavily at work—is that both the positing of problems becomes central in thinking, just as it is in the interpersonal process of refuting and defending in the Talmud, and considering the interpersonal refutations and counterrefutations, the site of such positing of problems becomes a rejected possibility. The positing of problems makes refuting (and with it interpersonality) both a viable and denied possibility as an element of the pure thinking. A reason for that exclusion might be that the positing of problems in Talmudic refutations does not simply indicate a "relative nothing" but rather turns on a "relative negation."

Relative negation is different from relative nothing. The former both posits and negates a position that is being refuted as a condition of the possibility for any valid position. If for Cohen and Soloveitchik pure thinking progresses from the positing of problems and the relative nothing that it creates toward a solution, whether or not it can be attained, then what is effaced by that move is relative negation, which entails no linear progress but instead insists on retaining the negated position as both valid and necessary for the problem to be posited in the correct way. Relative negation entails a refuted position, which is never to be left behind. The movement is therefore never progressive and must, by the progressivist logic of pure reason, be effaced.

More generally, if the thinking subject can still be understood as in terms of intersubjectivity at all, then pure thinking is radically impersonal, and the "formal man" however "personal" the term sounds, is radically impersonal, too. Pure thinking and the "formal man" implied by such thinking thus entail an even more radical effacement of the interpersonal. It is effacement because the "origin" of pure thinking might well have entailed the irreducibility of what is being refuted to its refutation, but it does not. Instead, pure thinking takes the route of "relative nothingness," "a known unknown" that either becomes something in a solution to the problem posited or becomes absolute nothingness in an antinomy. That both articulates and dismisses the possibility of relative negation and relative refutation, as distinct from relative nothingness. That possibility, and the interpersonal thinking that goes with it, becomes effaced from the horizon of pure thinking. As we have seen, the construction of the late ancient Talmud as an "old form" in the work of both critical scholars and traditional interpreters thus radically implies the subject's withdrawal for the sake of disinterested and objective analysis of the Talmud.

This construction involves the reduction of the main form of the late ancient Talmud to refutation, as if that were the Talmud's "natural" intellectual form. Both the Brisker Rav's and Soloveitchik's Cohenian views reinforce and reenact that construction, even as they replace the more conventional notion of the thinking subject with a more refined notion of pure thought. However critical and inventive these thinkers are in their construction of Maimonides as a medieval thinker, they follow the ways in which this medieval thinker himself constructed the ancient Talmud—as an intellectual form defined by rhetorical refutations.

The formal man, *Mensch*, whom both the Brisker Rav and R. Joseph Soloveitchik advance, thus means stripping the Talmudic tradition, and thus the tradition of the political it entails, from the role refutation plays therein, to promote instead a universal ontological value, that of the human as human as opposed to the human as an object alone; the value of humanity as both connected with and distinct from that of humankind. The latter includes racial, biological, or any other objective notions of man, while the former advances the formal notion of the humanity of a human, the notion of the formal man as a way to save the Talmudic tradition from Kant's criticism of Jewish tradition as "positive law." The price paid for that move was to reinforce a tradition in which the Talmud was first understood as bearing the form of refutation and counterrefutations and then stripped of that form in order to advance the allegedly philosophical content of it—the rational law, and formal man featuring the ontological equality of all humans as the one who is subject of and subject to that rational law. The resulting notion of the formal man meant reduction of the role of refutation in the Talmud to an extraneous element, thus meaning not only the victory of the apodictic over the irony (to use the terms describing the *Gornish*). Yet, as I will argue in the next chapter, it also meant both the proliferation and problematization of the medieval split between the law stripped from its form of the refutation and the narrative component of the Talmud, which I address while looking into other post-Kantian thinkers in the next chapter.

CHAPTER 7

Mis-Taking in *Halakhah* and *Aggadah* (Jewish Responses to Kant II)

In this chapter, I continue exploring post-Kantian element in the reception and construction of the Talmud, a process that, as I will argue, also entails the effacement of the interpersonal political in the Talmud in modern thought. I focus here on the intellectual and artistic continuum of philosophy and literature as articulated by modernist Jewish thinkers and writers produced in the period between the First and the Second World Wars. I examine notions of the implicit and, as I will show, the closely related notion of mistake in the work of Chaim N. Bialik, Walter Benjamin, Franz Kafka, and Franz Brentano as a case study in the construction of an, as it were, "authentic Talmud." This case study of illustrates the conceptual foundations the construction of the Talmud as "Jewish" and "law," articulates the limitations of that construction and thereby shows yet another way in which the effacement of the interpersonal in the Talmud has proceeded in the modern times. Here the post-Kantian element in modern secular Jewish literature not only continues to advance but also renegotiates the partitioning the Talmud into law, stripped of its rhetorical interpersonal form, on the one hand, and literary-poetic and in particular homiletic narratives as the counterpart to the "law" on the other.

The previous chapter showed how among tradition-oriented scholars, the interpersonal in the Talmud became effaced in the notion of a universal subject of reason, ultimately conceived of as pure thought and denying any intrinsic necessity of the intersubjective, let alone the interpersonal. This chapter attends to yet another move in the effacement of the interpersonal, now on the site of modernist philosophy and literature. At stake in this part of the story is once again the attempt to rethink of Kant's supersessionism in regard to positive law, but not by defending rabbinic tradition as transcendentalist. Rather, it attends to the modernist attempt to reassess the Jewish tradition critically by viewing it through the lens of post-Kantian thinking and simultaneously to rethink that thinking through such a reassessment.

The notion of the mistake is one site where such reassessment takes place. In a number of ways, modernist Jewish thinkers inherited (and reconsidered) the moves by which the late ancient Talmudic interpersonal became effaced in medieval and early modern rabbinic thought. Inherited from Maimonides, the partition of the Talmud into the legal and the homiletic or the legal and the poetic/literary became even stronger and more obviously involved in what informed that move: a new role for the mistake and mistaking in thinking the law and in shaping literature. The modernist thinkers this chapter treats attempted to rethink Kant's supersession in regard to positive law by showing that what now presents itself as the so-called positive law is to be called (in Chaim Bialik words, which I will later address in more detail) a homily (*aggadah*), not law (*halachah*). That meant for him that the Talmud is literature, rather than law, or law that becomes literature. As we will see, it is the literature of the inevitable mistake, without which neither law nor poetry can come to be.

The departure from neo-Kantianism attempted by these writers did not mean a cancellation of Kant's views on the Jewish Law as positive. In their thinking, the Talmud undergoes a critique in Kant's sense, but the Kantian assumption of the Talmud as positive law remains in place, even if it is criticized. Their critique of *halachah* as positive law does not undo the assumption that it is a positive law, as opposed to poetic or aggadic "parts" of the Talmud. These thinkers will attempt to criticize and even overcome the division of the Talmud into legal and poetic parts but will not deny the division in the first place.

This move, as well as the defense of rabbinic law as transcendental, as discussed in the previous chapter and the political ontology and political theology of Rancière and Schmitt, draw on and respond (each in its own way) to Kant's inevitably supersessionism-driven approach to positive law and its formal exclusion of those who adhere to it from conceptions of the human. A similar mechanism of the effacement of the interpersonal political in the Talmud is at work in each of these lines of thinking. It is in this context that this chapter attends to what perhaps is the most intriguing version of that effacement, the version of Jewish modernist philosophical and literary thinking.

Rethinking the Implicit: Mis-Taking (in) the Talmud

The term *implicit* refers to a whole range of thoughts, insights, or meanings that stand in opposition to those that are explicated. In the nineteenth and twentieth centuries, logicians appropriated the concept to philosophy. Retrieving the implicit from the realm of logic to the broader realm of rhetoric shows that a complicated structure of movements exercised by the mind and, indeed, by the whole person, interacting with a given expression, stands beyond what any logical notion of the implicit can describe.

In addition to its appropriation by philosophy, the concept of the implicit has been used broadly for the investigation of the nature of language as an object of linguistic science, where language is understood as an independent and self-regulating structure. (I use the word *structure* in order not to use *substance*, because structural linguists cannot agree to treat a *structure* as a kind of *substance* in the technical philosophical meaning of the term, yet *structure* shares with *substance* the important feature of self-sufficiency, if not immanence.)

Treating language as a structure is characteristic of both formal-mathematical linguistic approaches and formal-literary ones. The implicit is treated there as being strictly and definitely explicable at any moment of discourse. Thus, in formal-mathematical approaches, the ideal language is an artificial one; the implicit is strictly determined according to the formal rules of deduction and hence can be explicated easily at every point.

Similarly, formal-literary approaches deal with literature as with a language or form[1] that is subjected either to modification by creating a new "fact of literature," a *literarily fact*, as in the work of Yury Tynyanov, or to critical analysis of its poetics, as in that of Mikhail Bakhtin. Here, language is once again treated as a structure or substance, as something that can be either modified or revised. (Literature is a kind of "alchemy" of language.) In this approach, the implicit does not have any independent theoretical value.

In both approaches, meaning, including implied meanings, can be explicated, whether via the theory of language or in the form of a dictionary. However, if we do not understand the language as either a structure or a substance, we cannot continue to think of the implicit in terms of meaning that thus could be actually and explicitly determined for any particular unit of language. (By *unit*, I mean an expression, an utterance, a sentence, an argument, or even any particular language.) In this situation, the implicit becomes a complicated matter. The logical terms of the implicit become insufficient for elaborating the complicated topology of being implicit. Therefore, a new theoretical strategy is required.

We seem to have good resources for such a strategy, including taking into account the very *facticity* of the implicit "as is"—that is, ways to grant theoretical respect to the fact that the implicit in an expression has been *kept* implicit and has not been stated explicitly. However, this solution is not an easy one. If it is to be accepted, we have to elaborate a theory of how the status (the topos or location) of the particular sense of something implicit in it influences the sense of an expression. Walter Benjamin, Franz Brentano, and Franz Kafka seem to be thinkers who offer great resources for undertaking this task.

Criticizing the Linguistic Understanding of Language

Franz Brentano demonstrates a weak point of the linguistic-grammatical (substantialist) approach to language in his *Kategorienlehre* (translated as *The Theory of Categories*).[2] Brentano argues against the simplified distinction made by grammarians between the use of verb *sein* ("to be") as a main verb and as an auxiliary verb. He develops an important distinction between the thought of something *in obliquo* ("indirectly") and *in recto* ("directly"), which leads to an understanding that what is implicit (in his terms, *in obliquo*) need not necessarily exist.[3] Following his argument, we will see that consequently, the implicit must be strongly protected from being taken as *actually* and *evidently* existent on any plane of presence in an expression.

Here are the points of Brentano's argument that seem to be most important for our discussion of the effacement of the interpersonal in the Talmud by the modernist thinkers who draw on his program of rescuing thinking from the tenets of a linguistic game controlled by a universal grammar. As Brentano pointed, our grammarians would say that in the statement "A is," A is stated to exist. However, according to Brentano, "we are dealing with a simple affirmation of A thought of in the temporal mode of the present."[4]

Brentano takes us immediately from the grammatical dimension of substantial language to the dimension of "being thought of" as it is introduced by an utterance: "A is." This change is decisive. In many cases, where grammatical theory sees a kind of linguistic predication, Brentano discovers the expression for a kind of "thinking of."

"A is" is relatively a simple case of predication. More complex cases involve saying what exactly A is (e.g., "A is such and such") which would be an absolute determination, as opposed to a relative determination, in which A relates to B via a predicate. Comparative determinations (A is more . . . than B) would be an example of a broader class of relative determinations in which A is stated to relate to B in some way. The case of relative determinations is more complex than that of absolute determinations, which entail a claim that an A is something, or has a certain predicate. It is in his analysis of these more complicated cases of predication that Brentano points out the two distinct modes of "being thought of"—*in obliquo* and *in recto*, which will lead to a new notion of the implicit: "What distinguishes a relative determination from an absolute determination? The answer is this. Whenever one thinks a relative determination in *recto*, then one also thinks of something in *obliquo* at the same time. Thus, one who thinks of a person seeing is also thinking in *obliquo* of something colored that is seen."[5] Brentano continues by saying that a thing thought of *in obliquo* can be either existent or not. Its existence or nonexistence does not make a difference for thinking of it in *obliquo*.

Now we are ready for the next step. If the predications of grammarians in many cases turn out not to be predications, but rather *expressions* for being thought of, then what conclusions can we derive about the thoughts or "thinking of" expressed there? To answer, one should consider that Brentano's analysis is capable of dealing not only with the direct and indirect modes of thinking of a *thing* or an *object*, but also with states of thought itself. The thought of an object *in obliquo* is a thought that *is in obliquo*. Therefore, one is not obliged to read Brentano in terms of a reified opposition between the thought and the thing. Thinking *in obliquo* is a state or an act that is irrelevant to any classification in terms of actual existence or nonexistence.

Thus, it seems to be accurate to use Brentano's distinction for the description of states of thoughts. Doing so allows me to say that in terms of Brentano's discourse, the implicit is a thought *in obliquo* or that it is included in a relative determination. That means the implicit is given indirectly in a statement that only seems to be a predication, but instead turns out to be an affirmative expression of a state of thought—the state of being thought of.[6] Thus, the implicit is included in the relative determination of an expression, rather than in an absolute determination of predication.

For the present discussion, this means that to think of a relative determination is not necessarily to assume its existence. It therefore also means that implicit thinking (here understood as thinking *in oblique*) is not always fully present in a relative determination, nor can it ever be fully explicated therein. More generally, that is a first step toward seeing the implicit as never fully graspable by the process of explication. Explication cannot strip the implicit from its efficacy. Now, relative determination is the determination of thought itself, rather than of its object. The object of a relative determination is only an external determinative for the effect created by the indirect character of thought itself.

The most general conclusion to derive from the preceding exposition of Brentano's argument is that whenever we deal with an expression (as opposed to a statement or predication), there is some indirect thought included. It remains an indirect thought and remains irreducible to any explicit thoughts presented in the expression directly.

Brentano's discovery of what is "thought of," irrelevant to either the existence or nonexistence of either the objects described or the subjects manifested in an expression, reveals a new aspect of implicit thinking. His theory helps us to see an indirect thinking that hovers over any expression, however explicit or however "existent" the referents and the subjects of that expression might be. Such indirect thinking always accompanies direct and explicit thoughts in an expression. Brentano thus helps us see the irreducibility of indirect thinking or of thinking indirectly. And there is still more to thinking in that oblique register that can help us see how it both erases the Talmudic modes of thinking and leaves a trace thereof in the new notion of the implicit at which Brentano's view of thinking helps us to arrive.

A Way to Represent the Implicit

In Walter Benjamin's "Epistemo-Critical Prologue," the foreword to *The Origin of German Tragic Drama*, there is another very important aspect of the irreducibility of the implicit to any kind of existence and thus to any kind of explication. In this work, Benjamin suggests treating ideas as both separate from all the "phenomena of our world" and as separate from all the "concepts" of our theories that embrace these phenomena. Because ideas thus are prior to explicit concepts of theory, to represent ideas, one needs some specific form. For Benjamin, the form is that of a medieval tractate.[7] The notion of the medieval tractate is of a double importance for my argument here. It invokes not only philosophical writings in the Middle

Ages but also the Talmudic tractates as the media (both intellectual and material) in which the late ancient Talmud in its entirety presented itself to the medieval rabbis and from there on to the readers and "learners" of the Talmud today. Beginning with the Tosafists, the late ancient Talmud has come to be approached as a megatractate, a tractate consisting of tractates. This is in contrast to seeing the late ancient Talmud as a corpus of intrinsically unfinished discussions running one after another according to the order of the statements in the Mishnah, statements that these discussions examine, refute, and defend. This contrast thus highlights yet another path of erasure and effacement of the late ancient Talmud from the horizon of thinking from the Middle Ages to modernism.

More generally, a medieval tractate is often an extended letter or series of letters from a master to a student, often presuming that the student already has learned things directly from the master and thus has the requisite skill or knowledge that would allow understanding the letters correctly. The tractate often conveys esoteric knowledge that a student could grasp only by implementing that previously developed skill, knowledge, or aptitude in reading the tractate. All these general features apply to a medieval view of the Talmud as a tractate, as well, including even the "senders" of the Talmud as a megatractate, Ravina and Rav Ashi, as mentioned in the previous chapter.

The form of the tractate, reelaborated and implemented by Benjamin for his purposes, allows him to deal with ideas, even though these are never expressed directly, either in a concept or in a phenomenon.[8] The form of the tractate follows the idea, organizing concepts and phenomena without unfolding the idea in a concept, that is, maintaining it in the immediacy of the implicit. Benjamin's prologue emphasizes very strongly that the dimensions of the explicit and implicit are not convertible into each other and do not communicate with each other directly.

In his reading of Kafka, Benjamin further elaborates the point. In fact, Benjamin reads Kafka as someone who seeks to move from phenomena to their idea, but because the idea finally never can be embraced, is faced instead with the prospect of merely inventing new concepts, what Brentano called "spurious predications."[9] So instead, as Benjamin reads him, Kafka gives up the project of the transmission of truth by means of explicit concepts.

By Benjamin's definition, however, ideas cannot be fully explicated in concepts. Therefore, in attempting to grasp an idea, the concepts can only fail to grasp it. On the other hand, concepts are the only ways in which to approach the ideas, so that the failure of explication becomes necessary in order to access the implicit. This perspective would apply to the Talmud as a medieval megatractate, as well. Arguably, the Tosafists' commentary attempts to create—or, as they would have it, articulate—and repair failures in a commentary on the Talmud, the commentary of Rashi, to which the Tosafists are responding. This understanding of the importance of the role of the form of the tractate and of the role of failure therein allows me to come back to Benjamin's own treatment of failure of explication as he is reading Kafka.

Benjamin thus sees Kafka as a "failure": "To do justice to the figure of Kafka in its purity, and its peculiar beauty, one should never lose sight of one thing: it is the figure of a failure. . . . Nothing is more memorable than the fervor with which Kafka insists on his failure."[10]

This formulation seems to owe much to the essay "Halachah and Aggadah" by Chaim Nachman Bialik (1873–1934), poet laureate of the Hebrew renaissance, which Benjamin read in Gershom Scholem's translation.[11]

The terms *halakhah* and *aggadah* are Hebrew versions of the Babylonian Aramaic terms *aggadethah* and *hilkhathah*. In the Babylonian Talmud, the former Hebrew term generally refers to (interpretations of) a third-century document, the Mishnah, a compendium of pronouncements of those whom the rabbis in the Talmud consider sages. The rabbis refer to the sages as a group or to specific sages mentioned in the Mishnah and parallel apocryphal records of the sages' teachings by the name of a given sage. Collectively, that amounts to a set of instructions for rabbinic courts; more often than not, for the Rabbis in the Talmud, these instructions become both necessary and valid when common sense proves insufficient to resolve an issue between parties in conflict.[12] The first of the aforementioned Aramaic terms refers to homilies, stories, discourses, and narrations about earlier rabbinic authorities—their actions, interactions with others, and cases where their personal wisdom comes on display. The second Aramaic term refers to a clause in the Mishnah ascribed to a certain sage or a group of sages; it may also refer to interpreting a specific clause one way or another. Because, in the medieval period, the Talmud came to be treated as the source for the codes of the "Jewish Law" as system of rules, regulations, statuses, and decisions, the term *halachah* came to imply an impersonal rational code of law, thus making the "law" much more independent of any particular authority or sage mentioned in the Mishnah or Talmud, or "true" in its own terms. Such a change in the meaning of *halachah* led to presenting *aggadah* as contrasting to the universal propositional truth of the law. It also meant placing *aggadah* in the realm of poetic production of or about a wise person, as opposed to a philosophical, rational, systematic, and in any case impersonal account of "law," *halachah*. Needless to say, these changes also led to a much sharper division of the materials of discussions in the Talmud into *halachah* and *aggadah*, now understood, in keeping with the medieval effacement of the late ancient Talmud discussed in the previous chapter, as two different sources of authority, along with the marginalization of the latter in favor of the former.

In "Halachah and Aggadah," Bialik explains the generalized modern usage of these medieval terms:

> The words *Halachah* and *Aggadah* come from the Talmud . . . but from the point of view of their inner reality their meaning is capable of extension and enlargement to cover the whole range of related phenomena. . . . They are two different forms, two distinct styles that go together in life and in literature. To each age its own *Aggadah*; to each *Aggadah* its own *Halachah*.
>
> We are speaking not of this or that particular *halakhah* or *aggadah*. Our concern is with *Halachah* in general—with *Halachah* as a concrete and definite form of actual life, of a life which is not in the clouds, which does not depend on vague feeling and beautiful phrases alone, but has physical reality and physical beauty. *Halachah* in that sense, I assert, is but the inevitable continuation and sequel of *Aggadah*.
>
> The value of *Aggadah* is that it issues in *Halachah*. *Aggadah* that does not bring *Halachah* in its train is ineffective. Useless itself, it will end by incapacitating its author for action.[13]

In modernity, however, according to Bialik, "we are privileged to live in an age of pure *Aggadah*, both in literature and in actual life. The whole world is but *Aggadah* within *Aggadah*; of *Halachah*, in whatever sense, there is no trace and no mention."[14]

Aggadah fails without *halakhah*; wisdom fails without truth. Bialik can be interpreted more simplistically as suggesting that in what for him is modern times, people have forgotten about *Halakhah* and live "in the clouds," in the world of "vague feeling" alone. A more complex, but arguably also more refined interpretation suggests that in modernity, even those who live "according to *Halakhah*" live in the poetic world of a story. On that interpretation, instead of leading to *Halakhah*, *Aggadah* has consumed it. In either interpretation, *Aggadah* has failed and reigns in and through that strong failure. This is also how Benjamin describes the roots of Kafka's "beautiful failure": They are in Kafka's (and in part, in Benjamin's own) relation to tradition. Benjamin says,

> Kafka's work represents a sickening of tradition. Wisdom has sometimes been defined as the epic side of truth. Wisdom is thus characterized as an attribute of tradition; it is truth in its haggadic consistency.
>
> This consistency of truth has been lost. Kafka was by no means the first to be confronted with this situation. Many had come to terms with it in their own way—clinging to truth, or what they believed to be truth and, heavyhearted or nor, renouncing its transmissibility. Kafka's genius lay in the fact that he tried something altogether new: he gave up truth so that he could hold on to its transmissibility, the haggadic element.[15]

In terms of Benjamin's characterization of Kafka as a failure who gave up truth for the sake of its transmissibility, "failure" turns out to be the failure to go directly from a phenomenon to its idea. Even if such a failure is characteristic of modernity as a whole, as Bialik also claimed, Benjamin argues that it was only Kafka who lived it, experienced it in detail, and therefore grasped its beauty. Kafka's work thus seems to serve as an aesthetic or literary utopia for Benjamin's own epistemological project: in search of ideas, one fails, but lives in the beauty of that failure.

In Benjamin's terms, failure thus means that Kafka gave up the effort to reach the truth (that is, to arrive at ideas) directly or in explicit form—that is, in concepts—and instead transmitted ideas indirectly, in implicit form, without violating their indirect character. Like many others in modernity, Benjamin's Kafka thus found himself facing a choice between *aggadah* and *halakhah*, between the wisdom of ideas and the truth of concepts. Unlike many others, however, his solution was to change the conditions of the choice. Kafka gave up the project of arriving at transmissible truth (Benjamin's concepts) for the sake of preserving access to transmissible wisdom (Benjamin's ideas in the philosophical form of tractates). Thereby, Kafka won a new status for wisdom: as transmissible, but also as neither idea nor concept, wisdom is the only realistic form of the non-transmissible truth in our world, and the implicit is the way we have access to it. That is how wisdom becomes the foundation of the law, instead of being a secondary appendix to it, or in Bialik's terms, leads to the law, which is fundamentally the same. Benjamin's understanding of the law, which is for him is another name for ideas, exceeds the conceptual dimension of our world, but functions in our world thanks the forms of *aggadah* and the tractate. As an indirect mode of expression, *aggadah* becomes a fundamental representation of the law in our world. Benjamin says of Kafka: "His works are by nature parables. But their poverty and their beauty consist in their need to become *more* than parables. They don't simply lie down at the feet of doctrine, the way Aggadah lies down at the feet of Halakhah. Having crouched down, they unexpectedly cuff doctrine with a weighty paw."[16]

For Benjamin, however, raising a "weighty paw" against religious doctrine from a position of submission to it is not enough. Although the *aggadah* formally resemble the philosophical tractate, they still cannot organize any positive representation of ideas. "That is why," according to Benjamin, "in Kafka, there is no longer any talk of wisdom." Instead, "only the products of its decomposition are left." Benjamin, however, wants to do what Kafka's strategy of failure cannot: express the law in the world in a positive way—that is, represent ideas themselves, but implicitly, by employing the failure of their explicit representation in the form of the tractate.[17]

What that means, however, is that Benjamin sees Kafka as resisting the medieval partition of the Talmud into law and narrative wherein both belong to "this world," defined by poetic forms (*aggadah*) and legal-philosophical or conceptually definable forms (*halachah*), according to Maimonides. He instead promotes ideas that exceed this world but that, unlike in Kant's epistemology, are not totally out of reach—precisely because the concepts productively fail. Failure is the way to ideas. It therefore effectively could also be seen as an attempt to recover the Talmud from the *halachah/aggadah* partitioning. However, as the next section will show, this attempt only complicates the erasure of the Talmud.

Of Tradition

The implicit plays different roles in Kafka's "haggadic" pieces and in rabbinic tradition. First, consider Kafka's parables that "need to become *more* than parables" in terms of that need and the failure to fulfill it. In Kafka's short story called "On Parables," an anonymous voice, the narrator of the story, complains that the words of the wise are mere parables, incompatible with our everyday world. A parable bespeaks the inconceivable, which is beyond our world and cannot help us here: the complaint is that a sage, the narrator of a parable, bespeaks the inconceivable by means of a parable because she does not have any direct knowledge of the inconceivable. Whoever relates a parable is simply saying that the inconceivable is inconceivable—"*und das haben wir gewusst*," "and that we have already known," the complainer notes bitterly. A different voice responds to that complaint that the best possible result of the sage's telling of the parable is in becoming aware that parables deal with the inconceivable, with what is incompatible with our everyday world. What for the complainer is failure, the failure to connect the inconceivable with our everyday world, is a productive act for the sage and his followers. The complainer seemingly wins in reality, but in fact loses the inconceivable as the intrinsic part of the real. That is, the sage's performance is a success precisely because it is a failure to conceive the inconceivable.

The success of a parable cannot be measured in terms of achieving the goal that the sage narrating of the parable has in telling it. Rather, it is based on the work of a device that none of those involved in making use of the parable—neither the sage who tells it nor the complainer about it—can control. The parable is a machine for learning from failure. One starts it and lets it go. In the words of the parable that "On Parables" goes on to supply, "Concerning this a man once said: Why such reluctance? If you only followed the parables you yourselves would become parables and with that rid yourself of all your daily cares. Another said: I bet that is also a parable. The first said: 'you have won.' The second said: 'But unfortunately only in parable.' The first said: 'No, in reality: in parable you have lost.'"[18] Victory in reality is loss in the parable. That is how the machine of learning from a failure works. Such a failure is not a mistake. Mistakes can be corrected. Actual failures cannot.[19]

At least that would be the first, and therefore rough, approximation of the relationship between a mistake and a failure. In light of what will become clear at a later stage of analysis, this understanding of the relationships between failure and mistake would be both more complex and more precise. It will also tell more about both the invocation and erasure of the role of failure and mistake in the Talmud in how Benjamin and Benjamin's Kafka approach the virtues of failing. The relationship between mistaking and failing would be not so much one of difference as of imbrication and/or consequence. Mistakes produce failures, but "failing" an interpretation would seem to, in effect, "correct" the mistake by revealing it as such and leading to its abandonment[20] and thus to some new understanding that always also could be a mistake. Failure becomes a way to reveal and thereby correct the mistake without ever turning on any version of dialectical progress in either negative dialectics or in that of sublation and even less so in the sense of any kind of circular movement. In other words, this relationship would not be dialectical in the usual philosophical senses of dialectics.

Yet, can this machine generating failure produce more than despair? Kafka's and Benjamin's answers differ. For the complainer in the Kafka's story, there is only a negative way of relating to the inconceivable: by failing to conceive the inconceivable. That failure is the only real way to relate to it. For Benjamin, however, both the failure to conceive the inconceivable and the positive results of that failure are parts of one form—of one machine: that of the tractate, in which both "reality" and "parable," both law and homily, *halakhah* and *aggadah*, are intrinsically interconnected. From Benjamin's standpoint, the failure of parable or *aggadah* to conceive the inconceivable leads to the reality of what is addressed in the law or *halakhah*. To understand this, we need to examine the nature of Midrash *aggadah* as well as explore the relationship it to Benjamin's reading of the role of failure and mistake.

Midrash Aggadah

As a genre, Midrash *aggadah* is a form of exegesis of biblical phrases and passages. The characters in Midrash *aggadah*, often nameless narrators, initially present the audience with what seems to be an incoherence in the divine utterances in the Bible, then show them the ultimate coherence of these utterances as reconstructed and defended in the Midrash. Jill Robbins offers as an example the Midrash *aggadah* on Genesis 22, the story known as "The Binding of Isaac" in the Jewish tradition or as "The Sacrifice of Abraham" in the Christian tradition.[21] As a character in that story, Abraham makes a mistake, a mis-taking or misapprehension, in that he understands the divine order "bring him [Isaac] to (the) sacrifice" as "slaughter Isaac," a command that to Abraham seems "incoherent" with earlier promises G-d made to him. On this reading, shocked by the discrepancy between this command and the earlier promise G-d had made in Genesis 17 about Isaac's future, Abraham does not pay sufficient attention to the ambiguity of the phrase "bring him to sacrifice." The divine utterance also might have meant "bring him to the place of slaughtering," Robbins points out. Instead, she argues, following the Midrash, Abraham commits a "mistake of hearing," which is later corrected by the angel. The "mistake of hearing" is a detail that the Midrash *aggadah* adds to the story to restore the coherence between the earlier divine promise to perpetuate Abraham's seed through Isaac and the new command, which strikes both the audience, and therefore also Abraham, as incoherent with the earlier promise.

This mistake of hearing, however, has an intrinsic temporal element that the Midrash *aggadah*, as Robbins reads it, does not address, but Kafka does. For Kafka, the mistake is a necessary part of the story, not just a way to explain a seeming incoherence in the Bible. It is an essential part of the temporal structure of the story's narrative form. For Kafka, as she interprets him, at the beginning of the story, Abraham "heard," or paid attention to, only the first meaning only ("slaughter Isaac") and he understood the second meaning (in effect, "take him to the altar") only at the very end, standing, as he did, in front of the altar, with his hand outstretched to kill his son. According to Robbins, whereas the Midrash *aggadah* reveals the "mistake of hearing" only to restore the coherence of the biblical text, that is, merely to correct a mistaken understanding of the command, Kafka defends the fundamental character and necessity of such a mistake. For Kafka, in her interpretation, in order for the story to work, Abraham cannot avoid this mistake at the beginning, even if by the end he has realized it was a mistake. Otherwise, there is no story.

A mistake that cannot be avoided is one of the features not only in Kafka's work, as we have seen, but is also a feature of Talmudic discussions. Recognition of the importance of making a mistake in studying the Torah finds an explicit expression in an *aggadah* about two Talmudic sages in which a winner of the argument consoles his losing friend (and, potentially, himself as well, since he might have been the loser): "one can understand the words of the Torah only if one gets mistaken about them." The original language is also translatable as "by them," to mean that it is the words of the Torah that make the sage mistake their meaning. The original wording, *nikhshal bahen*, represents the middle voice, which is neither exactly passive nor precisely active, but rather is either neither or both. In the middle voice, there is no active subject of the action; neither "the words of the Torah," nor "the sage" appear as the subject and/or cause of the mistaking. In the light of this rule of the mistake, the mechanics of the story run like this:

1. Abraham previously was promised that "in Isaac shall thy seed be called" (Genesis 21:12).
2. Abraham was tempted ("tested" as most of the English translations have it). He heard an utterance that he could understand either as a command to bring Isaac as a burnt offering or as a command to bring Isaac to the place of burnt offerings.
3. Even if Abraham understood the ambiguity of the command right away, from the start of the story, by the end, with his hand outstretched, he intimates his own willingness (or his own understanding of the divine will) to sacrifice the son, which proves different from the action commanded by the utterance, even in the

> sense of bringing Isaac to the altar. Of course, Abraham's choice to sacrifice, rather than simply to bring to the place of sacrifice, is still related to the utterance "bring him to sacrifice" as one possible interpretation, but his understanding no longer depends on the sense conveyed.

This double bind—relation to an utterance without dependence on it—substantiates the essential role that the "mistake of hearing" plays here. It is the machinery of mis-taking, or misapprehension, that reveals to Abraham the sense implicit in the divine utterance beyond Abraham's hearing it. Because of this machine of mistaking, the divine word is revealed to the audience of the Midrash *aggadah* in isolation from Abraham's interpretation of and acting on it. Two meanings in one utterance create the necessity of choosing one of them. Abraham's interpretation, along with the necessity of a mistake in interpretation, are what make for the moving force of the story, as the audience for it can clearly see but Abraham cannot.

In action, that is, "in reality," Abraham wins: He fulfills both meanings by approaching the altar and stopping there at the very last moment, thereby showing the audience the true meaning of one's relation to the divine. However, "in the parable," that is, in his interpretation of the utterance, that is, in what guides the actions of Abraham as a character, he loses, no matter which way he interprets the utterance at the start. If, at the beginning of the story, he interprets the divine words as simply a command to bring Isaac to the altar, he is missing the other possibility of interpretation, and thus he is mistaken. However, if, at the beginning of the story, he interprets the utterance as a command to slaughter Isaac, he again is mistaken, as becomes clear at the end. If, in yet another way of interpreting the command, at the beginning of the story he had understood fully the ambiguity of the utterance and interpreted it both ways, this also would have been a mistake, because from the beginning, having to act on the double interpretation automatically would mean choosing the weakest one, that is, dismissing the command to slaughter Isaac altogether. In yet another way, Abraham understands the ambiguity of the command from the start and moves forward up to the point where he stands with his arm stretched, no longer able to continue without sacrificing one of the meanings of the divine command. In this case, Abraham fails, too, because by that stoppage, he still sacrifices one of the meanings. At the beginning of the story, Abraham cannot control the end of it. Any attempt to control the end would be and must be a mistake. To arrive to the end of the story "in the parable," Abraham must commit a mistake and must lose "in reality." To arrive to the end of the story "in reality," he must fail "in the parable." This inevitable mistake leads Abraham to winning his future and that of his descendants either "in parable" or "in reality."

There is yet another reading of this story, however. It is closer to Benjamin's account of the implicit than to Kafka's. Yet it approximates the rabbinic tradition of Midrash a*ggadah* no less than Kafka's view does, even if from a different angle. This reading has to do not only with time, but also with the timeless—not only with the irreversible, although retraceable working of a time machine in which mistakes must occur to make a story work, but also with what Benjamin saw as the timeless ideas that are approached in that story.

Abraham, in one of the readings above, was capable from the start of seeing both possible interpretations of the divine utterance "bring him to sacrifice." However, a new understanding comes to Abraham and to the audience only after, and as a result of, the mistake he commits—the understanding that the divine utterance stands beyond and above any graspable interpretation. Otherwise, the character of Abraham would have to be read along the lines of Kierkegaard's Abraham, that is, as one who must simply make a leap of faith.[22] For Benjamin, however, the divine utterance is an idea, which means that although it stands beyond any graspable sense, it remains implicit. To borrow Brentano's terms, this utterance is a relative determination, rather than an absolute one. What is more, it is a relative determination in which the determinants are not stable; it can mean "thinking of" a situation when it is more about bringing to sacrifice than it is about sacrificing, or vice versa; nor do the determinants make any claim to existence, that is, make a direct command. This means that as a parable, "The Binding of Isaac" does not reveal what the divine idea behind the story actually is; neither does it make any claim about either the existence or nonexistence of the inconceivable or about any knowledge or lack of knowledge about the inconceivable. Rather, and much more powerfully, it creates and induces in the reader the initial "thinking of" of the inconceivable that is approached by the story.[23]

The machinery of misapprehension maintains the implicit character of the initial divine utterance, that is, what is excluded from its initial interpretation ("sacrifice Isaac") at the beginning. Nor is what is implicit in the utterance fully explicated when the story ends. All the end of the story does is reveal the implicit to be implicit.

Failure as Proof in the Talmud

From both Benjamin's and Kafka's perspectives, the story of Abraham and Isaac is the symbolic birthplace of the rabbinic rhetoric of the mistake, and Kafka's and Benjamin's manner of dealing with the mistake and with misapprehension pertain not only to reading (or should I have said misreading?) this biblical story, but also to some passages in the Talmud, as well. As I will immediately illustrate, the general statement that "one can understand the words of the Torah only if one gets mistaken about them" in the Babylonian Talmud is not just something that one rabbi tells another in the course of a polemic, because misapprehension plays a much more serious role as both a heuristic device and as an instrument for proving, and, more to the point, in failing interpretations. The rabbis self-refute and thereby, indeed only thereby, act politically, even if their action becomes latter invoked and missed, that is to say erased in the notions of irony and well-structured uncertainty, as we have seen in other examples in the previous chapters. We can even find a Talmudic hero of mistake making, ironical or even more precisely satirical, though that hero proves to be, who on different readings, in accord with the logic of the middle voice, either teaches or learns the beauty and importance not only of making mistakes, but also of entering a true interpersonal relationship with the other. The name of this hero of the interpersonal (or of the hero of mistake, if one thinks in Benjamin's terms) is Raba Bar Rav Huna; and it is in his story, narrated in a passage from the Talmudic tractate *Gittin* (Divorce Writs),[24] that we find the dictum:

> One can understand the words of the Torah only if one gets mistaken about them.
>
> אין אדם עומד על דברי תורה אלא אם כן נכשל בהן

Misapprehension is a condition for success in doing Torah. I will summarize the story of Raba Bar Rav Huna in what follows, assuming that the text displays a coherent argument, rather than being an anthology of the three or four independent fragments loosely connected by association or by similarity in style, names, or characters. I will also presuppose that in the story there are no purely "ornamental" figures of speech.

It is important to begin with the broader context of legal discussion pertaining to the story. The story is set in a society in which there are not only free individuals, who therefore can marry and who bear the financial responsibilities of doing so, but also slaves, who are not financially responsible and therefore cannot legally marry. Most important for the story, in such a society, there can also be individuals who are half-slaves and half-free. This legal condition arises when two owners own a slave and one of them sets his or her part of the slave free. Also, in this society, a free person may have and be responsible for more than one wife.

This situation creates a series of legal issues. If a slave belongs to two owners and one has granted him freedom, then the half-slave, half-free man works one day for his owner and another for himself, a group of sages proposes in the Mishnah. A much more difficult question is whether such a person can marry. The Mishnah says a half-free man "cannot marry a free woman," because he is partly a slave, nor can he marry a slave woman, because free people do not marry slaves, and he is partly free. On account of these legal difficulties, the other group of the sages in the Mishnah proposes that a court should require the remaining owner free the half-slave with an obligation to pay that owner back at half the price of a slave. This becomes a solution that the first group of sages, too, agrees to accept.

Centuries later and miles away from the point of Mishnah's composition, the nameless characters in the Talmud, interpretable as rabbis and students in Babylon, are challenged to reconfirm the recorded memory of the Mishnah. If the Mishnah is available for them only as recorded memory, is this record automatically accurate? Following the tactics of refutation and counterrefutation, these rabbis and students explore a possibility that the Mishnah does not mention and therefore would seem to deny: the possibility of a man who is half-slave legally marrying a woman who also is half-slave. Is this possible, even though the Mishnah, as recorded, omits that possibility? If so, the text of the Mishnah is not remembered correctly, is corrupt, and needs to be amended. So what is at stake here is the accuracy and therefore the authority of the Mishnah itself.

The task is thus to test and dismiss the possibility of marriage between people who are both half-slave and half-free, focusing in particular on marrying a half-free woman. The strategic goal of the rabbis is to prove that such a marriage would not be readily allowable, not just even if but also precisely because it is not explicitly considered in the Mishnah. Tactically, however, the characters in the Talmudic discussion begin by testing and dismissing possible legal grounds that would allow such a marriage. Unlike other models of relationship between tactics and strategies, for them, a tactical failure means strategic success.

In a sequence of arguments, the anonymous characters in the Talmud consistently follow the tactics of successful refutations and even, at one point, make the elusive nature of the failure of a series of proofs into the theme of a story in one of the proofs in the series.

The literary structure of this series is as complex as it is unusual for modern readers. The series includes conversations between nameless characters who, in making their arguments, often cite not only the pronouncements of earlier, named authorities, the rabbis of the earlier generations, but also whole conversations and discussions of such authorities about the pronouncement of yet another, older authority. There are citations of conversations between other nameless characters as well. To articulate this complex interplay of arguments and citations occurring at different times and places, but all brought together sequentially, I will summarize a fragment of the series in the form of a theatrical script, with a main stage, where the main conversation between nameless characters is taking place, and two secondary stages, where the cited conversations occur. If I were to give a name to this theater, I would call it the theater of memory, for the action is all oriented toward thoughtful investigation of the traditions remembered in order to assure the reliability of their memory. I would further call it a theater of satire, in reference to the political informing the interpersonal relationships performed on the stage.

The main stage is a rabbinic academy in Babylon—call it a rabbinic school of rhetoric. The time is a morning circa the seventh century C.E. A *tanna*, an entry-level or an intermediate-level student whose role is the mechanical memorization and recitation of the teachings of the Palestinian Rabbis, of the third century or before—the "sages"—reports as follows. The sages had a legal problem: a slave was owned by two masters. One of the masters freed his or her part of the slave. What is the slave's legal status now?

As the *tanna* recites it, one school of the sages, the House of Hillel, proposed that the slave becomes a half-slave, half-free person who works one day for himself and another day for his owner. The sages of a competing school, the House of Shammai, objected. "You have taken a good legal care of the master, but not of the new half-free person."[25] In other words, you created a legally untenable situation, an impasse, as follows: "He can marry neither a slave woman, because he is partially free, nor a free woman, because he is partially slave, whereas G-d created the world for procreation and commanded the free man to procreate."[26] Because this person is partially free, he is subject to divine commandments, and procreation is one of them. Yet he can legally marry neither a slave woman nor a free woman. That means, you, the sages of the House of Hillel, have become responsible for the violation of the commandment of procreation.

To avoid these difficulties, the sages of the second school, the House of Shammai, offered an alternative solution: The court must require the remaining owner to let the slave go free with an obligation to pay back his owner for his freed half. Having heard that, the sages of the first school, the House of Hillel, renounced their solution and accepted the solution of the second school, or so the *tanna* reports this amazing story of the law in the making.

Next, the scene on the main stage shifts, and new characters appear there, the teachers and advanced students in the rabbinic academy. Their concern is the accuracy of the *tanna*'s memory. Strategically hoping to defend the memory of the *tanna*, they tactically notice a potential flaw in his account. For them, the *tanna*'s account of the argument of the second school, the House of Shammai, against the first school, the House of Hillel, sounds refutable, and thus the recorded memory of the victory of the first school might be wrong as well. The *tanna* thereby must be dismissed as a witness. This is because there is a tacit exclusion. Indeed, the argument of the second school tacitly has excluded the possibility that a half-free man could marry a half-free woman and, what is more, the other school, the House of Hillel, has tacitly agreed with that tacit exclusion.

The characters have identified an issue of refutability in the *tanna*'s testimony about the Mishnah, and they now attempt to verify the defensibility of that tacit exclusion. For them, if the implied possibility of marrying a half-free woman is not legally defensible as viable, the *tanna*'s record can be accepted as accurate; if it is defensible, the authority of the text he recites is in jeopardy. Consequently, as the characters probe the refutability and defensibility of the implied exclusion of such a marriage, tactically, they want the possibility of such marriage to be defensible, but strategically, they want the defense to fail, thus proving that the tacit exclusion was correct. This conversation on the main stage about a half-free person marrying a half-free woman goes as follows.

> —You might argue that the marriage is approvable by analogy with the case of an Israelite man who said to an Israelite woman "You are betrothed to a half of me" [and she accepts], which makes her legally betrothed to him.
>
> —Yet this analogy does not work, because, as a free person, that man was fully available to marry her, however a half slave is not fully available for marriage.

—[On the contrary,] you might argue it is not approvable by analogy to another case, that of an Israelite man attempting to betroth half a woman, which [as established elsewhere] invalidates his betrothal.

—Yet this analogy does not work, either. The only reason the betrothal does not become legal is that he attempted to acquire less than he could (which indicates he is not acting in earnest.) That is to say, if it went through, such a betrothal would have left another half of the woman marriageable, and it is impossible to be marriageable and not marriageable at the same time, which thus makes his offer not earnest. Unlike that, if a half-free person offers to marry a [half]-free woman, he offers to acquire as much as he can [all of her, that is].

The characters on the main stage thus ask if a half-free man can marry a free woman, and based on how they treat the question, they imply that the woman is only half-free as well. Also, the case of the wholly free woman is seemingly explicitly ruled out by the House of Shammai in the *tanna*'s account and thus is beside the point at this juncture.[27] In the preceding exchange, the characters attempt an analogy proving that a half-free man can marry a half-free woman, but end up by refuting the analogy. Then they attempt another analogy to prove that he cannot do so, and they fail that, too. That creates an aporia.

Tactically, in order to resolve the question positively (to say that a half-free man can marry a half-free woman), the characters attempt recalling a certain legal ruling along with its discussion elsewhere. The recalled ruling and the discussion of it concerned a half-slave killed by a domestic animal. The ruling prescribed a "fine" payable to his "survivors." The discussion of the ruling concerned to whom exactly the fine is payable. Think of that recalled discussion as happening on a second stage erected in the background of the main one. The second stage now comes to fore, and the action goes as follows.

—Let's [then] derive the answer from the following teaching, "[one who's animal] killed someone who was half free and half slave will have to pay half of the fine to the master [of the half-slave] and another half to the [half-slave's] survivors." If you argue that a betrothal in question is not legally valid, how come the half slave has legal descendants?

For the main-stage characters, if that works, contrary to the Mishnah's explicit statement, and contrary to the prior aporia, a half-slave can have been legally married.

Yet that claim fails. The discussion on the second stage is a fight between named rabbis, Rav Adda bar Ahava and Rabbah, about the reliability of the memory of a ruling about a half-free man killed by an animal. In their discussion, the former tries to bend the language to say that the "survivors" referred to the half slave himself, meaning the ruling addressed a wounded half-slave, not a dead half-slave, so that the "fine" is payable to him. The second named rabbi in this discussion, Rabbah, quotes an earlier rabbinic authority, Rabbi Shimon Ben Lakish, to make a point that the language of "fine" presumes the half-slave was indeed dead and not merely wounded. Having thereby refuted Rav Adda bar Ahava's defense of the ruling, the second rabbi, Rabba, offers his own defense instead. "The fine would be payable to the legal descendants, if there were any."[28] Even if the result of that second-stage discussion of the ruling is ambiguous, the ruling is still defended, and even if the defense might sound weak, the intrinsic goal of the characters on the second stage is achieved. There, the ruling about a half-slave who was killed is proven to be defensible.

Yet what was a victory on the second stage becomes a tactical defeat on the main one. For the purposes of the question with which the characters on the main stage are dealing, in light of the recalled discussion of it that appeared on the second stage, the ruling provides no sufficient proof of the possibility of a half-slave having had legal heirs and thus having been legally married to any woman, half-free or wholly free. For "if there were any" does not prove there indeed could have been heirs. With that the second stage fades to black.

That leaves the characters on the main stage with the understanding that the question of whether a half-free man can marry a half-free woman remains unanswerable in the case of a half-free woman. (And for the case of the wholly free woman, the recalled story is of no help, either.) That means the aporia still stands. So the characters on the main stage now understand that the tacitly excluded possibility for a half-slave man marrying a half-slave woman yields a rhetorical aporia—an aporia that threatens to be the definitive refutation to the testimony on the Mishnah—with no analogy or tradition that allows them to solve it one way or another and thus with no way to make a counterrefutation. It looks as if the *tanna*'s testimony on the Mishnah is to be dismissed. Yet as the further action on the stage proves, that was not the end of the game.

As their next step, the characters on the main stage put that understanding to a further test by juxtaposing it with the recollection of another argument attributed to one of the same characters, Rabba, who has already emerged on the second stage. The main-stage characters now recall a new teaching of Rabba's:

> —Rabba said, "Just as if one betroths a half [a] woman, this woman is not considered betrothed, so also betrothing a woman who is half slave, half free does not make her betrothed either."

And this is trouble. Seemingly contrary to the understanding just attained, that there is no solvable result for the question of marrying a woman if she is half free, Rabba is now recalled to have argued by analogy and explicitly that marrying a half-slave man to a half-slave woman is not legal, just as a free man marrying half of a free woman is not. That recollection means that instead of there being an aporia, Rabba has a clear-cut solution, negative though it may be.

Because Rabba is the same character as in the recalled discussion on the second stage above, the main-stage characters find their current understanding that there is an aporia and thus a refutation of the Mishnah in jeopardy. After all, the same name of a rabbi cannot be used for rendering the question irresolvable and at the same be recalled as having provided a direct resolution for it.

As a way out, the characters on the main stage recall a story about two other rabbis, one of whom, Rabbah bar Rav Huna, sounds almost verbatim like Rabba on this issue of this troubling teaching. As they do so, a new secondary stage comes to fore. On it, appear the true heroes of mistake-making in this (satiric) theater of memory, Rav Aba Bar Rav Huna and Rav Hisda.

As presented on this new second stage, the story recalled there proves helpful for the main-stage characters, because in that story, that Rabba-like teaching, so troubling for the main-stage characters, is accepted, but accepted ironically, if indeed, not sarcastically, so in the reality that the second-stage story conveys, it is reduced to an absurdity. (It yet remains to be seen what that does in reality as conveyed on the main stage.)

The story on the new second stage is about misapprehension, failing, and self-refutation. In Bialik's terms, but perhaps not in accord with his thesis, the story functions as *aggadah* and *halakhah* at the same time, not only with one leading to other but also with one becoming inseparable from the other. (It is precisely because Bialik's terms apply, but his theory of *aggadah* barren of *halakhah*—or of *halakhah* having become *aggadah*—does not, that one can see how the interpersonal theater of Talmudic satire becomes effaced in his view.)

The story on the new second stage is thus a narrative about rabbinic authorities of the past in their attempts to refute each other's proofs by proving they are self-refuting. As is already clear, in the way the story is positioned, narrated, and explained in the Talmud, the story also represents a reading of the story by the anonymous rabbis and students in the Babylonian academy, who are the main-stage characters. Because the story not only performs the tactics of failing proofs, but also makes the refutation of proofs its theme, the story is the most interesting case of such tactics in the whole sequence. The story goes as follows:

> Raba Bar Rav Huna inferred (דרש): just as "a [free] woman is not betrothed to one who betroths only a half of her," so also "a half-slave, half-free woman who was betrothed is not [legally] betrothed" [which is nearly[29] identical in content with Rabba above].
>
> Rav Hisda objected to him: [Your analogy is too fragile and therefore it does not work!] What's in common [between the two]? There [in the antecedent] a free man would have been able to get the [free] woman in whole, but here [in the consequent] the female half slave could not have been taken in whole at all!
>
> Rava Bar Rav Huna held back [stopped his discourse], and put in front of him an *amora* [the reciter/announcer of post-Mishnaic legal materials] to recite [after him] as follows: "The verse in *Isaiah*, "When a man shall take hold of his brother of the home of his father, saying, Thou [hast clothing, be thou our ruler, and *let* this ruin *be* under thy hand],"[30] suggests "*let* this ruin *be* under thy hand" to mean no one can [properly] take the words of Torah, unless one gets mistaken about them (אין אדם עומד על דברי תורה אלא אם כן נכשל בהן). Even if there is a tradition saying that one who betroths half of a woman does not make the woman betrothed, still if a woman was half-slave, half-free person, and she was betrothed, her betrothal is legally valid.[31]

The rabbis and students in the rabbinic academy comment on that as if in the name of Rava Bar Rav Huna, and, in fact, even mimic the objection of Rav Hisda:

> —What was the reason [for Rava Bar Rav Huna's final conclusion]? There [in the antecedent] a free man was able to betroth the woman in whole, but here [in the consequent] a female half slave cannot be taken in whole at all![32]

This exchange is a part of the tactics of failing proofs and of self-refuting. As complex as these tactics already are, in this exchange, the relationship between failure and success is even more complex, but also even more clearly articulated.

Rava Bar Rav Huna suggests that just as a free man cannot betroth himself to a half-free woman, a half-slave cannot do so, either. Rav Hisda denies the analogy, because the two cases are not comparable. In the former, the man could have betrothed himself to a wholly free woman, but did not; however, in the latter, the man could not do so.

In the story, if it is read with no irony, Rava Bar Rav Huna begins (like Rabba above); Rav Hisda objects; and Rava Bar Rav Huna simply accepts the objection. Yet the reality that the story conveys is actually full of irony, albeit not of Socratic irony. In other words it is full of sarcasm and satire. Rava Bar Rav Huna's acceptance is not an acceptance at all, but a reductio ad absurdum as a means of self-refutation, showing as it does that in the reality of the secondary stage, the objection is self-refuting, because it leads to an absurdity. "Just look where we get if I accept your objection," says Rava Bar Rav Huna to Rav Hisda, as it were: From, as it turned out, too fragile an analogy between a half-free and fully free woman we get to a conclusion, which one cannot even call an analogy, not even a fragile one. For the main-stage characters, that means Raba Bar Rav Huna offered a Rabba-like analogy; Rav Hisda broke it apart; and Raba Bar Rav Huna ironically concluded with a resulting self-refuting "analogy" that did not hold up at all, and thus was not even fragile. The seeming but not effectively real victory of the Rabba-like position on the second secondary stage makes Rabba's (negative) resolution of the aporia self-refuting on the main stage, as well, thus restoring the aporia, if not as well-structured uncertainty as medieval Aristotelian commentators of the Talmud might have seen it, then as a move toward an impasse, which is the strategic direction the main-stage characters have been consistently taking.

That renders the aporia of half-a-slave man marrying a half-a-slave woman genuinely unresolvable. A seemingly definitive negative resolution of it in the words of Rabba (such a marriage is not legally possible) is now neutralized by Rav Hisdah having objected to Rabba-like statement of Raba Bar Rav Huna, followed by Rav Hisda having ironically accepted but realistically undermined the power of that objection. The main-stage result of the irony on the secondary stage casts is that Rabba's position can be neither fully refuted nor fully defended. In turn, for the main-stage characters, that explains and justifies the silence of the Mishnaic authorities on the matter, thereby keeping the testimony of the *tanna* in play.

The logic of the irony (not to say satire) of self-refuting on the secondary stage is crucial for attaining such a result on the main stage, as well.

The irony is also in the relationship between the two stages. The irony of the pretended defeat needed to show Rava Bar Rav Huna's devastating victory on the secondary stage transforms into real victory on the first stage. Ironically, that irony is necessary, because without it, the first stage was threatening to present the *tanna* as the ultimate looser in failing to consider the possibility of half-a-slave man marrying a half-a-slave woman. Had that happened, the rabbinic system of authority would have been in the much more severe danger of rendering one of its traditions indefensible and therefore unreliable. Ironically, only the irony on the secondary stage prevents that from happening.

This is why the logic of irony (again, not to say satire) here takes over those who participate in its dance. The two rabbis, Rav Hisda and Rava Bar Rav Huna, collectively participate in their interpersonal discovery of and recovery from the necessary irony of mistake making by making the scriptural verse support them in their partnered journey of failing the refutation. Their dance is not that of a fight in which one of the parties wins and the other either loses or is won over. It does not involve dialectical irony or an intersubjective encounter. Rather, it is a dance of interpersonal arguments performed in the middle voice in which productive failure is impossible without both parties taking part. In the story, it thus is Rava Bar Rav Huna's proof that has failed, but in the reality that the story conveys, the winner is Rava Bar Rav Huna, even if his victory is masked as defeat.[33]

The new second stage now fades. What happened there has provided enough for the main-stage characters to preserve the aporia, to save the *tanna*'s testimony on the Mishnah, or to maintain that even if the *tanna* did not explicitly mention a possibility of a half-slave marrying a half-free woman, that was because the legality of such marriage remains irresolvable, which makes the testimony both refutable and defensible, or again, in the view of medieval Talmudic logical Aristotelianism of the *Gornish*, it provides a well-structured uncertainty that keeps the *tanna* in the courtroom. The outcome is that the *tanna* was silent about a certain issue because the issue could be neither ruled out nor approved explicitly, as far as legal argument is concerned. The *tanna* was silent not because he forgot, but because the authorities, the sages whom he transmits, encountered an aporia and thus did not have anything to say.

Rather, because the issue was aporetic, it is to be kept where it is, in the realm of tacit exclusion: that is, in the realm of the implicit. As a result, even if the *tanna*'s account does not explicitly rule out marrying a half-free man to a half-free woman, the account keeps that option implicit, because the possibility is aporetic. However, and most importantly, the implied aporia continues to inform the Mishnah in accordance with the aporia's nature, that of an irresolvable implicit, which therefore would have to remain where it is, in the implicit.

Of course, such a form of the implicit is actively at work. It both informs and defends the position of the sages of the House of Shammai in the Mishnah in their objections to the sages of the House of Hillel. It also informs and defends the position of the House of Hillel in their otherwise suspiciously obedient acceptance of the position of the House of Shammai. Therefore, the implicit aporia ultimately defends the accuracy of the memory of the ruling in the Mishnah recited by the *tanna* as well.

Elevating what seemed to be the forgotten possibility of a half-free man marrying a half-free woman into a legal aporia is one of the strategies the main-stage characters employ to justify the accuracy of the memory inscribed in the text provided by the *tanna*. Their understanding is that the possibility was omitted precisely because it was irresolvable. In a legal ruling, the aporia cannot be explicated precisely because of its nature as an aporia, leading to no ruling one way or another. From that point on, the main-stage characters continue the discussion, which I have summarized only thus far.[34]

Irony, Mis-Taking, and the Implicit

In this account, the difference between the reality of the characters on the main stage and those of the second stage is important. The ironical (again, not to say satiric) reduction of Rav Hisda's argument to absurdity tells the main-stage characters that Rabba's solution forbidding for a half-free man to marry a half-free woman was not final. Even if, in the story on the second stage, the question of who failed is handled ironically, in a playful manner, in the reality of the main stage, the role of the failure is entirely serious there. The irony helps to reconfirm what needs to be reconfirmed: The Mishnah was right to avoid committing to one or another answer on whether the half-slave man can marry a half-slave woman. For the main-stage characters, the ironical gesture on the second stage tells them that they went too far in their reasoning, reaching to a point at which the Mishnah's memory can no longer be defended. If there is a way to marry a half-slave woman, and a half-slave man can do so, the *tanna* had to have mentioned it, and the other school of the sages, the House of Hillel, should not have agreed to comply with the House of Shammai.

Failure is the indispensable tactic for arriving at that conclusion. Failing the refutations of the Mishnah in reality, disguised as refuting one's own proof in the story, remains necessary for success both in the story and in reality. In the story, the Mishnah is defended against the allegation of error in its recording, and in reality, the authority of the Mishnah is reaffirmed.

As already highlighted, in the new second-stage story, not only do proofs fail, but also their elusive nature becomes a theme that the characters on the main stage enjoy seeing. That means different readers can read the whole series in different ways. For the main-stage characters in the Talmud, the story of Rava Bar Rav Huna and Rav Hisda not only reconfirms the problematic nature of answering whether half-free people can marry (and hence confirms that the Mishnah is defensible in omitting that as an option—precisely because there is no way to determine legitimacy of it), but it also illustrates the heuristic role of failure, in particular, of misapprehension, mis-taking, and of self-refutation in debates about the matters of the Torah. What for Bialik is an element of *halakhah*, legal discussion, and what is for him an element of *aggadah*, storytelling, thus illuminate each other. In the eyes of rabbis as readers of the story, if *aggadah* and *halakhah* were separated in it, the story could not work. For other readers, if *aggadah* and *halakhah* were separated in it, the story might suggest that Raba Bar Rav Huna admitted his mistake and changed his opinion in favor of his opponent's, also with an undesired implication for the main-stage characters. To yet others, it might suggest that in their interpersonal interaction, Rav Hisda proved that Raba Bar Rav Huna held a self-refuting position, thus applying the rule of mistakes not to himself but to his opponent. Yet for the anonymous rabbis and students in the Talmud, as readers of this second-stage story, only the latter reading is possible, at least given what they say explaining Rav Hisda's argument.

Because they support different readings, the arguments made in failing proofs are open to attempts either to show that a proof did not fail or that it fails in a different way. Medieval Talmudic commentaries show how that can be done, and early modern commentators even show how studying the arguments of failing proofs may also involve the need for heuristic failure on the part of the student of the Talmud.[35] As a result, the text of the Talmud, too, becomes accessible only through failure to grasp what it means. In the passage we have just seen enacted, readers see the ruins of argument created by misapprehension and erect new arguments on these ruins. The ruins created by misapprehension serve as the basis for a conclusion, either ironical or taken seriously, that itself also constantly threatens to be proven a mistake. Misapprehension, and in particular, proving to another that he or she has mis-taken—that is, simultaneously took and missed—something thus stands at the very core of this process of construction and constantly haunts its results. It cannot be eliminated from either the process or its results, either.

At stake in both the process and the results of understanding pursued by misapprehension is the silence of the implicit and of validating that silence as a source of authority: keeping the implicit implicit. If the Mishnah's silence on the issue of whether a half-slave man can marry a half-slave woman was indeed an omission, the authority of either the Mishnah or of the memory of the Mishnah is in danger. If the Mishnah was silent because the aporetic nature of the issue, that is, if the issue was a possibility implicitly well considered and implicitly excluded as untenable and, in particular, as undecidable, the memory of the Mishnah is correct. There consequently is no way to explicate the Mishnah's silence as working either against or for the Mishnah. The implicit must remain implicit and silent in order to do its work.

The function of irony in Rabba Bar Rav Huna's response to Rav Hisda by either quoting or quoting and expounding the scriptural verse about failing and failure as the way to master the hidden subtleties of the Torah is to explain the silence in the Mishnah: an implicit way to keep the implicit implicit. It reaffirms the Talmud as the locus of the inconceivable while at the same time and by the same token (re)establishing the full authority of the Mishnah.[36]

The Implicit and the Political in Modernity

It is the trace of this valorization of self-refutation, of the resulting well-structured uncertainty and mis-taking, that remains in modernity, despite the effacement of the personal and the interpersonal by the subjective and the intersubjective and the demand for certainty as a central philosophical value. It is the trace left by the erasure of such characteristics of the political form of the Talmud from the horizon of political theology and political ontology after Kant that also makes the political in the Talmud discernible.

In its rhetorical form, the Talmud is comparable to what Benjamin called the form of the tractate, in which access to ideas occurs by effectively failing to grasp them. What the Talmud means becomes accessible to its readers only through a series of carefully performed failures to understand what it means. What Benjamin would call the "ideas" that are implicit in the Talmud never can be approached in any final or definitive way. In addition to being a tractate in its rhetorical form, the Talmud also occupies the status of an idea, which for the readers of the Talmud will always be imminently grasped, but never grasped in any final way.[37]

However, because Kant's subject of reason requires intersubjectivity, defending the Jewish Law against Kant entails suppressing the interpersonal and with it the interpersonal form of the political that is found in the Talmud. The result is a formal conception of the political that is structurally identical to that advanced by Schmitt. As modernists, Bialik and Benjamin introduce the machinery of mistake and of misapprehension as the only way of encountering the power of the implicit, which for them is the power of the "law." Because this power controls but is not controlled by all acts of administering the law and permeates all other acts in all other spheres of human life, the power of the implicit is by definition a version of the political. Grounding the law in the political understood as the implicit effectively defends the *halachah*—understood by these thinkers as the "Jewish Law"—against Kant's criticism of positive law, because "positive" law is associated only with the explicit regulations that the *halachah* imposes on its subjects, not with the implicit power of the law over them. Limiting the always explicit regulations of *halachah* by the power of the implicit law thus serves, for these thinkers, as a general defense against allegations of the "positive law."[38]

For these modernists, a mistaken view of the law or a misapprehension of the law simply becomes an experience that a subject undergoes. Both advancing and reconsidering Kant's concern for the limits of rational conception, these thinkers introduced a never avoidable misapprehension of ideas or the elusive power of poetic narrative that the *aggadah* represents in one's relation to the law or "truth" (Bialik).[39] The individual subject, lonely, even if not necessarily alone, as the subject must be after Kant, thus stands "before the law," to borrow Kafka's language, both in the sense of being judged and in the sense of not having arrived at the law yet—or else in the sense of having fatally missed it. In any case, that subject is tacitly opposed to and subversively suppressive of the form of the interpersonal political discernible in the Talmud—the interpersonal form in which it is the role of a person (as an individual or as a group) to listen into the voice of the other person and thereby to refute the other person. In other words, the subject develops, or at least strives to develop, intersubjectivity at the expense of the suppressed interpersonality.

From the position occupied by the subject of reason, with regard to the implicit, the only thing one can do and at the same time cannot plan on doing is to make mistakes—to fail to grasp the implicit in a negative sense. But in the Talmudic story, the uncertainty of misapprehension has a positive aspect: The mistakes made by Raba Bar Rav Huna and Rav Hisda are the basis for reaching new conclusions. Unlike failing to grasp the ungraspable in Benjamin's assessment of Kafka, Talmudic mis-taking not only moves the discussion forward but also constantly threatens its outcomes. Misapprehension is a perpetual process, but not a negative one in any sense of the term.

The preceding has focused on only a particular aspect of the replacement of interpersonality as the mode of interaction between the characters in the Talmud with intersubjectivity as a way of interaction between Kantian "subjects of reason" and the elision of the refutation of a refutation from the horizon of ontological and theological thinking about the political. Clearly, however, what is involved here is the much broader scope of the relationship between philosophy and Talmud as traditions of thought and the erasure of the conception of the political in the Talmud. In the concluding chapter, therefore, I broaden the question of the relationships between the political in the Talmud and in political ontology and theology by examining philosophy as the possible and in particular impossible horizon of thinking of the political. As will become clear, the broader scope of the analysis of the political in the Talmud vis-à-vis the modern versions of the political in political theology and political ontology will require questioning the relationship between the Talmud and pre-Socratic thought and philosophy. As will also become clear, the philosophy of Gilles Deleuze will provide a viewpoint from which to proceed with the inquiry about pre-Socratic, Talmudic, and philosophical displays and effacements of the political.

To conclude this chapter and to invoke, for a moment, the example of Rabbi Tzadok and the noble lady I addressed in Chapter 3, let me emblematically highlight another rabbinic possibility of reading the Abraham and Isaac story. As a result of effacing interpersonality by intersubjectivity, the possibility of reading Abraham and Isaac story remains beyond the horizons opened up from Kafka's, Benjamin's, and Bialik's points of view, defined as they are by subjectivity and in particular intersubjectivity, by the bestowal of nonbeing and being, and by uncertainty and the misapprehension of certainty, rather than by refutation, counterrefutation, and self-refutation as foundations of interpersonal political action and in particular of an action in the area of justice.

That reading arises in light of the Talmudic interpersonal version of the political. Instigated by Rashi's commentary on Genesis 22,[40] but also by the story of Rabbi Tzadok and the noble Roman lady, this alternative rabbinic interpretation suggests that Abraham not only understood the ambiguity of the command "bring your son to (the) sacrifice" from the very start, but also used that understanding at the end to self-refute whomever have given him that command. Abraham continued to act within the limits of the ambiguity while ambiguity was still possible. He stopped with the knife in his hand, precisely when any continuation—either slaughtering Isaac or to refusing to do so—would violate, or if one prefers, "sacrifice" one of the sides of the ambiguous command. Abraham thus enters into an interpersonal relationship to the command giver through the argument of self-refutation: with the knife in hand, he says, as it were: "From now on, in any way I proceed, I violate one of the aspects of your own command." Therefore, the creation of the angel was either an expression of or a response to the argument of self-refutation. It was expression of the argument of self-refutation, in which case Abraham was the one who created the angel. Alternatively, it was a response to self-refutation argument, in which case G-d sent him the angel. Similar to Benjamin's and Bialik's perspective, the version of the political Abraham has turned on is predicated on the notion of the implicit as the law accessible in no other way except by mistake and misapprehension. Yet, dissimilar to Bialik and Benjamin, the mistake and misapprehension is not an experience of an isolated post-Kantian subject. Instead it is an effect of the intrinsic interpersonality of one's engagement with oneself—for example in the way in which Abraham treats himself in deciding how to proceed on the first morning after receiving the command. It is also interpersonal in the sense of engaging others: Isaac or the command giver, as well as the audience of the narrative. On this reading, Abraham preserves the ambiguity even in talking to his son and also with the others, which in this case include both the command giver, G-d, and the narrators and readers of that account of the past, from which the narrator and the reader have to decide to depend or possibly not.[41] In short, Abraham constantly self-refutes.

However, all the preceding readings of Abraham story both invoke and miss another possibility, the possibility of intrinsic interpersonality. In this case, this is the interpersonality of relationships between G-d and Abraham. On that reading, Abraham self-refutes G-d by reducing the divine command to absurdity. Abraham understood the ambiguity of the command from the start. He could therefore have dismissed it as refutable from the start, too. (The command is not precise—it means either "slaughter" or "take to the altar" and thus is not worthy of acting upon, or perhaps may not even come from G-d, who cannot be inconsistent.) Instead, Abraham suspends any attempts to determine if the command is from G-d or not. Rather, he provisionally assumes the command is from G-d and decides to take G-d to a point where G-d will realize that Abraham cannot fulfill the command without violating it.

The temporality of the interpersonal relationship between Abraham and G-d is most crucial here. Abraham moves ahead in the story (donkey, wood, Isaac, Mount Moriah, binding, knife) as long as each of his actions fulfills both of the meanings of the command. Abraham stops only when any step further will sacrifice one of the meanings to the other: He has his knife in his hand, his arm stretched, and he cannot continue. At this point, slaughtering does not fulfill (overdoes) the command to take to the altar, and withdrawing the knife does not fulfill the command to slaughter. Abraham corners, or more technically, self-refutes whomever it is who has given him the command. (This reading also explains why he is stopped by the "Angel of Lord," not by "G-d": He has cornered G-d into a self-refutation and thereby has created the Angel. On that reading, it is not only and not primarily a movement of failure through which Abraham goes; rather, it is a movement in which "in the story" G-d is self-refuted and thus loses, although G-d wins in reality, because Abraham has withstood the test. Losing in the story means, for G-d, victory in reality.)

A missed but invoked possibility here is precisely what Benjamin's and Kafka's readings effaces—the interpersonal political at work between Abraham and G-d. In that relationship, G-d loses in the story to win in reality, and Abraham wins in the story, but perhaps (or so other rabbinic interpretations suggest) loses the trust of his son and the life of his wife in reality. What is effaced is the temporality of the interpersonal political, in which the outcome of the story is out control of either G-d or Abraham, but is absolutely precise as long as both G-d and Abraham employ the interpersonal power of self-refuting.

Of course, this reading, too, is only a possibility, but the one that the horizon of the intersubjective political, and by extension, of the political theology and political ontology can only suppress, while at the same time and by the same token making it possible to discern.

The preceding chapters have shown specific correlations between rabbinic and philosophical modes of thought: intersubjectivity versus interpersonality; refutation as the truth criterion versus *being* of what-is (as opposed to nonbeing of what-seems-to-be) that plays the role of the truth; orientation to disagreement and well-structured uncertainty versus striving for the ideal of certainty both in the knowledge and in the action; and the resulting understanding of the disagreement as that which is either excluded from or reluctantly but necessarily tolerated in anything worth of the name of the political. These specific juxtapositions suggest and even necessitate a more general question of relationship between the Talmud and philosophy as two distinct but interconnected modes of thought.

If, speaking in the broader scale on things in the analysis in the preceding chapters, the effacement of interpersonal marks the birth and strengthening of the intersubjective approaches to the political, then the question of the political displayed in the Talmud needs to be asked in a broader framework of the complex relationship between Talmud and philosophy. That framework would suspend medieval partitioning of the Talmud into legal and poetic elements, *aggadah* and *halakhah*, at the expense of the obscuring the view of the ironical and satiric forms as forms of the political in the Talmud. Even more important, this broader perspective would shed a new darkness on the question of the political, now beyond the confines of differences between the Talmud and philosophy. At stake is the darkness, and, as the next chapter will begin charting, Earth as the matter of the political. This second matter needs to be carefully attended well before Socratic irony and/or post-Socratic satire emerge on the stage.

Instead of conclusion and by way of highlighting the direction of the development that project has charted so far, the next chapter begins to respond to that necessity of addressing Earth in relationship to the political at a point that logically precedes the effacement of the interpersonal political by the intersubjective political. This point will have to do with pre-Socratic thinking about Earth.

CHAPTER 8

The Earth for the Other Others

This chapter explores an implication of the question of effacement of the other others, which this book advanced, for and in thinking the earth. In a sense, mobilizing the question of the other others to think the earth anew is no more but also no less than an articulation of yet another, perhaps the most important part of the question: How, or is it possible, to think the earth in the first place? Advancing this problem means moving beyond the hitherto predominant paradigms of linear otherness, in which the other and the question of belonging to a territory have been inextricably connected one to another. Is that connection between other and territory necessary, and what does that connection preclude from the view?

I began this study by developing the ways in which philosophers as different as Carl Schmitt and Jacques Rancière share a common formal element regarding the question of the political as articulated in the philosophical discourses of political theology and political ontology. However, there is another common denominator shared by Rancière, the thinker of the political philosophy of disagreement, and Schmitt, the theorist of the political theology of decision. That element is thinking, acting, and living in the "daylight"—in the steady light of day where the being of things together is lost in the distinctions between them as often as confusions result between what a thing is and what it merely seems to be. In the light of day, chimeras emerge. Political theology and political ontology originate in the daylight, and the daylight always remains a necessary condition for them—and for philosophy as such. As philosophers, Schmitt and Rancière both think in the bright and steady light of day.

This is in contrast to living a life illuminated by bolts of lightning,[1] when it is only things on their being as such are briefly to be glimpsed, beyond any conceptual grasp. This difference between the daylight and the illumination of lightning leads to an even more radical distinction between both of these and the "ungraspable and void," the earth, the biblical תהו ובהו, or *tohu-bohu*, a translation that brings the original exactly to what it means in the context—a state of confusion.

Without seeing things with the clarity of daylight, disagreement would not be possible. It is only in that light that uncontrolled disagreements appear, and not only radical disagreement, but also the power of decision, based, as it is, on the representation of representation, would be impossible without daylight. Neither can operate when the contours of distinct things are blurred at night, and the sharp contours of the earth both emerge and disappear in a momentarily flash of lightning. In the daylight of the *agora*, some things merely *seem to be* just, and some *are* just, and in a *Biergarten*, some people only *seem to be* friends, but *are* enemies. Such a clear (and clearly blinding) initial sense of the appearance of things in their distinctions one from another, from which any further distinction between seeming and being can stem, is possible only in the daylight. At night, however, all contours merge and blur, and lightning does nothing but bring that blurring to light by illuminating the ungraspable that is the earth.

Through the examples and/or instances addressed in the preceding chapters, I have argued that the Talmud, both despite and including the tradition of its interpretation, emerges as an authentic counterexample opposed to both political theology and political ontology. However, as is also consequent upon the pages above, the political is not readily visible in the Talmud's pages when read only philosophically, in the clear light of day. It is displayed through performances of the characters in the Talmud, but its traces are to be discerned there only in flashes—the preceding chapters exemplify this—it having been effaced by the philosophical effacement of the rhetorical. It thus both lurks and vanishes in the interval between the political and ontology, the political and theology.

In the light supplied by these flashes, it becomes possible to ask broader questions about the never final erasure of the political in the Talmud that philosophy performs. At stake at this more general level of the question of the political in the Talmud and philosophy is the relationship between the Talmud and philosophy as ways in thinking of the political in its connection and in particular disconnection from ontology and theology in relation to the earth.

What does it mean that I have engaged and continue to engage with philosophy when asking about Talmud as way of intellectual life, and more specifically as a form of the political? In *Geophilosophy*,[2] Rodolphe Gasché asks a similar question of the complexity of the engagement of philosophy and literature that informs his reading of Gilles Deleuze and Félix Guattari's preoccupation, in *What Is Philosophy?* with the earth.[3] By way of another intersection with Gasché's argument, that also becomes a question about the earth—–in contradistinction to the traditions of philosophy, asking about the biblical earth (ארץ) in its radical distinction from both ground and land (אדמה). Engaging with philosophy when asking about the Talmud as a form of the political and asking about the biblical earth in its radical distinction from both ground and land provides a heuristic opening through which to approach the question[4] of the overall relationship between the Talmud and philosophy as it concerns the question of the political. And this, in turn, provides a way to return to and understand the status of the other others, those who are ontotheologically excluded from being and who can never "get back to where they once belonged."

There are various ways of thinking about others. The most readily is by linking them to a territory, a piece of land, a place different from "mine" or "ours." A more politically sophisticated understanding of the other treats the other as an enemy who is not only in or threatens to be in "our" territory, but who also has no territory of her own and who therefore pretends to be one of "us" but in fact only appears to be so. An even more sophisticated and much more ethically responsible way of approaching the other is as a face that "I" recognize as such, well before "I" can "decide" either to treat the other as a genuine person or to objectify it as a mere function. This is an ethical position that includes recourse to what makes this primordial face what it is, the neither present nor absent G-d and/or immemorial past that has no representation, but for which face is the trace. However, it is only by regarding the face understood in this way as still too strongly delineated by the steady light of day and by that of which the face is thought to be a trace that we arrive at the question of the other others—others plural, and as distinct from the indistinctly plural or singular G-d or immemorial past.

What needs to be asked about these other others is the question of the face. In view of their plurality and of the almost satirical instability of the interpersonal relationship they perform, do not the other others entail a version of the political relationship to the earth for which the face as a foundation for ethics might be as insufficient as it is necessary? For in an interpersonal encounter with and about the earth, the face might be no more and no less than an effacement. Such a face/trace might still belong too strongly to the monotony of long and slow exposure to the steady light of day.

In lightning, by contrast, faces do not appear, or they do not appear for long enough to afford enough time either to objectify them or to treat them ethically. As the preceding pages suggest, to begin this rethinking is to ask about the other others whom the face effaces by giving these others a face. The interpersonal political that the pages above introduced is not an intersubjective encounter, nor is it a move beyond the subject, for the interpersonal dance does not begin from the subject in the first place. The interpersonal thinking, acting, and living that the characters in the Talmud perform moves too fast and thus is too unstable to allow any stable face of the other to suffice to represent any of them. In judging, the characters in the Talmud do not look into a face, but listen into the voice of words. They radically bypass the ontology of what is versus what seems to be versus what is otherwise than being in the Platonic sense. Perhaps understanding their work in a broader context requires a recourse to a pre-Socratic sense of the otherwise than being, a sense in which otherwise than being refers not to nonbeing in the sense of a function of seeming to be, but rather, if at all, to the being of all things together that lighting brings forth. However, as the analysis in this chapter will begin to show, this recourse to a pre-Socratic sense of nonbeing would not be enough, either. The interpersonal and the other others to which it gives voice—but gives no face—will require us to advance asking if, and if yes, how, the face effaces these other others, those who have neither a way to "get back" as well as those who have no place "where they once belonged." Instead, these other others entail a radically different relationship to the earth, a relationship that this chapter begins to articulate.

D&G: A Derridean Reading of Deleuze

Gasché's *Geophilosophy* turns on a dialogue that never took place empirically but might have always going on intellectually, the dialogue between Jacques Derrida on the one hand and Gilles Deleuze and Félix Guattari on the other. On Gasché's reading, in the classical opposition between immanence and transcendence, Deleuze and Guattari take the side of immanence, even if at the same time undoing the distinction between the two. In the first approximation, their argument has to do with reevaluation of the history of philosophy. For Deleuze and Guattari, it is a history of the emergence, loss, and (still endangered) reemergence of philosophy's singular nature, which is a concern with the immanence in the name of the earth, as opposed to transcendence in the name of Heaven. Despite the historical distractions and/or intrusions of either imperial impulses, the scriptural traditions of the Bible and its interpreters, or of other powers of transcendence, philosophy's main and most unique concern continues to be immanence. The concern with the earth and with the thought devoted to and arising from the thinking of the earth orients Gasché's critical reading of *What Is Philosophy?* as he translates the work from its more technical language into a more accessible *koine* of contemporary Continental philosophy.[5]

Gasché condenses Deleuze and Guattari's names in the abbreviation D&G to highlight the virtuality of the book's second writer, Guattari, and by the same token to express the virtual characters of the both. For not totally dissimilar reasons, and with regard of the other motives I will soon explain, I take the convenience of coincidence to make the same abbreviation suggest that at certain junctures, the "G" in D&G designates the agency of Rodolphe Gasché as a critical interpreter of D&G, while in the others, Gasché's readings in Derrida interfere to form a heuristic dissonance in the "D," resulting, productively, in a new overtone, suggesting, still spectrally, not only Deleuze and Guattari but also Derrida and Gasché. I will be listening to that dissonance and to that overtone to isolate turning points around which to map or to show impossibility of mapping the political displayed in the Talmud vis-à-vis thought about the earth, which as D&G argue is the main concern of philosophy.

In its tone, Gasché's reading of *What Is Philosophy?* is a critique, to a point where faithful interpretation and internal critique become indistinguishable, not only in the sense that his exposition addresses the explicit or implicit polemics D&G have with other thinkers—with Heidegger or with other versions of postphenomenology, but also in the sense of asking the critical question that D&G do not explicitly ask. Precisely due to its nature as critique, in Gasché's reading of D&G, the limits of such critique become heuristically visible and even palpable, limits that will also raise the most difficult question of the relation between the Talmud and philosophy. That question arises when philosophy and Talmud emerge as two distinct but interconnected traditions of thought engaging and creating the political not only as their object but also as what cannot be objectified but that informs, defines, and orients D&G's thought in the first place.

Land, Territorialization, and Reterritorialization

The earth arises for D&G as what conditions the possibility of transitioning from either agricultural, autochthonous land or from the always both mobile and steady territorialization of nomads to the political territory of either a city-state or an empire. This transition from land or nomadic movement to political territory depends on a condition that has no objectification and that therefore D&G would call the earth coinciding with Thought in which it cannot be objectified, and thus named Earth-Thought. Because of both the impossibility to objectify that condition and the necessity of having it, philosophy as thinking the earth becomes both necessary and possible. Yet, before getting into details, let me dwell for a moment on Gasché's positioning as an interpreter of D&G.

The questions for us here, in and after Gasché's critique of D&G, are these: If for D&G the primary and ultimate concern of philosophy is with immanence construed as Earth-Thought, as distinct from and related to either autochthonous land, nomadic move, or political territory, and if Earth-Thought becomes attainable for a philosopher *only after* or looms large into his or her life *only because* the earth frees itself either from any native (and therefore possibly even transcendent) specificity of autochthony or nomadism and from any abstract, but objectifying thinking about the earth as territory or as the matter of cartography, geometry, astronomy, mathematics, or any other objectifying science, as well as from any artistic ways of thinking the earth as an inexpressible affect connecting one to elusive "land," then a more general question arises, a question concerned with the relation of the Talmud to philosophy. Is the Earth-Thought of D&G also the primary and ultimate concern of the Talmud as thought? Or is it alternatively the case that the Talmud broaches a new path distinct not only from scientific objectification and from its alternative, artistic expression, but also distinct from philosophy as geophilosophy?

It is my argument here that the Talmud as thought not only embraces Earth-Thought, but also at the same time circumscribes it within a broader orientation of thought, which in my previous work I have proposed to identify as an orientation toward memory and remembering in which memory orients thought, not the other way around. To take the example of D&G's term "Earth-Thought" and to coin a similar one, one could call that alternative orientation Memory-Thought, thought that reach beyond the earth of philosophy, while at the same time not quite involving the earth of the sciences or arts. So a shorter but narrower form of the question posed above would be: Does Earth-Thought remain an intrinsic part of Memory-Thought?[6]

To think through the latter possibility, I proceed with that narrower question. It concerns two respective formal procedures, orientations, and/or tasks in thinking and/or remembering: memory and the earth, in their relationship to one another. The demarcation between the earth and memory would have to do with refutation as the form of remembering in its relationship to and in distinction from what D&G address as "territorialization," including deterritorialization and reterritorialization, "relative" and "absolute."

"Territorialization," which leads D&G to claim that the earth is the primary concern of philosophy, is an originary way to structure an elusive presence, "human presence" (including even "animal presence") either collective or individual, either agricultural or nomadic. The limits of what habitually has been called by that name in modernity can be seen in the Lascaux paintings, which, as Georges Bataille argued, were archaeologically and chronologically first known works of art and therefore, for him, the first signs of human presence, because as Bataille persuasively insists, it is the work of art, rather than tool-making that originally marks a new "presence," which he automatically and perhaps too hurriedly calls "human." Tools, for him, still leave their users chained into the sequences of physical causes and effects, resulting in no (new) presence, even if, perhaps, featuring some more advanced capabilities for survival. In contrast, Bataille's argument suggests, Lascaux drawings are evidence of artists released from the forceful chain of causes and effects.

Following his interpretation and speaking in modern terms, in those paintings, there is what can be easily mistaken as mere "representations" or schemas/images of bulls and hunters. The images on the walls of the Lascaux cave are not representations of mighty bulls as bulls, but instead, a set of rather unusual self-portraits. The "bulls" on the wall are if not the first, then the most preferable body images that these artists give to themselves as what they want to be as opposed to what they might be in the physical chain of cause and effect, a presence that is prior to, in advance of and independent of any particular body image. It does not matter if this image is a bull or a figure with tiny hands, legs, and head. In giving one's body a body image (no matter what), the artists articulate or present themselves, rather than being articulated by the always secondary re-presentation entailed by the physical chain of cause and effect. That is, they bring themselves into presence for the very first time.[7]

As the proportions and details of the Lascaux bulls suggests, the artists privilege the body images of the bulls at the expense of much smaller and comparatively poorly developed body images of the hunters. Alternatively, both by and despite the logic of Hegelian speculation, which for Bataille was not totally foreign, even if perhaps completely reversed, the Lascaux drawings show how the poorly developed body images of the hunters become the well-developed body image of bulls that artists find or develop for themselves. On either reading, to apply Bataille's interpretation to illustrate D&G's notion of territorialization, the majestic bulls of Lascaux, along with the walls of the cave, are the first territorialization, the way to produce and structure a primary "presence" that Bataille—again perhaps too hurriedly—calls "human."

(Human) presence is thus always territorialized. For D&G, such territorialization also entails "reterritorialization." Although no longer by any Hegelian necessity, the originary territorialization or presence can be suspended and/or undone by "reterritorialization." This process introduces another presence, or more precisely, another kind of presence, this time through an image or sense of geometrically rather than empirically (or "arithmetically") graspable territory. It now is territory that is marked, partitioned, or divided up as an abstract object conducive to mapping, rather than a primary foundation/expression of presence.

As a result, if there is an initial, "chthonic," nomadic, and/or agricultural presence, it transforms into a new, political or "geometrical" one, while at the same time maintaining continuity with the first: the image of a territory brings forth a certain new sense of presence in Bataille's sense, as well. It may be no longer a self-portrait, but it is the presence of a cartographer or a geometer, someone who is present by producing a map and thus the respective political territory, as opposed to chthonic land or nomadic move.

Unlike territorialization, reterritorialization has to do with the political. As already briefly mentioned it involves the foundations of either a city-state or an empire and their respective territories, rather than lands or other primary territorializations per se. In an example that D&G use, the Greek city-state introduces a new, political territorialization; it produces "friends," the liberation of "opinion," and the "fractalization of Greece." The first refers to friendship that is always also rivalry. The second elevates opinion as not only what must be allowed to be expressed freely, but also as what, through the competition of freely expressed opinions, liberates friends from becoming slaves to themselves or to anybody else in the city. The third term, the "fractalization of Greece," bespeaks the openness of the Greek city-state to foreigners in a free marketplace where the freedom of opinion is achieved through exchanges with foreigners. By the same token, a free citizen becomes a foreigner for himself or herself by entertaining the views about the citizen that the foreigner expressed: The inside becomes the outside, and the outside moves inside; thus the term "fractal."

"Friends," "Liberating Opinion," and "Fractalization of Greece" also name three chapters in Gasché's book *Geophilosophy*. In their own right, the terms and their meanings deserve a much more detailed analysis, yet, for the purposes of my argument here, I limit myself to a brief comparison with some figures in rabbinic literature, and in particular, in the Talmud.

"Friends-rivals" most readily map onto rabbinical texts as fellows (*chaverim*) in a rabbinic academy, as city-based as such an academy typically is assumed to be in the Talmud. The *chaverim* differ from the "people of the countryside" (*'am ha-aretz*) and from "idiots" (*idiota*), who are assumed not to be educated enough and therefore are not reliable enough in the matters of observance (for example, for the purposes of taxation.) Beyond the *chaverim*, Greek "friends-rivals" also translates into rivalry relationships among the sages in the Mishnah and among those in the Talmud. Here, as in an emblematic story of Rabbi Yochanan and Resh Lakish, having a rival-friend becomes a question of life and death.[8]

Mapped onto the Talmud, "liberating opinion" transforms from opinions competing in the *agora*, where their bearers win and lose to each other into a competition between the presumably valid, but conflicting opinions of the past, compared with the moment at which the characters, the rabbis and students in a rabbinic academy fight to ensure the infallibility (that is, the refutability and counterrefutabiliy) of each opinion delivered through tradition.

The "fractalization of Greece" maps onto the Talmudic "conceptual figures" (Gasché's and Deleuze's term) of outsiders or foreigners in the Talmud—emperors, noble Roman ladies, heretics, who all, ironically, speak in rabbinic parlance and even rather proficiently cite Scripture, as well as engage in and typically lose disputes to the rabbis. There of course is an obvious difference: These foreigners represent the dominant power, and the rabbis model the leadership of a colonized or "Hellenized" community. However, that difference notwithstanding, these still are the "conceptual figures" of the outside on the inside and the inside on the outside. What is more, when thrown against one another in the Talmud, the rabbis and the emperors help to create an inside within the inside in the Talmud: the inner circle of students in the academy, so that students can cleave to their teachers. A typical scenario is when the students know better than the foreigner does how to object to a rabbi, but these students still let rabbi win over the foreigner and only after the fight is over approach the rabbis with their objections and receive satisfactory answers. By the logic of these inner fractals, the outside becomes the inside and the inside the outside, because the inner circle of students and rabbis is attainable only via the point of view of the foreigners, that is, from the outside. Significantly, the rabbis and students in this fractal assume the outsiders' view of them as "Jews" (*yehudaya*), even if without necessarily accepting that view as a self-definition, using instead "Children of Israel" or, when appropriate, fellows (*chaverim*), for that purpose.

With the parallel Greek and Talmudic "reterritorializations" established, we can now proceed to what D&G describe as "absolute deterritorialization," a characterization that renders all the territorializations and deterritorializations described so far "relative." In D&G, the term "relative" presumes there also are "absolute" deterritorializations. For D&G, in order to have transitioned from an initial "presence" (to use Bataille's term) to political territory, there must be a step in between, which, however, marks no territory. To move from (1) originary territorialization or "(human) presence" toward (2) the political territory of a city-state or empire, one must have already uprooted oneself from (1) before arriving in (2.) The content of (1) and the (2) can vary and are relative to one another, as well. They are thus termed "relative deterritorializations," departures from a particular chthonic or nomadic "presence" and then "relative reterritorializations," arrivals in a political territory. For another example, it is a move from empirical arithmetic, which relatively deterritorializes everything from the hunted prey to gathered grain by transforming them into lists and numbers, to geometry, which accounts for pieces of land using notions such as square roots or tangents that are arithmetically ungraspable, but which make possible counting what has no empirical equivalent.

"Absolute" deterritorialization indicates for D&G what enables the transition from arithmetic to geometry. It is "absolute" because it has no empirical territorial equivalency, neither arithmetic nor geometrical, and it is a "deterritorialization" because it marks a departure both from arithmetic and from "(human) presence." To dwell on this example a bit longer, one can manage additions, subtractions, and even divisions and multiplications within "natural numbers" by still thinking about numbers as objects—say, eggs. It does not matter what one is to count arithmetically—eggs or elephants. This is why one can still count elephants thinking about them as if they were eggs. We are still within original territorialization here.

Yet when it comes to proportions in a triangle or to calculating a square root, eggs or even elephants can no longer be helpful. One has to think numbers, not digits, and this is nothing empirical, although no less "real." How was the transition from counting eggs or elephants to thinking numbers possible? "Absolute deterritorialization" is the answer, or more precisely, it is the intermediary step on the way from elephants to numbers, and even more precisely, it is a challenge that only philosophy can address properly, D&G argue. To have arrived at numbers, one must have already "deterritorialized" elephants and must have done that "absolutely"—with no, eggs, rabbits, or even digits, let alone any other empirical objects in play. To have come to thinking numbers or, to come back to Rancière, to have come to thinking justice, yet another nonempirical matter, one must have "absolutely deterritorialized" from one's "(human) presence" or from the original territorialization and from relative reterritorialization of arithmetic.

These relative deterritorializations and reterritorializations are therefore secondary phenomena. As explained in D&G's "10,000 B.C.: The Geology of Morals" in *A Thousand Plateaus*, "what is primary is an absolute deterritorialization, however complex or multiple—that of the plane of consistency . . . (the earth, the absolutely deterritorialized). . . . There is a perpetual immanence of absolute deterritorialization within relative deterritorialization." Immanence is what names absolute deterritorializations, for D&G. The name also explains why it is absolute: it does not depend on or perhaps does not even have anything "outside" it. The earth, the absolutely deterritorialized, "knows nothing of differences in level, orders of magnitude, or distances. It knows nothing of the differences between the artificial and the natural. It knows nothing of the distinction between contents and expressions, or that between forms and formed substances."[9] The earth, thus, knows nothing about either the arithmetical or geometrical orders.

This is why, however well that the above conceptual figures of the three "Greek" reterritorializations map on the texts of the Talmud, both the originals and the mappings, according to D&G, are no more than examples of "relative" and therefore only sociopsychological reterritorializations. In the Greek case, it was the deterritorialization of original agricultural land and/or of autochthony that consequently reterritorializes in political space as "friend," "opinion," and "fractal."

However, it is important to note that the Talmudic relative reterritorializations, similar as they are to the Greek ones, do not directly indicate any such initial chthonic and/or agricultural stage, nor are they originary nomadic territorializations, say, on the body image of either horses or sheep. Their Abrahamic past, as it makes sense to the rabbis, begins from a denial of a settled existence, an existence at which the Tower of Babel was an attempt. The constitutive event for Israelites, as the rabbis think them, is the Exodus from Egypt toward a political reterritorialization on the Promised Land. Those who exited Egypt and became Israelites for the rabbis were not nomads, neither no longer nomads nor nomads in the first place, nor were they settlers. They came from one of the best lands in Egypt, a land they were permitted to use, the Land of Goshen in the Nile Delta, and they traveled to another land, a land that was only promised to Abraham, Isaac, and Jacob: Israel. What was promised, however, was afforded to their progeny, who did not have either a nomadic or a settled experience, only the experience of the move to the promised future. This explains not only why either a settled or a nomadic starting point is moot when it comes to reterritorializating the Promised Land. Most important, it explains why this land, which always remains what it is called, "Promised," is "permitted" only on the conditions of the Covenant, which includes an eviction clause. Even more important, it explains why, although the Talmud constantly refers to the moment when Israel is on its own land (*admatan*), this moment is always simultaneously both in the past and in the future, not just and exclusively in a past that is over and done with, as in Greece.

What that means, however is that the Talmudic figures of relative reterritorialization, as diasporal and colonized as they might be, presume no particular originary territorialization, either nomadic or chthonic. Rather, the constitutive movement of the Israelites is a move toward a reterritorialization that is fundamentally either in the future or in the past, so that even when it is attained in any moment of the present, the powers of the future and of the past always exert their influence, constantly threatening any present reterritorialization, or if I may say so without jumping ahead of myself, constantly gesturing toward the powers of the earth as greater than the powers of any reterritorialization on land.

That highlights an important, perhaps even fundamental difference as compared with D&G's thinking about Greece: the Israelites break with their past of nomads just as they break with their past of the subjects of the Egyptian king, but they do not arrive at any relative reterritorialization that would be intrinsically final, even if the reterritorialization at which they arrive is not exactly relative, because it always belongs to either the past or the future. That means that unlike "Greece" they do not have any constitutive starting point. They have neither nomadic nor chthonic originary territorialization from which an initial relative deterritorialization would have started, even if such an initial stage is presumed in D&G's reconstruction of Greek political history. The movement of the Israelites is toward the Promised Land, not from any originary territorialization that can be either privileges or broken with. There is no "getting back," either to Egypt or to a nomadic life.

In other words, even at the sociopsychological level, there is a difference. In the Greece of D&G, relative reterritorialization follows the initial step of relative deterritorialization—the departure from agricultural and/or autochthonous land. In the Talmud, however, the departure from the land is never full, and that land is more of a territory anyway, with variable body images of nomadic sheep, settled calves, or no image in particular, when it comes to the generation who cross the Jordan and reach the Promised land for the first time ever. In other words, there is no initial relative deterritorialization. As we will see, that difference makes a difference.

From Land and Territory to the Earth

Because there is no relative deterritorialization, the "Children of Israel"—the name under which the rabbis see themselves and their communities, in biblical narratives and in how these narratives read by the Rabbis—emerge in the Egyptian context as "foreigners," *ksenoi* or "those who came from the other side" (*'ivrim*, Hebrews). Neither designation implies any positive specificity. Notably in this respect, "Egypt" is a name of a political territory that names neither "land" nor "the earth." These designations do not appear in conjunction with *mitzraim*, or "Egypt," in biblical narratives. The Children of Israel thus first emerge neither from a chthonic connection to an agricultural land nor from a nomadic move, but rather as foreigners, a status that in the Talmud they retain in the Hellenistic political territory of the Babylonian "diaspora." Like Egypt, Babylon, too, remarkably, has no designation as either land or the earth,[10] and again, not unlike Egypt is a political territory. Of course, there is a difference. In Babylon, the rabbis and their communities have a more distinct political-territorial identity as "Jews" or *yudaiyos*, perhaps derivable from the political territory of Judah by which they might have been marked or identified from an outside point of view. This is, again, not their own self-definition as the Children of Israel. The connection, if any the Children of Israel have developed to either Egypt or Babylon would be a connection to the earth, which extends beyond any political connection with territory and does not coincide with any chthonic and/or agricultural connection to land. Similar to what D&G say about the earth, this connection lurks between land and territory and, because of its lack of objectification, it requires and gives birth to philosophy to think it. However, the connection to the earth here does not involve any initial connection to land. Neither does it always lead to an investment in a political territory. At some points it of course does, but the connection to the earth remains constant, or as D&G would have had it, absolute, a matter of either the past or the future. In contrast, relative political reterritorialization is a matter of the present, including the present in the past (*praesens historicum*) and the present in the future (*praesens futurum*), but not the matter of the initial connection to the earth rather than to either land or territory. In addition to philosophy's connection to the earth through absolute deterritorialization, the Children of Israel live and think what in the closest approximation to D&G's terminology would amount to an *absolute reterritorialization*, in which the transformation of the earth into territory is never fully complete, either in the past or in the future.

In what follows, I will explore the advantages and limitations of thinking the earth in terms of absolute reterritorialization. I see this exploration as a way to thinking the relationship between the Talmud and philosophy in terms of the political and more specifically as an important entrance to thinking the other others.

I therefore provisionally submit that on the absolute plane, unlike "the Greek" case of D&G, in the Talmud, the earth is not only and not primarily an absolute deterritorialization, but also and more important an absolute reterritorialization, a reterritorialization that always involves a surplus over any political territory that any relative reterritorialization produces. That absolute reterritorialization is never objectified, not even in a geometrical, let alone in arithmetical way. It is to the earth as absolute reterritorialization that the Children of Israel aspire in their movement toward "the Promised Land," beyond any relative reterritorialization in a geometrical order of either a city-state or empire.

Needless to say, the standard translation of ארץ as a "land" is misleading in this context, for two reasons: "territory" would be better than "land," but even a territory does not and cannot fully comprise the earth. Rather, the promised land (ארץ, earth) is therefore always either in the future, as in the five Books of Moses, or both in the past and in the future, as in the Rabbinic texts. It is not exactly in the "now," as per the Talmud or Mishnah. Similarly, in the other scriptural books of the rabbinic canon, in the *Prophets* and *Writings*, the land (ארץ, earth) is at best in a conditional present, premised as it always is on the Children of Israel's observance, rather than on any political territory per se. The "land," or more precisely "the earth" (ארץ) of Israel therefore is always firmly promised, but a territory is never permitted[11] unless the conditions set forth in the Covenant are all met. Even when in possession as a political territory, the earth can be permitted only on the condition of observing the commandments, which means the always imminent possibility of the permission being suspended, even if never ever permanently removed.

In light of the comparisons of the social and psychological conceptual figures in the city-state and in the rabbinic academy, the Children of Israel in the Talmud surely both undergo and undertake only a relative reterritorialization, even if with modifications. The Children of Israel do not leave the agricultural land in the past in favor of a political territory. Rather, both in the past and in the future they both relatively deterritorialize from a political territory (Egypt) and reterritorialize to a political territory, either the "Promised Land" or another land—Babylon. As already explained, that involves a mode of temporal and conditional relationships with G-d and with the earth, rather than with any kind of political territory per se.

In this context, deciding on the applicability of D&G to the Talmudic performance of the political decisively depends on D&G's most crucial notion, that of absolute deterritorialization, which is how D&G arrive at the concept of the earth.[12] The latter is what philosophy and only philosophy attends to, D&G argue. The earth, for D&G, even if it emerges on these "relative" grounds, does not stem from them in any sense of causality. The earth opens up on the way from the initial deterritorialization of either autochthonous agricultural land or nomadic move to the relative reterritorialization exemplified in (divisible) political spaces, or as Schmitt would have it, in the "*nomos* of the Earth."[13]

Earth-Thought and Absolute Reterritorialization

Because the core of the issue at hand concerns the earth as absolute deterritorialization for D&G, that notion comes to the center of the attention. To get from relative deterritorialization to relative reterritorialization, an intermediary step, however momentary, and however nonempirical and, most importantly, noncausal,[14] must have always taken place.[15] That step is absolute deterritorialization. It opens up the earth prior to and beyond any relative territorialization, be it the chthonic bull of Lascaux or political territory embracing both dry land and the sea. To understand where it places the Talmud, a closer look at absolute deterritorialization is needed.

The necessity, the lack of external causality, and therefore also the absolute immanence implied in D&G's notion of absolute deterritorialization collectively open up not only philosophy, but more broadly thought as Earth-Thought. As a nonrepresentable intermediary step between a relative deterritorialization and a relative reterritorialization, absolute reterritorialization is necessary. However, it is not a cause of relative reterritorialization, for absolute deterritorialization does not belong to the same plane as the relative deterritorialization. It is immanent and depends on nothing external to it, either by way of causation or by way of representation.

Absolute deterritorialization comes in three main shapes, as Gasché highlights. The first is philosophy, or thought in concepts, that is to say, in problems (*aporias*) and their creation. The second is science, or thought in "functives" that always target answers, rather than questions/problems and that thus have a referential component, which concepts (as *aporias* or "problems") do not intrinsically have to have. The third is art or thought in "percepts" or "affects," wherein referents can never be fully explicated and thus must always remain implicit. Philosophy, science, and art as ways of thinking absolute deterritorialization come in that order, which Gasché critically highlights and disagrees with on the grounds that, I will suggest, he finds in Derrida. As Gasché has it, for D&G, the creation of concepts/problems—that is, philosophy—seems to enjoy a tacit privilege over the other two forms of thought.

The privilege of philosophy over the sciences and arts in accessing the earth is, for D&G, due to philosophy's intrinsic independence from reference and representation. Science must solve problems and thus must have referents. The arts also must have referents even if, and precisely because art approaches them as inexpressible. Only philosophy focuses on the problems per se, and thus does not have to have any referential content. This is why D&G criticize many schools of philosophy as not living up to thinking the earth properly.

There is no point in mentioning here any explicitly religious philosophies in which G-d would be a referent, however elusive and/or transcendent, even on the verge of becoming an object of "art" in the terms above. Rather at issue are the less obvious, but more important targets of D&G critique of philosophy: Husserl's and Merleau-Ponty's phenomenology. For D&G, despite the phenomenological bracketing of the existence of all referents, subjects included, these philosophers, too, fall short of satisfying the requirement of intrinsic independence from reference. Freed from dependence from objects and in particular from subjects, these philosophers still must entertain an indirect point of reference from which, as from a ground, they approach all other points of reference. This has to do with their connection between life and the earth understood as such a "ground" of experiencing all objects or subjects.

Here, I approach a very important point for understanding the place of the Talmud in the equation, and will therefore advance more slowly, proceeding by taking as examples of philosophical thinking of the earth in Husserl's and Merleau-Ponty's respective notions of *Urdoxa* and of a non-objectified but always intimately felt body, *Leib* as a foundation of all experiences.[16] *Urdoxa*, a primordial "opinion," is prior to any reference to any content. This primordial empty opinion is given in every *doxa* or opinion in the regular sense of the term. *Leib*, or the body as nonrepresentable and even wild "flesh" is distinct from any body image. *Leib* is the "ground" for experiencing all other, objectified bodies, but cannot be objectified. In both the *Urdoxa* and *Leib*, however, there still remains a residue of reference, even if empty or formal, or even "wild." For D&G, that residue of indirect reference is what shows that phenomenology has not lived up to the task of philosophy as Earth-Thought.

However, for D&G, the pre-Socratics, along with few other instances in the history of philosophy, do live up to Earth-Thought. The "Greek" philosophy of the pre-Socratics creates concepts that run and are being run through the chaos by the "plane of immanence." The philosophy of Spinoza as a panentheism of immanence, as well as Bergson's concept of duration, along with D&G's own oeuvre are the only other instances in which philosophy lives up to its proper task, that is to say, to Earth-Thought.

Among other philosophers outside of this list, D&G privilege Heidegger's Being as a much more agreeable approximation of philosophy to the task of thinking the earth. However, as it becomes clear in Gasché's analysis, being remains neither easily classifiable nor fully satisfactory in terms of its relationship to Earth-Thought. For D&G, the problem with Heidegger is that thought of the earth as thought of Being harkens back to the Greeks' presumed residue of the autochthonous—the "Greek" (or rather, in Heidegger's case, the "German") chthonic relation to land as *the* way to and in *Being*, in the sense of what shines through all particular entities by running[17] them and having them being run through chaos as beings, thus leaving their particularity and/or referentiality behind or and by the same token making reference irrelevant.

But the chthonic residue of land poses the question: Does asking about Being mean thinking the earth? Gasché's subtly expressed critique of D&G leaves it crucially open as to whether or not D&G's stipulation about the chthonic residue in Heidegger is enough to free the earth from Heidegger's concept of Being. Per Gasché, the tipping point and/or the hesitation here is that harkening back to ("Greek"/"German") "land" rather than to a universally open the earth may or may not be an intrinsic, rather than extrinsic, element in Heidegger's thought of Being. This hesitation becomes much more pressing when Gasché concludes the analysis in *Geophilosophy* with the question of whether or not the earth leaves any room for "the World"—that is, what for Gasché would be open not only to philosophy, but also equally to the arts and sciences, without privileging the philosophy of immanence above them.

If I read *Geophilosophy* correctly, Gasché is drawing here on Derrida's analysis of the complexity of the relationships between philosophy and art. He deploys that analysis in order to criticize D&G for privileging the philosophy of immanence over the always elusive forms in the arts, and in particular in literature, and by extension over the sciences. The proper discernment of the display of the political in the Talmud in terms of the earth and the World has everything to do with how Gasché deploys Derrida to criticize D&G.

The question of the World versus the earth concerns autochthonous land. On my reading of Gasché's argument, that suggests the problem of the universality of the Earth-Thought in the face of an always given locality (including the military expandability) of the land as both the source and the object of possession, even if on behalf of all humankind and/or humanity.[18]

If Gasché's reading suggests that D&G's view of philosophy fails to take adequate consideration of the world of arts and sciences by privileging the creation of concepts over the creation of affects and "functives," that reading allows and even requires us to come back to the implications of Gasché's critique of D&G for missing the significance of the world for the question of the relationship between the earth, territory, and land as this problematic applies to the case of the "land"—or more precisely, the ארץ or earth—"of Israel." To do that, I first need to work through the background of Gasché's critical reading of D&G in some more detail in order to isolate yet another force at play in his thinking.

The force I discern at work in Gasché's critical reading of D&G is *différence*, Derrida's prevalent mode of thinking.

Derrida and D&G can be easily seen as incompatible. Indeed, D&G insist on immanence as privileged way in Earth-Thought and criticized transcendence as the political equivalence of empire or religion, wisdom or despotism, in opposition to democracy of friends, fractals, and liberating opinion. They therefore saw transcendence as taking philosophy away from what it uniquely and singularly is thought of immanence, Earth-Thought. At best, D&G allow for transcendence as a function of or a negative projection of immanence.

The most interesting counterexample of that, which however only reinforces their point, might be Kant's notion of the transcendental, rather than the transcendent, for Kant is remarkably not included in D&G's list of philosophers who think the earth. For Kant, the transcendental is what operates strictly within the limits of human experience but is independent of it. Kant's transcendental, thus, amounts to the "transcendent within," or to immanent transcendence. That, however, only reconfigures but does not undermine the opposition between the immanent and the transcendent, because for D&G, Kant's argument still depends on reference, the data of experience, through which the subject arrives at the transcendental foundations of experience.

On this point, Derrida is different, because Derrida's *différence* is different. In contrast to Kant, who purported to solve the problem of the opposition between the immanent and the transcendent by introducing the transcendental, Derrida's *différence* grounds, undermines, and escapes the opposition between immanent and transcendent in the first place. Positing that transcendence must proceed from within immanence—what immanence differs from at the same time is must be infinitely deferred as unthinkable in order to make immanence thinkable—makes the valorization of pure immanence impossible.

In the context of Gasché's critical reading of D&G, that is precisely what leads to the question of the world in distinction from the earth, the territory, and the land: Earth-Thought occurs on the plane of immanence, yet Derrida's *différence* undermines the distinction between immanence and transcendence. The result is that absolute deterritorialization, on Gasché's reading, is closer to *différence*, including the difference between transcendence and immanence, than to the plane of immanence per se. Derrida and Gasché, this other D&G, thus argue that not seeing the proximity of absolute deterritorialization to *différence*, D&G's Earth-Thought has no access to what is open not only to philosophy, but also to the arts and sciences without privileging the philosophy of immanence—that is, no access to what Gasché calls "the World."

Yet the two other ways of thinking Earth-Thought, the arts and sciences do have their access to the world, and this is precisely where D&G as Derrida and Gasché offer a critique of D&G in the sense of Deleuze and Guattari. The critique is not only that by privileging philosophy over the arts and sciences, D&G as philosophers block access to the world, but also that their privileging philosophy is not possible in the first place, because, as Derrida and Gasché have it in regard to philosophy and literature, philosophy cannot control literature, but literature by its very nature lays no claim to controlling philosophy or anything else. For Gasché, by the logic of Derrida's *différence*, the loss of the world to philosophy is a luxury that neither philosophy nor arts or sciences can afford.

The Earth of the Talmud, between the World, Territory, and Land

Gasché's critical attempt to rescue the world for the arts and sciences from D&G's earth and the privileging of philosophy via immanence helps us map the Talmud as thought and to ask about the role of that thought in regard to the question of the other others. Where exactly does the Talmud as thought stand in relation to Earth-Thought and Being? In terms of relative reterritorialization and its "conceptual figures," its outsiders and foreigners, its emperors, noble Roman ladies, and heretics, the question is: Where does the political that the characters in the Talmud perform vis-à-vis philosophy, the arts, and the sciences in relation to the earth and/or the world. In terms of absolute deterritorialization, the question concerns the never full and never final reterritorialization of the earth as political territory.

At this point these questions assume the following form: Where does the Talmud as thought stand in relation to Earth-Thought and Being? Where is the Talmud in relation to the world, which finds no place in immanence? Toward the end of the *Geophilosophy*, Gasché asks, "What about the world?"

> With their respective concerns with the Earth, Nature, and the Cosmos, philosophy, science, and art have parceled out three concerns that in early Greek thought were ultimately interlinked. But what about the world? The problematic of the world arises in *What Is Philosophy?* in the context of what D&G call a belief in this world, in an unconditional yes to the world as it is. This affirmation of the world is

> the philosophical gesture par excellence, which sets it squarely apart from wisdom and religion. Is the world, that is, is this world, then, the over-arching unity in which the earth, nature, and the universe-cosmos are distributed, or in view of which philosophy, science, and art create? Is "world" the broader philosophical concept in which the Earth as philosophy's proper concern, in so far as it is one form among other forms of thought, is shown to have its place, together with Nature and the Cosmos? Is it not through this [sic!] concept of world, that philosophy, rather than science and art, has surreptitiously guided D&G's inquiry into the three so very different forms of thought that are philosophy, science, and art?[19]

As already established, the question is: Is the world the earth, or is it the Cosmos and Nature as well? If indeed only philosophy has the access to the absolute deterritorialization or the earth as what has no representation, then what are art and science doing? On the logic of D&G, they fall prey to either geometric or residual representation. If, on the contrary, they, to, have access to the world, then the world must be different from the nonrepresentational the earth, and philosophy's nonrepresentational thinking must not have the privilege that D&G gave to it.

In this way, Gasché's critique discovers an aporia in D&G's thought. Is there a resolution? Following Derrida's model of the relationship between literature and philosophy, Gasché seems to refuse the possibility of privileging either philosophy, or science and art in relation to the world. The logic of the Derridean model is that while literature undermines philosophy's claim of superiority in thinking the earth, literature cannot claim its own superiority, either. The question "what about the world?" thus reveals a limitation in D&G's understanding of philosophy as geophilosophy.

And in the light of that limitation, another one comes to view. What if Earth-Thought is not exactly a nonrepresentational precondition of all subsequent representations in the arts, sciences and the political territories that the latter two chart? In other words, what if the earth can be more than an absolute deterritorialization? I have begun suggesting that the Talmud exemplifies the way in which the earth can be understood as a movement of absolute reterritorialization, a movement as "absolute" as philosophy, and that the Talmud performs the "reterritorialization" characteristic of the arts and sciences at the same time. The Talmud exemplifies a discipline of thought that employs all these modes of thought to access the world as its infinite task. That task is not only and not primarily that of representing or charting a political territory, but first and foremost, one of remembering the world in excess of not only representation, but also of absolute deterritorialization.

Absolute reterritorialization differs from absolute deterritorialization, first, because it comes from a different context—that of relative reterritorialization. The preceding step, the relative deterritorialization of the chthonic, agricultural, or nomadic does not occur. The conceptual figures in the Talmud involve neither chthonic nor agricultural land or nomadic movement as a starting point, but instead always imply an always already politically charted territory—either Egypt as a point of forced departure or forced exile in Babylon, expressed, in particular, in the figure of "Israel on its land," which is a figure of a Babylonian political chart. The absence of either chthonic land or nomadic movement at the start leads to a different conclusion as well. Reterritorialization (absolute reterritorialization) then is either in the past or in the future and is never fully reached, so that even a futurist resurrection from death at the time of Messiah's coming is neither completely denied nor positively affirmed in the Talmud.[20] In other words, any relative reterritorialization on the political territory of a "Promised Land" is never complete. Even when the relative reterritorialization is charted as land and/or ground in any temporal mode, the earth as ארץ remains as a surplus. It functions as a power that undoes any relative—and therefore always temporary—reterritorialization. What is more, on the absolute level, Earth-Thought does not necessarily threaten to undermine reterritorialization in either the city-state or empire, but instead is supposed to condition their fruition. But the ארץ does. The biblical ארץ as approached in the Talmud includes the earth as the infinite task in light of which the world is to be remembered rather, than exhaustively charted in any political reterritorialization.

The Talmud's ארץ thus is related to, but does not coincide with D&G's conceptions of land, territory, and the earth. Instead, ארץ is positioned at the center of the relationship between land, territory, and Earth-Thought. The Talmud's ארץ makes it both necessary and insufficient to project the task of thinking, living, and remembering ארץ onto the task of nonrepresentational philosophy, as well as onto the respective tasks of the representational, even if only the residually representational, in the arts and sciences. In this view, if the Talmud exemplifies a discipline of remembering in excess of any representation and in excess of any relative political territorialization. If so, then following from Gasché's critique of D&G, the Talmud can be reduced neither to philosophy nor to art, let alone to science. On the other hand, the Talmud as a discipline and as an example of the task of remembering Talmud's ארץ could not be graspable without its always insufficient but necessary projections in philosophy, the arts, and the sciences.

Thus reintroduction of the Talmud as a site of the political, a site of the absolute reterritorialization of philosophy, the arts, and the sciences back into the World, a site where none is privileged over the others, opens up a way to let the other others back into thinking, acting, and living in the political, both beyond, before, and after the currently dominant conceptions of the political in theology or ontology, conceptions that continue to efface the other others from the face and depth of the earth and from the World, thereby continuing the effacement—and thereby the return—of the political in the Talmud back or for the first time to the World.

ACKNOWLEDGMENTS

I would like to express my sincere gratitude and appreciation for many conversations with many people at different stages of this book's development. These conversations were stimulating, productive, provocative, and always heuristically helpful. Among my most important interlocutors were David Bates, Daniel Boyarin, Jonathan Boyarin, Richard Cohen, Kenneth Dauber, James Diamond, Oona Eisenstadt, Rodolphe Gasché, Chaya Halberstam, Aaron Hughes, David Johnson, Nitzan Lebovic, Vivian Liska, Ron Mayers, Edouard Nadtochi, Noam Pines, Ron Reisberg, Bruce Rosenstock, Paula Schwebel, Shai Secunda, Zvi Septimus, Moulie Vidas, Ewa Ziarek, and Krzysztof Ziarek. I am grateful and deeply indebted to Bud Bynack for his always helpful editorial interventions. I did not always respond to his suggestions directly, but I always attended to issues these suggestions indicated. I am immeasurably thankful to my spouse, Lilia Dolgopolskaia, and to our daughters, Polina Dolgopolskaia and Elen-Sarrah Dolgopolskaia, for their existential support during the time of my work on this book. Preparation of the book for publication was made possible with the generous support of the Gordon and Gretchen Gross Professorship in Jewish Thought at the University at Buffalo, SUNY.

I dedicate this book to the memory of Helen Tartar, whom I will never be able to thank sufficiently for her gift of an editor—a gift to help a book, including this one, to become what that book was asking to be.

Earlier and differently framed versions of the materials in this book appear in the following venues: "Jews, in Theory," in *Jews and the Ends of Theory*, ed. Shai Ginsburg, Martin Land, and Jonathan Boyarin (New York: Fordham University Press, forthcoming); "Tosafot Gornish Post-Kant: The Talmud as Political Thought," in *Talmudic Transgressions: Engaging the Work of Daniel Boyarin*, ed. Charlotte Fonrobert (Leiden: Brill, 2017), 74–105; "Rethinking the Implicit: Fragments of the Project on Aggadah and Halakhah in Walter Benjamin," in Words: *Religious Language Matters*, ed. Ernst van den Hemel and Asja Szafraniec (New York: Fordham University Press, 2015), 249–268; "I Will Regret Later: Personhood, Repentance, and Time in Neoplatonic Thought and the Talmud," *Philosophy & Rhetoric* 48, no. 1 (2015): 73–98; and "Constructed Denied: 'The Talmud' from the Brisker Rav to the *Mishneh Torah*," in *Encountering the Medieval in Modern Jewish Thought*, ed. Aaron Hughes and James Diamond (Leiden: Brill, 2012), 177–200; and "Remember the Past or Know What Was: The Political Philology of the Talmud," *Judaica Petropolitana* 3 (2014): 162–180. I thank the respective presses for allowing me to use these materials in the book.

NOTES

INTRODUCTION: HUMANS, JEWS, AND THE OTHER OTHERS

1. The political, that is to say, is not about institutions. This distinction is as subtle as it is crucial. The book as a whole does not focus on the state, nor does its final chapter focus on the contemporary State of Israel, even if pertinent implications about both could be drawn from its argument. Considering any (modern) state would have meant shifting away from analyzing the political as such, which is the book's focus, to analyzing the condition of particular political institutions, which is programmatically not the book's main theme, question, and/or concern.

2. Jacques Rancière, *Dis-agreement: Politics and Philosophy*, trans. Julie Rose (Minneapolis: University of Minnesota Press, 1999).

3. Carl Schmitt, *The Concept of the Political*, trans. George Schwab (Chicago: University of Chicago Press, 1976); Schmitt, *Political Theology: Four Chapters on the Concept of Sovereignty*, trans. George Schwab (Chicago: University of Chicago Press, 2005).

4. Or even "political form," the concept by which Carl Schmitt approached the political in his *Roman Catholicism and Political Form* (Westport, Conn.: Greenwood Press, 1996). In this work, he links the political with the theological, as the work's title suggests. And Martin Heidegger, a thinker commensurable with Schmitt in epoch, scope, and influence, enabled making a similar linkage between the political and the ontological, because both, for him, were inspired and led by the question of being. The present book both heuristically applies and ultimately renegotiates these hitherto predominant linkages of the political with theology and/or ontology. Needless to say, that does not mean a return to relinking the political with economy, as Marxist tradition would suggest.

5. For a critical account of the state of the field, see Yair Lobrerbaum, *Disempowered King: Monarchy in Classical Jewish Literature* (New York: Continuum, 2011).

1. THE QUESTION OF THE POLITICAL: BACK TO WHERE YOU ONCE BELONGED?

1. The approach to the other others I take here is different from Levinas's or Lacan's approaches to alterity in their respective juxtapositions of an-other who is empirically confronted (the "petite object *a*" and the "face of the other," respectively) and the other Other, the big or "divine" one. Both Levinas and Lacan assume the superiority, indeed, the domination of (respectively) the divine Other. What is more, while for Levinas the divine Other is neither present nor absent, and thus is exterritorial and transcendental, then the other other I detect and address in this argument is perceived by the subject as territorial, namely, as falsely rooted in the subject's territory, while having possibility of getting back to where it once belonged—an unbearable situation for both the subject and the other other. Similarly, Lacan's real and dominant Other, as an unknown, is unproblematically deterritorial, even if and precisely because the territory, or precisely the terra it occupies must remains terra incognita for the subject. Not dominating but rather repressed and not able to get back to where it once belonged, the other other therefore calls for a mode of analysis reaching beyond the domains that either phenomenology or psychoanalysis are designed to reach.

2. See Carl Schmitt, *Römischer Katholizismus und politische Form* (Stuttgart: Klett-Cotta, 1984 [orig. 1925]) and English translation, Carl Schmitt, *Roman Catholicism and Political Form*, trans. G. L. Ulmen (Westport, Conn.: Greenwood Press, 1996 [orig. 1923]). Schmitt writes: "The Catholic Church is the sole surviving contemporary example of the medieval capacity to create representative figures—the pope, the emperor, the monk, the knight, the merchant. It is certainly the last of what a scholar once called the four remaining pillars—the House of Lords, the Prussian General Staff, the *Académie Française*, and the Vatican. It stands so alone that whoever sees therein only external form mockingly must say it represents nothing more than the idea of representation (*so einsam, dass, wer in ihr nur äussere Form sieht, mit epigrammatischem Spott sagen muss, sie repräsentierte überhaupt nur noch die Repräsentation*). The eighteenth century still had some classical figures, like the 'législateur.' In view of the unproductiveness of the nineteenth century, even the Goddess of Reason appears to be a representative" (original, 32; translation, 19). Even if there of course is some content, the "external form" does not go away, and is arguably more important, and most certainly more invariable than any content, as circumstantial, fluent and changing as it might be. The form therefore is all important even beyond the "mocking" or more precisely, beyond the "epigrammatic." "Representing nothing than"—G. L. Ulmen adds, "idea of"—"representation" is of course precisely this: representing nothing else but representation, a representation of

representation. Marginal, and again "*epigrammatischen*" or as Ulmen has it "mocking" or, perhaps better "epigrammatic" as this definition of the political form is for Schmitt, it nevertheless affords him very strong, perhaps even strongest grounds for differentiating political representation—whether he supports it outside of the mystic content of Catholic church or not—from techno-economical representation, which he dismisses as distorted notions of representing.

3. What is more, representing G-d takes precedence over any particular person's claim to be that god. Anyone's claims of being a flash and blood god must yield to the power of an organization, say Church, which is representing G-d, and thus, paradoxically becoming G-d's body. (See notes following.)

4. Ironically just as that representation takes precedence over the personal traits and/or positions of a given Church official, so too the function of representation of Christ takes precedence over any particular individual claiming to be Christ in flesh and blood, who have just come back. I both develop and explain this irony further in the next chapter. See also the next note.

5. As Kathleen Biddick recent work helps understand, translated into terms of the medieval theology in understanding the Church as that which is represented through its officials, Schmitt follows a tacit medieval theological equation of *corpus mysticum* (understood as Eucharist) with *corpus christi* (understood as Church), in contradistinction from *corpus verum*, the "true" or "historical" body of Christ, however absent, as the Gospels said that corpus was, from the tomb. (Biddick, "What Does 'Deconstructing Christianity' Want? The Institutional Imaginary of the Incarnation," unpublished manuscript). See note 28 on the agency of these concepts in Schmitt's theory.

6. Schmitt, *Roman Catholicism and Political Form*, 19: "[The Catholic Church] stands so alone that whoever sees therein only external form mockingly must say it represents nothing more than the idea of representation." From the standpoint of "external form," the Church, including, on my reading, each official thereof, "represent . . . the idea of representation." Reluctant as this admission about "external form" may sound in Schmitt's words, it precisely the "form" that he brings forth in the title of his essay, and it is this form that he is isolating as the core of both the political and of Catholic Church properly understood, for him.

7. See Kathleen Biddick, *Make and Let Die: Untimely Sovereignties* (Goleta, Calif.: Punctum Books, 2016.)

8. This external point of view may well be not Schmitt's own point of view as a devout Catholic, but it is the conception of representation that

Schmitt develops on his way to the concept of political form in the work and of political theology in his later writings.

9. Added in English translation to alleviate the opaque but crucial original language, "representation of representation."

10. The "law" is of course understood here as the "positive law" in the sense in which Kant criticizes that law for being imposed "from the outside." For one context in which that critique finds continuation, see Nancy's essay "Church, State, Resistance," *Journal of Law and Society* 34, no. 1 (March 2007): 3–13.

11. In the example of the Church, such a sovereign would be Christ, who suspends the techno-economical "law" of the "Old Testament," as well as the pope in the capacity of the highest Church official, who designates friends and enemies (such as heretics, pagans, and importantly for a later stage in my argument, Jews, who become the figure of exception par excellence, because the Church cannot place Jews in either "heretics" (to qualify one must be a Christian) or "pagans" (which would undermine the very foundation of the Christian Church). Being such an exception, "Jews" only help to create the rule—the normative Church, whose first sovereign, Christ, proclaims the exception from "the law of the Jews" and whose other sovereigns proclaim exception of Jews from the Law, including, as was more recently done, partial allowance to admit them in that suspension of Law.

12. The who and the what coincide here because the enemy loses personal qualities of a human, let alone of a free citizen. The enemy can be reduced to an animal, to a natural power, or as a better fit to the logic, to that which must not exist if the emergency is to be treated in full. At this point, the political theology and political ontology meet one another: the denial of the status of an existing thing for an enemy, reducing him, her, or them to an appearance, say an appearance of a human, but also of a were-wolf, of a zombie, etc. That appearance must be eliminated in order to eliminate the emergency.

13. Carl Schmitt, *The Concept of the Political*, trans. George Schwab (Chicago: University of Chicago Press, 1976), 26.

14. The triplet easily gets reduced to a couplet of what-is versus what-only-seems-to-be; for the true opposite of being is seeming, rather than nonbeing, with the latter explained as only a prosthetic device to maintain separation between the first two. Thus, the question about ontology in relation to the political would be as follows: Can dividing into friends and foes work without sorting out who is and who only seems to be a friend? To attempt answering for Schmitt, a true distinction between someone and her enemy has to do with the very "existence and/or life-style" of an individual or a group threatened by the foe. On empirical grounds, that alone establishes

inseparability between the political form and the fight for existence, thus making the political form always full of ontological and/or life-bound content.

Yet beyond that empirical connection between political form and the content of the human existence, there is much more to the relation between the political and the ontological in Schmitt, and by extension in modern thinking about the political. That "much more," however, is much less obvious. It has to do with transcendental rather than empirical dimension of Schmitt's conception of the political. To make it even more complicated, it concerns the third element in the equation, the theological aspect of the relationship between the political and ontology. In this equation, the theological often comes in the disguise of the secular. In that context, "secular" means "Protestant" by virtue of the implied opposition between "religious" (in the sense of institutional) and "secular" (in the sense of noninstitutional), which features Protestantism's criticism of Catholic Church's focus on institutions, hierarchies, and offices as opposed to personal faith (and in particular lack thereof) in each individual in society. This complex interplay of religious and secular, faith and institution, Protestant and Catholic, conflicting theologies makes it even harder and even more pertinent to discern the theological component of the connection between the political and the ontological. A register when that connection becomes most available for analysis is the transcendental dimension of Schmitt's ontology of being versus seeming in his conception of the political.

15. Structurally, the other other is paradoxically similar to Levinas's divine Other, who is neither present nor absent but only traced by the subject on the face of the first-order other, the person (human or animal) whom the subject confronts. Denied existence as either humans or animals, and thus refused the status of either present or absent, the Jews at the time of the "Holocaust" structurally fall into the same category, in the eyes of the perpetrators. The difference is of course is that the Divine other makes no appearance, and Jews—as exemplified among other figures by that of Selig, are assumed to have only appearance and never being or existence.

16. Jacques Rancière, *Dis-agreement: Politics and Philosophy*, trans. Julie Rose (Minneapolis: University of Minnesota Press, 1999), xii. Translated by "disagreement," *mésentente* connotes, in Rancière, an inevitable speaking past each other, which the different groups of society inevitably commit, when their words are the same but matters brought forth through the words are different, or are seen differently by each group. This meaning of disagreement differs from other meaning of the terms I will deploy in this book, but it retains an important common denominator—unavoidability of

the difference in positions. In any version of disagreement there always are different parties involved, and the differences between them cannot be eliminated, sublated, or eradicated in any other way, whether or not these parties, or someone on their behalf understand the differences between them.

17. The term *mésentente* is more specific in meaning than its generic translation as "disagreement." *Mésentente* involves and is involved in a version of homonymy: the same words used in the same meanings address radically different things, and the difference cannot be easily explained to those who address the matter that concerns them with the same words. Entrapped by homonymies, the different parties keep speaking past each other, because they use exactly the same words, and they understand the meaning of these words, too, but the things these words address do not coincide. They cannot, because one thing replaces another "unbeknownst" to each of the parties. In an extreme and therefore very telling case, "saying something else entirely" can even reach a point that the other party cannot comprehend that the words are the same at all.

18. Rancière, *Dis-agreement*, xi.

19. Ibid., xii. The utterance "These dates are good" provides an example of a misunderstanding that can be clarified. If X says this, talking about certain days of the month, and what Y hears involves fruit, there is a simple semantic misunderstanding that which can be clarified. But if Y cannot see the object that X presents to him and does not even believe the X speaks meaningful words introducing that object, even if Y still understands each word, we have the extreme case of disagreement. X sees the object and presents it in words; Y does not see the object and does not recognize the words that X used as meaningful.

20. The terms "useful" and "harmful" are from Aristotle, and Rancière locates unavoidable disagreement already at work in the Greek city-state, arguing that the disruptive power of disagreement remains condition sine qua none for the modern version of the political as found in nation-state. He thus counters the view in which the political begins in the modern period, with the advent of nation-states. Carl Schmitt's political theology exemplifies this position, even if—and as—it takes root in Rousseau's and Hobbes's theories of society. I will get to this competition between political ontology of Rancière and political theology of Schmitt in a moment.

21. Ibid., 15.

22. Ibid., 9.

23. Ibid., 18.

24. Ibid., 15.

25. Ibid., 14.

26. Ibid.
27. Ibid.
28. Ibid., 21–22.
29. Of course, just as the empirical designations of who is a friend and who is an enemy in Schmitt, as well as specific configurations of disagreements about what is just and what is not in Rancière can constantly change, so too the claims of who exists and who seems to can evolve and even flip from one side on the other. By implication, that makes the political power never glued to the hand of those who exercise it. The political is therefore always taking off from an empirical ground, even if never leaves that ground behind.
30. Kant, *Critique of Pure Reason*, A141.
31. Ibid., A146.
32. Kant both constructed and criticized Jewish Law under the rubric of "positive" law, which can be taken or practiced by its subjects either dogmatically or relativistically. Most immediately, "Jewish Law" would mean, for Kant, the Old Testament, yet by extension, it would include modern versions of Jewish Law rooted in the Talmud and also other forms of religious dogmatism and/or relativism (or as Kant would have it, deism and anthropomorphism) as unwelcome elements of the Christian doctrine. All these norms involve either dogmatic of skeptical/relativist responses to the positive law. The positive or posited and imposed norms can make their subjects respond by way of dogmatism, teaching how to obey them with enthusiasm, or by way of skepticism or relativism, teaching how to evade those norms. Either scenario is superseded by Kant's transcendentalism and his expression of the law as the categorical imperative. Jewish neo-Kantians, in particular Hermann Cohen in his philosophical work and R. Josef Soloveitchik in his writings on "Jewish law" (*halakhah*), responded to Kant's critique of "Jewish law" as merely positive as opposed to transcendental by reversing the argument. They reclaimed the Jewish law as transcendental rather than positive. The reversal, however, raised the price that the medieval Aristotelian commentators and interpreters of the Talmud already had begun paying long before by rereading the Talmud accommodate the intellectual norms and concerns of medieval and modern versions of rationalism. See Leo Strauss, *Philosophy and Law* (Albany: SUNY Press, 1995). For both Soloveitchik and Cohen, that rereading entailed disconnecting Talmudic refutations of refutations from their relationship to the task of memory and remembering. To counter that disconnection of refutation from memory is to highlight the price it entailed.
33. On the face value the reduction of seeming to be to nonbeing can be counterintuitive. If I seem to be happy, but deep down I am sad, I nevertheless

remain in being. A wolf in sheep's clothing is not nothing; it is a wolf. In the agora, those things that only seem just are still something else, not nothing, and those who seem friends, but are enemies, indeed still *are*. Yet, the happy me does not exist in this case, nor is there a sheep. Things which seem to be just but are not comparable to a square triangle, and object, which can be described in words, as I just did, but can only seem to exist, not to exist indeed. Nor does one who only seems to be friend have to be something else. Indeed, in Schmitt, being enemy precisely means seeming without being, a nonbeing of which needs to be cashed as "nonbeing' through the extermination of its seeming-to-be.

34. Heraclitus 64: τὰ δὲ πάντα οἰακίζει κεραυνός, "Lightning steers the universe" (Diels's translation); τὰ πάντα in both Heidegger's and Fink's readings refers not to "the universe" but to all things together without accentuating any clear-cut differences between them, but without denying their multiplicity either. In a flash of lightning, things are clearly many, but they are not clearly distinct one from another. See Heraclitus Seminar, Martin Heidegger, and Eugen Fink, *Heraclitus Seminar* (Tuscaloosa: University of Alabama Press, 1979), 4ff.

35. Of course, an argument can be made that both Heidegger's "being" and Schmitt's "representation of (the idea of) representation" emphasize the finitude of being in view of nonbeing as more fundamental than the *being* versus *seeming* of each individual thing or matter. That argument would go along the following lines. Just as "representation of (the idea of) representation" does not have any intrinsic relationship to any particular content (but is instead a "pure form," even if it is always coming with and visible only through *an*—extrinsic—content attached to it) so too, Heidegger's being does not have any intrinsic relationship to any particular being, to a particular thing, which *is*. It does not, even if, for Heidegger, being is always and only available through an extrinsic connection to an individual thing; or even to all such things together. In other words, intrinsically, being is only opposed to nonbeing, not to the being of a particular thing. Yet, the arrival to nonbeing as authentic horizon of being, or to nonbeing as that which, along the lines of Heraclitus, man bestows on the things, fully depends on triangulations of being, seeming, and nonbeing. It is either the case that seeming equates to nonbeing, or it is the case that being contracts nonbeing, whereas seeming is left behind, but kept as negated. In either case, however, seeming remains at play, even if only as a term to bypass, and in this sense to negate.

36. It is equally possible that, in moving backward from Plato to pre-Socratics, being becomes night, as it does in Levinas's critique of ontology;

however, this version of being is still predicated on the opposition between being and seeming as the dominant one.

37. That mechanism of exclusion can work in reverse as the mechanism of inclusion as well. Thus, the figure of exclusion remains at work in its more recent form of "tolerance" that allows for the inclusion of the deviant others. Examples of the included excluded would be the groups defined by homosexuality, disability, obesity, transgender, misogyny, racism, ageism, public control of birth or abortion, or "racial deviation," exemplified before and at the time of the World War II by the persecution of Gypsies as deviant Indo-Europeans or by the planned but never carried out persecution of "deviant Germans" for the purposes of promoting the political fantastic of the "Indo-European race."

38. The interpersonal component of the Talmudic discussion is central for the Talmud, in contrast to a philosophical (Hegelian) perspective on satire, which remains marginal for philosophy, leaning instead toward irony, even if the latter is understood, in Hegel's case, in interpersonal terms. In that regard, one might consider but will have to reject a possible analogy of "the interpersonal" with Hegel's *bacchantische Taumel* (Bacchanalian revel) in the preface to the *Phenomenology*. In interpersonal relationships, "negated," or, more precisely, "refuted" does not mean "false." This therefore could be confused with Hegel's similarly sounding principle that "negated" does not means "false." For Hegel, however, it is about Bacchanalian ecstasy at a drunken party. Just as such a party is going on, even as some participants come and go, phenomena come and go, but the flow of coming and going remains stable and true to itself in that stability. That prevents the negativity of becoming from being merely the process of showing phenomena false. Seeing a phenomenon vanish does not mean claiming it is false, for it belongs to "the true" (*das Wahre*) to the paradoxical stability of coming and going, which itself does not come and go. In other words, Hegel's principle that "negated" or "negative" does not mean "false" belongs to the register of constant becoming, to the Bacchanalian ecstasy of each phenomenon, which nevertheless is a part of overarching tranquility that reigns over any Bacchanalian night. The ecstatic negations contribute to the tranquil process of their becoming followed by their vanishing. However, and just because of that, each "member" (*Gleid*)—each phenomenon—is fundamentally indifferent to every other and to their coming and going. Nobody cares about anybody else in particular in this party more than they do about both drunk and tranquil spirit (*einfache Ruhe*) of the party itself. In short, the principle that "negativity does not mean falsity" translates, for Hegel, as "the participants may go, but Bacchus remains."

However, the interpersonality of Talmudic refutations is radically different from the Bacchanalian revel. Equally ecstatic in their satirical or sarcastic mood of needing to keep the refuted strong and around in order for the refutation make sense, the Talmud's ecstasy, satire and/or sarcasm remains totally sober. By this alone it is not a Bacchanalian revel of truth in a Hegelian sense. A sober satire has nothing to do with a Bacchanalian night. The interpersonal relationships in Talmudic refutations do not hold negative, or more precisely, "refuted" positions to be false, for refutation is never a negation in the sense of an annihilation or in the sense of making the refuted disappear completely. On the contrary, to have something refuted by a statement or a position makes the statement or the position true. A position is false only if is obvious and refuting nothing.

39. See Christine Elizabeth Hayes, *Between the Babylonian and Palestinian Talmuds: Accounting for Halakhic Difference in Selected Sugyot from Tractate Avodah Zarah* (New York: Oxford University Press, 1977).

40. See Daniel Boyarin, *Socrates and the Fat Rabbis* (Chicago: University of Chicago Press, 2012).

41. Ibid.

42. Chaya T. Halberstam, *Law and Truth in Biblical and Rabbinic Literature* (Bloomington: Indiana University Press, 2010).

43. See Rodolphe Gasché, "Λόγος, Τόπος, Στοιχεῖον," *Internationales Jahrbuch für Hermeneutik* (Tübingen: Mohr Siebeck, 2009), 147–169.

44. Part of the reason why this concept is difficult is that U.S. legal system does not work in this way. It is the prosecution that makes the determination of how to characterize a putative crime, and while a judge may have some say in explaining the alternative ways to characterize it (if any) to a jury, it is up to prosecution to determine how the defendant is to be charged and up to the jury to determine if that or another, different crime has been committed. It is not a subsuming an established action under a rule or law it violates, but it is probing the accusation of having violated a certain law or rule in the first place.

45. "Possible" here opposes the necessary. The deduction reveals the conditions of possibility, not conditions of necessity, even if Kant move have been understood along the lines of necessity too, the core of transcendental deduction concerns the possible, rather than necessary, and thus fundamentally invited rhetoric into play—not in the sense of metaphors and metonymies, as Paul de Man would attempt to recover rhetoric in Kant, but rather in terms of the possible as opposed to either impossible or necessary.

46. Among examples of such modifications would be Nancy's notion of inoperative community in Jean-Luc Nancy, *The Inoperative Community* (Minneapolis: University of Minnesota Press, 1991), as well as Luce Irigaray's

thinking in *To Be Two* (New York: Routledge, 2001). On a separate note, the modern view of human society as intersubjective is no more and no less than an anthropomorphic deviation from the Kant's intersubjective society of the subjects of reason. Its anthropomorphism (Kant's terms) consists in confusing a human as an object recognizable through a schema of human (just like a dog is recognizable through the schema of dog) in the First Critique with the human as the only known but in principle not the only example of the subject of reason in the Third Critique, where human (and G-d alike) is a symbol but not a schema. In that sense, the Talmudic interpersonality differs from both anthropomorphic (schematic) and from symbolic understandings of the humanity of the humans.

47. In the modes of either being-together, or of "being two," or of being an "inoperative community."

48. That does not have to be dogmatism, of course, or relativism of truth. For the intersubjective model of the political, transcendentalism does much better.

2. JEWS, IN THEORY

1. Jean-François Lyotard, in *Heidegger and the "the jews"* (Minneapolis: University of Minnesota Press, 1990), to whom Philippe Lacoue-Labarthe is responding in *Typography: Mimesis, Philosophy, Politics* (Cambridge, Mass.: Harvard University Press, 1989). I write Jews, Jew, and Jewish with a capital "J" and without quotation marks in order to indicate full-fledged reality of the Jew as a modern *type*, in Lacoue-Labarthe's terms, translated into and de facto politically inscribed on the flesh, blood, and psyches of the people, whose genealogy goes back to the biblical, Talmudic, and medieval Israel. The capitalized "J" and the erasure of the quotation marks from the "Jews" is of course not a regression to what Lyotard suspends as a naturalist view of Jews. Rather, the erasure and capitalization only indicates the full-fledged reality of the flesh, blood, and psyche of the modern Jews as what Lacoue-Labarthe helps us understand as type, in the technical sense of neither natural nor figurative, as I will elaborate. To express that technical sense of Jews as a type means to avoid understandings insisting on the dichotomies between a natural, biological, racist view of humans and thus of the Jews on the one hand and the "religious" view of Jews as a religious group on the other. To indicate a departure from that dichotomy, if I could, I would both use and erase quotation marks when writing "Jew," "Jews," or "Jewish." Because that is not graphically feasible, I instead use Jew, Jews, and Jewish, thus indicating the excess, the (im)possibility, or at least problematic character of these dichotomies between "natural" and "religious" in application to Jews and to things Jewish.

2. For example, the mathematical notion of a point is a fiction, at least in the sense that it can never be empirically real, and it is a necessary fiction without which geometry, that particular domain of reason, cannot operate.

3. See Erich Auerbach, *Figura* (New York: Meridian Books, 1959).

4. Hegel, of course, is yet another thinker for whom *Gestalt* functions a specter, this time of an "organic whole" in which members are not parts but rather organs, and in which therefore a member embraces or "reflects" the "whole" of the organism; so that, to come back to men and women, that organism proceeds through differing implementation of one and the same set of organs, which are developed in different degrees in individuals of different sexes.

5. Precisely because "specter" only exemplifies *Ge-stalt*, in certain contexts it is more important to note that a specter is a *Ge-stalt*. In such contexts, I use these terms together or interchangeably.

6. One might apply here Rodolphe Gasché's notion of singular universal, a singular that serves as a universal. See Rodolphe Gasché, "Piercing the Horizon," *Journal of French Philosophy* 17, no. 2 (Fall 2007): 1–12.

7. As Jonathan Boyarin has suggested, that sounds remarkably reminiscent of Abraham Joshua Heschel's interpretation of the Chasidic thought of Menachem Mendel of Kotzk (1787–1859). See Abraham Joshua Heschel, *A Passion for Truth* (New York: Farrar, Straus and Giroux, 1973).

8. Haunting as these objects or subjects always are, specters lurk and lure in dispelling them. In contrast, concepts may work without ever presenting themselves as either objects or subjects. They instead can inform thinking and action without ever thematically emerging in them.

9. See Daniel Boyarin, *Carnal Israel: Reading Sex in Talmudic Culture* (Berkeley: University of California Press, 1993).

10. The Jew is a figure of exception from both the old and the new law. Theologically, "the Jew" is a figure that enables Christians to consider the New Testaments as an exception, that is, famously both the suspension and the supersession, but not the cancellation of the Old Testament, which therefore renders the Old testament as "Jewish Law." In that sense, the Jew is a figure enabling the New Testament as an exception from the Old Testament. Additionally, theologically, "the Jew" is also an exception from the New Testament. The latter does not cancel the Jews, nor does it allow judging them according to the new law. That is, Jews cannot be judged as either heathens or heretics, which are the standard or, as it were, "linear" others of those who adhere to the New Testament beginning from the creation and formation of the concept of the New Testament from the third century onward.

11. For the analysis and complication of that dynamic relationship in medieval Jewish, Christian, and Muslim identities, see Steven F. Kruger, *The Spectral Jew: Conversion and Embodiment in Medieval Europe* (Minneapolis: University of Minnesota Press, 2006).

12. For much earlier, Hellenistic negotiations of the borders of humanity, see, for example, "The Universe of the Human" in Jonathan Boyarin, *The Unconverted Self: Jews, Indians, and the Identity of Christian Europe* (Chicago: University of Chicago Press, 2009), 70–90. As Boyarin argues, the rhetoric of kinship (which in Lacoue-Labarthe's terms is distinct from fictive productions of reason in the form of *Ge-stell*) remains heavily at work.

13. Pavel Florenski, "Idei i sudjba christian [Idea and Fate of Christianity]," letter to V. V. Rosanov, October 26. In V. V. Rosanov, *Sacharna: Obajatelnoje i osjasatelnoje otnoshenije evreev k krovi* (Sensor and Tactile Relationship of Jews to Blood) (Moscow: "Respbublica," 1998), 363: "Indeed, there is nothing to say. Is there anything at all you can do with Jewish advocates? And why do you think we will learn from them. . . . something deeper than the art of advocacy? Noteworthy, *advocacy*, and 'Enlightenment' in general—is *their* [cursive in the original] invention. It was they who stirred the controversy around the Catholic Church. Humanism derives from the Kabbalah. More generally, Jews used to and will continue to keep secrets for themselves, and they used to and will continue to give out only the shells: a white tie, 'Russkie Vedomosti' newspaper, cheap charities, and our right to supply newborns for them. Jews have always turned to us, the Arians, with that side of theirs to which we, due to our lack of religiosity, have always been *seducible;* and they then always took advantage of such a situation. They taught us that all people [*lyudi*, men] are equal,—in order to take advantage of us [lit.: sit on our neck]; they taught that all religions are superstitions and atavisms of the Middle Ages (which they, by the way, dislike so much precisely because of its integrity, because, then, one knew how to deal with them),—in order to take away our power—our faith; they taught 'autonomous' morality, in order for them to take already existing morality away and to substitute for it what is banal and vulgar. If they just wanted to make us Jewish, that would be only a half-trouble. Yet the problem is that they have perfectly understood and still understand the value of every religious principle, and ultimately, its power to unite people, thereby secretly keeping their own religious principle for themselves" (363, my translation).

14. In *Origins of Totalitarianism* (New York: Meridian Books, 1958), in the section "Between Pariah and Parvenu," Arendt develops a complex interplay between "mankind" as an always repressive attempt to reduce the plurality of humanity to a unity, and "humanity," which is always pluralistic

and inclusive of (as she critically quotes Herder), a "new specimen of humanity," which is not exactly a specimen, but rather an insider who is an outsider and an outsider who is an insider and who cannot always be certainly told who he was, or who is, in one simple word: a Jew. Arendt thus insists on her being treated as a Jew within humanity, rather than as a pure "human being" among other human beings, the members of mankind. Humanity, thus, for her, does not predicate "human being" as its component. Because she was persecuted as a Jew, she demands to be respected as a Jew, rather than as a "human being." That defines humanity as a way of treatment of the other other in public discourse, rather than as a definition of private beings united in a group, say, in a nation-state, bypassing the public political dimension, as Schmitt, in this respect not totally unlike Arendt, also indicated in his critique of the modern capitalist nation-states. On these grounds, which are of course rather different from those of Florensky, Arendt arrives at a strikingly similar conclusion: that treating Jews and everybody else as "human beings" is politically impossible. Despite the fact that Florensky conceptually replaces "human being" with "religion" and Arendt with "humanity," both thinkers arrive to the conclusion that treating the Jew, and thus everybody else, as a "human being" is problematic, because it erases the political (Arendt) or religious (Florensky) dimensions of the life of society.

15. Hannah Arendt, *The Jew as Pariah: Jewish Identity and Politics in the Modern Age* (New York: Grove Press, 1978).

16. This is confirmed not only and not primarily by the emptiness of the leaflets. Instead, whatever the content of his protest might be, the grounds on which he protests are that of a universal human being (a subject of rights, in one dimension of it), fighting for the universal and for Jewish values at the same time.

17. In what follows, I will begin renegotiating these theoretical concepts to think about "the political form" of the Talmud (to continue to use—polemically—Schmitt's terminology from his earlier work) and in turn to apply an understanding of that "form" to gaining an even better view of Rabinovitch as a political figure. As I hope this helps to argue, the Talmud showcases the political as an authentic and therefore elided counterexample of Schmitt's political form, as distinct from what Schmitt offers as a counterexample for his notion of the political: the rule of law, and endless liberal disputation with no decision when law cannot help to decide.

18. *Darstellung* is a fiction, an act of mimesis that obscures reason, even if reason cannot function without another fictioning, that of *Vorstellung*.

19. I borrow two major terms from Heidegger's *Being and Time* but also refer to other ideas of futurist time from Cohen to Bergson and via Heidegger to Levinas and Derrida.

20. For a preliminary gloss, *Vorstellung* introduces agency representing another agency (for example, an ambassador representing a country) without any claim of semblance involved. *Darstellung* introduces an image as a representation claiming a resemblance with that which is represented (for example, a painting claims both a resemblance and a dissemblance with the object it reproduces and/or constructs).

21. "Rethinking the Implicit: Fragments on Aggadah and Halakhah in Kafka, Bialik, and Benjamin," in *Words*, ed. Ernst Van Den Hemmel and Asja Szafranniec (New York: Fordham University Press, 2015), 249–268.

22. Lyotard's "what" also belongs to the plane of representation alone. Lyotard's treatment of the affect in *Discourse, Figure* as the pure "what" without the "who," the "to whom," or the "about what" is still taking place within the level of representation: the zero degree thereof. This is important in the context of this essay because of the contrast of Lacoue-Labarthe's position to Lyotard's *Heidegger and "the jews."* This connection, however, would require a separate treatment.

23. Is the Talmudic refutation of a refutation "decisionist" in Schmitt's sense? Or is it a version of what he criticizes as "liberal debate" about creation and application of rules with no end or decision ever attained? The refutation of a refutation does not involve a spurious infinity but is instead cumulative in a way that differs from the dialectics of cumulative sublation (*Aufhebung*) as well. Instead of either a spurious infinity of negation or dialectical synthesis, after each completed step of refuting and counterrefuting, the memory of the past (and thus of oneself as a function of the past) advances a step forward, thus affording a just action, which after each step is more precise than before. In contrast, "liberal disputation," as Schmitt sees it, reaches no decision because it is spurious and because, for him, it lacks political form and therefore has no political will to interrupt a spurious multiplicity of opinions under discussion. The desire for certainty, claimed to be guaranteed by knowing what is, both drives "liberal disputation" and at the same time and by the same token, due to the multiplicity of claims about what is, the debate comes to no resolution.

24. Refutation therefore is not just a fourth dimension on the plane of signification, manifestation, and denotation, in Deleuze's terms in *Logic of Sense*, but rather is an altogether different plane, a dimension that circumscribes the level of representation on which the first three occur.

25. See, for example, b. Quiddushin 70a.

26. A common denominator between Roman Catholicism and the Talmud in terms of political form has to do with the infallibility principle. In the case of the Church, it is the infallibility of the words of the pope delivered ex cathedra. In the Talmud, it is the infallibility of the words of the authorities, say, in the Mishnah, an early third-century code of instruction for rabbinical courts, or of the post-Mishnaic masters collectively named *amoraim* in the Talmud after those who repeated their words aloud in the public space of a rabbinic academy in Babylon that is implied in the text, as opposed to the nameless rabbinic students in discussions archived in records and compositions, which since the Middle Ages have been called the Babylonian Talmud. In the case of the Church, the infallibility principle is an axiom. In the Talmud, however, while the authorities of the past are still infallible by axiom, the memory of their words and deeds is infallible only when proven so by accumulating mimetically mutually exclusive but politically complementary versions of what these words meant, that is, what they were refuting. In the Talmud, one begins with a heuristic attempt to refute the accuracy of the memory of a tradition or teaching and ends up refuting that refutation, repeating and developing the process further. Furthermore, as already indicated, refutation serves not only as the vehicle of remembering, but also as the truth criterion of what is remembered, as well as a main mode of delivery and thus the main character trait of the nameless students in the Talmud who argue about their teachers in earlier generations, to whom the students also ascribe the same character traits.

27. The refutation of a refutation is both similar to and different from the Platonic genre of dialogue. Despite seeming openness in terms of content, Platonic dialogues follow the path of irony to direct the audience to a formal end. The latter is known in advance: the victory of the philosopher of being over his deeply confused interlocutors, immersed, unbeknownst to them, in the limbo of seeming, of mimesis, which also leads them to evil, mistake, and illusion. Unlike the genre of the Platonic dialogue, the process of refutation and counterrefutation is always complete, but is never over. Yet even if the refutation of a refutation is complete, it is intrinsically not closed, because it promotes uncertainty as a basis for just action, rather than striving for certainty envisioned as determining of what is or what was.

28. I am borrowing Lacoue-Labarthe's terms here.

29. Both Schmitt and Heidegger are future-oriented. Schmitt's political thought follows the same lines as Heidegger's in the treatment of the intimate relationships between being and time, where time is first and foremost the form of having a future and only secondarily a form engaging the past and the present. At stake in Schmitt's understanding of the political action is one's existence and one's lifestyle (*conatus*, in Hobbes's terms),

which can be at stake only if the figure of having future is at work. Needless to say, both in Heidegger and in Schmitt, the future-orientation of human existence—or more precisely and more generally, of a person's existence—artificially diminishes the importance of the past, reducing it to the fiction of a starting point and directing both thinking and memory toward being, eternal for Plato, which leads to ideas and theory, or temporized for Heidegger, which leads to replacing the theory by critique framed in terms of *Ge-stalt* as *Ge-stell*. (For the purposes of this argument, I bracket the question of Heidegger's return to pre-Socratic moment. His discernment of being in pre-Socratics is guided by understanding being through time, future-oriented as it generally remains for him.)

30. The refutation of a refutation differs from negative dialectics. A technical difference, one that medieval Aristotelian commentators of the Talmud noted, is that in a chain of refutations, the second refutation, call it the "counterrefutation," idiomatically termed by those commentators *terutz* or *peruk* (respectively "excuse" or "dismantling,") is expected to be weaker than the first refutation. If the counterrefutation were to succeed, the whole process of refuting would lead to nothing, and the process of Talmudic argumentation would have to start from ground zero. Instead, the second refutation builds on the first one. The result is a more reliable and more elaborate memory of the traditions, teachings, of accounts of the law. The process of refuting and counterrefuting is thus heuristic. After the process of refuting and counterrefuting, the initial traditions are remembered better both in terms of neutralizing the mistakes of mechanical transmission and in terms of the implications (or more precisely, the *inventions*) that the rabbinic traditions are understood to have had. Needless to say, the result of refuting and counterrefuting is not Hegelian dialectics of *Aufhebung*, sublation, nor is it a Platonic clarification of confusion. The outcome of the refutation of a refutation, the building up of memory and remembering is not a synthesis of contradictions negating and suspending each other. It is so not only because, like Aristotelian hermeneutics and rhetoric, the Talmudic refutations operate not with contradictions but with contrarieties, but also, and more important, because the process does not to have to take one direction only. Refutations of refutations can branch out and even go rhizomatic, starting, as they often do, not with a tradition at hand, but instead with another tradition, not immediately obviously related to the tradition currently considered in discussion. Branches and rhizomes of the refutations of refutations introduce a register of refuting that enriches memory by building it up on refutations of refutations in more than one way, along the lines of more than one trajectory of analysis, which the dialectics of cumulative *Aufhebung* cannot afford.

31. For Chaim Luzzatto, an effort to remember through an enactment threatens to forget the importance of remembering through intellectual engagement even with things that might seem obvious otherwise. See his introduction to *Mesillat Yesharim* in Chaim Luzzatto and Abraham Shoshana, *Complete Mesillat Yesharim: Dialogue and Thematic versions* (Cleveland: Ofeq Institute, 2010). Luzzatto's example of such forgetting through reenactment is a religious group that forgets the importance of fear of heaven or of divine love through constantly enacting these things in the rituals.

32. See Giles Deleuze, *Expressionism in Philosophy: Spinoza* (New York: Zone Books, 1990).

33. As Deleuze argues in his reading of Spinoza, just as Spinoza's "substance" can be expressed only through an attribute but can never be reduced to any particular attribute, so too, more generally, by the tripartitioning logic of the expression as distinct from the dual logic of representation, what is being expressed ("substance") is always more than what is actually expressed ("attribute") in any particular ("modus") of expression.

34. I refer here to De Libera's work on subjectity and subjectivity, *Archéologie du sujet. I. Naissance du sujet* (Paris: Vrin, 2007), and my previous engagement with his argument in *The Open Past: Subjectivity and Remembering in the Talmud* (New York: Fordham University Press, 2013.)

3. TALMUDIC SELF-REFUTATION (INTERPERSONALITY I)

1. See, for but one example, David W. Halivni, *Sources and Traditions: A Source Critical Commentary on the Talmud: Tractate Baba Metzia* (Jerusalem: Magnes and Hebrew University of Jerusalem Press, 2003).

2. See Daniel Boyarin, *Socrates and the Fat Rabbis* (Chicago: University of Chicago Press, 2009). See also Richard Hidary, "The Agonistic Bavli: Greco-Roman Rhetoric in Sasanian Persia," in *Shoshannat Yaakov: Jewish and Iranian Studies in Honor of Yaakov Elman*, ed. Shai Secunda and Steven Fine (Leiden: Brill, 2012), 137–164.

3. See Martin S. Jaffe, *Early Judaism: Religious Worlds of the First Judaic Millennium, Studies and Texts in Jewish History and Culture* (Bethesda: University Press of Maryland, 2006).

4. M. F. Burnyeat, "Enthymeme: The Logic of Persuasion," in *Aristotle's Rhetoric: Philosophical Essays* (Princeton: Princeton University Press, 1994), 3–56. See also his essay on *peritrope*, "Protagoras and Self-Refutation in Plato's Theaetetus," *Philosophical Review* 85, no. 2 (April 1976).

5. Burnyeat, "Protagoras and Self-Refutation in Plato's Theaetetus," 172.

6. Kaufman MS (A50): 116–117.

7. bQid. 39b 40a. Oxford Opp. 248(367). The translation is from the Schottenstein edition of the Babylonian Talmud, heavily amended.

8. Such a question becomes possible because both fragments of the Mishnah in play are not marked by the names of specific sages and thus allegedly represent teaching with which all the sages in the Mishnah agree.

4. CONCEPTIONS OF THE HUMAN (INTERPERSONALITY II): THE LIMITS OF REGRET

1. An earlier and shorter version of this analysis was published as "I Will Regret Later: Personhood, Repentance and Time," *Philosophy & Rhetoric* 48, no. 1 (2015): 73–98.

2. For the lack of less theologically charged terms, I continue using "pagan," and later "monotheist," if only in quotation marks.

3. Alexey Losev (1893–1988), a classical philologist, philosopher, and musician by education, combined a revised version of Platonism with the teachings of Eastern Church Fathers in the framework of Russian Orthodox Church. He was particularly interested in the Imyaslavie movement, which developed in Russia in the first decades of the last century to resist both modern "Western" forms of Idealism and the Russian communist philosophy of dialectical materialism (while seeing the latter as an outcome of the former). Losev's lifelong project of "taxonomy" of ancient aesthetics could be explained as an application of the modern idea of aesthetics developed in Baumgarten and Kant (see the last section of this essay) for rethinking the late ancient philosophical heritage in order to reinvent Russian Orthodoxy through the philosophies and theologies of the West. Losev's intellectual and practical-religious positions came together when, in 1929, at the time of political triumph of dialectical materialism, he and his wife took a practical step of secretly accepting monks' vows. They consequently used their marriage as a then-necessary camouflage for their lives as orthodox monks. For Losev's critical intellectual biography, see V. V. Bibikhin, *Aleksei Fedorovich Losev; Sergei Sergeevich Averintsev* (Moscow: Institut filosofii, teologii i istorii Sviatogo Fomy, 2004).

4. Alexey Losev, *History of Ancient Aesthetics*, 8 vols. (Moscow: Iskusstvo, 1963–92).

5. "Jewish Rhetoric" represents here a more general rubric under which rabbinic rhetoric becomes subsumed in modernity.

6. The need to embrace (and to complicate) the relationships between rhetoric and philosophy in studying the Talmud requires no justification. By definition, rhetoric as a discipline stands in complex and never stable relationships to its disciplinary other, philosophy. The Talmud historically has fallen prey to that instability—sometimes fully alienated from philosophy

and sometimes interpreted as a version of rhetoric. However, in the last century, in a competition between modern rhetoric and new philosophical disciplines such as ontology, anthropology, and phenomenology for the status of the truly "fundamental" discipline, the relationship between rhetoric and philosophy has taken a new shape, allowing us to reevaluate the Talmud as an independent discipline in its own right having a no less complex standing in regard to the disciplines of philosophy and rhetoric. As the analysis in this chapter helps illustrate, that competition suggests reconsidering the role of the discipline of aesthetics, as well, by turning back to the ancient versions of it as a way to map and better understand the complex relationships between the disciplines of rhetoric, Talmud, and philosophy.

7. Emmanuel Levinas, "Is Ontology Fundamental," in *Basic Philosophical Writings*, ed. Adriaan T. Peperzak (Bloomington: Indiana University Press, 1996), 1–10.

8. Paul de Man, *Allegories of Reading: Figural Language in Rousseau, Nietzsche, Rilke, and Proust* (New Haven: Yale University Press, 1979). Worth mentioning is David A. Frank's article, "A Traumatic Reading of Twentieth-Century Rhetorical Theory: The Belgian Holocaust, Malines, Perelman, and de Man," *Quarterly Journal of Speech* 93 (2007): 308–343, which puts Perelman and de Man into conversation as responses to the Holocaust and the crises it either caused or made evident.

9. These theories build on Levinas's critique of Heidegger and ultimately on Husserl's notion of *Abbau*. See Rodolphe Gasché, "Nontotalization without Spuriousness: Hegel and Derrida on the Infinite," *Journal of the British Society for Phenomenology* 17, no. 3 (1986): 289–307.

10. The Talmud and its study have already emerged in different capacities at different stages of the fundamentals debate. First, the Talmud emerged as a subject of study in the neo-Kantian tradition of philological-historical and philosophical-theoretical analysis of cultures and texts (Herman Cohen, David Daube, Max Kadushin). "Translated" by Levinas into the language of philosophy, the Talmud then became the model case for his ethics of the subject's infinite responsibility toward the Other, emerging as a basis for Levinas's resistance to Heidegger's claims of fundamental ontology. Scholars also have claimed the Talmud's congeniality to deconstruction and to its Americanized view, "poststructuralism." Against these backgrounds, Losev's work opens up a yet another way in which the Talmud can emerge in that context, this time through the perspective of ancient aesthetics.

11. See note 10.

12. See note 3.

13. That dissolution in the face of the Other also means that the question of ethical responsibility in Levinas's sense of the term does not even arise. There is no time for it. For Levinas, the face of the other hits "me" before I can do anything about it, and I am therefore responsible to and for what is out of my control (Richard A. Cohen's term). For Losev, instead, the timing is radically different: "I" dissolve before I can even think about "objectifying" the face.

14. Unlike Levinas's *face*, which maintains the distance from the other, thus surely limiting but still preserving the existence of Cartesian subject, Losev's look absorbs the viewer in the personhood to which that look is leading.

15. See Pavel Florenksi, *Iconostas* (Saint Petersburg: Russkaya Kniga, 1993).

16. Losev, *History of Ancient Aesthetics*, 7:271.

17. Ibid., 7. The paradigm thus becomes embodied in life and thereby paves the way to reverse the process, that is, of the return of becoming to being (the growing pine tree to a pine as a tree, in the earlier Iamblichus example). His reading of aesthetics highlights embodiment in two distinct roles—as a way to keep the three parts of the triplet both apart and together and as a way for the paradigm to enter into and return from the "unfortunate" circumstances of becoming, or "life." Importantly, the process of embodiment in no way implies personification, a moment that Losev makes particularly noticeable by indicating in his reading of Amelius that Iamblichus, as a more "advanced" Neoplatonist, differentiates between the demiurge (a person) and the paradigm as only one aspect of the triplet. What that means, however, is that the mind is not intrinsically a person, even if in the ways of becoming it can manifest in personification. In Amelius, the mind is thus not intrinsically personified, but if it is personified, it is only as a multiplicity of personae. This will prove equally important for understanding personification and embodiment in Talmudic thinking as well.

18. That again presents aesthetics as "fundamental," notwithstanding the fact that there, grounding leads to a ground in which none of the elements is possible without the other two.

19. Different positions in the critical study of the Babylonian Talmud revolve around different combinations of the concepts of person, meaning, and writing. Combining the notions of person and meaning in the concept of intention, romantic literary criticism and, among Talmud scholars, David W. Halivni, hold that a person (either a collective person, or an individual, called "*stammaim*") historically precedes writing. Locating intention thus understood in the writing, the New Criticism and, among Talmud scholars Shamma Freidman, advance the method of close reading. Roland

Barthes and, in Talmud scholarship, Martin Jaffe (who holds that the audience is the author) dismiss the notion of intention, considering meaning a part of writing revealed to the person of reader, who is also a part of the writing. Paul de Man's rhetoric of reading, and in Talmud study, the earlier work of Daniel Boyarin and part of Shamma Friedman's work, consider rhetorical figures as intervening in the seeming mutual transparency of writing and meaning, logic, and grammar. Jacques Derrida, and, in Talmud study, Boyarin's work on "intertextuality," and, if I may include it, my own recent work, show that rhetorical figures cannot control the transcendental production of meaning, thus necessitating the engaging an explicitly philosophical and/or theoretical perspective in the critical analysis of the Babylonian Talmud, as well as using the Babylonian Talmud as a ground for rethinking the history of philosophical tradition.

20. See Shamma Friedman, *Talmud Arukh: Perek Ha-Sokher et Ha-Umanin: Bavli Bava Metsia Perek Shishi—Mahadurah al Derekh Ha Mehkar Im Perush Ha-Sugyot* (New York: Jewish Theological Seminary, 1990).

21. See David Halivni, *Sources and Traditions, Mekorot u-Masorot: Beurim Ba-Talmud—Masekhet Bava Metsia* (Jerusalem: Magnes Press 2003); Jeffrey L. Rubenstein, *The Culture of the Babylonian Talmud* (Baltimore: Johns Hopkins University Press, 2003).

22. Shamma Friedman's work (see note 19) is definitive in approaching the formation of the Babylonian Talmud as a transformation of the earlier materials—the sayings of the sages of the Mishnah and earlier masters of the generations following the Mishnah's completion in 220 C.E.—into a later form of anonymous dialectics between the characters on the stage. Dialectics not only is a new, later genre of anonymous conversation in the Talmud, but also a new form in which sayings or fragments of the sayings of the earlier—named—masters reappear as speeches or part of the speeches of the anonymous characters in the Talmud; conversely, some of the speeches of the anonymous characters take the shape of pronouncements or parts of pronouncements attributed to the names of the earlier masters.

23. See the argument on Friedman's and Halivni's approaches in Sergey Dolgopolski, *The Open Past: Subjectivity and Remembering in the Talmud* (New York: Fordham University Press, 2013), preparing aspects of asking about and renegotiating the concept of personhood in application to the Talmud undertaken here.

24. The phrase indicates a direction that his project has taken both breaking from and continuing the line of thinking I began in *The Open Past*, now turning, along with other scholars, to continuities and discontinuities between rabbinic and "pagan" traditions of thought.

25. Needless to say, previously contemplating regret is not one of the statutory sins, and as such it is not considered sinful. The only question that the characters address is whether or not such a claim of regret, after having been previously contemplated, can still be successful.

26. The question whether it would work only once only for a certain sin or for any sin whatsoever remains outside the discussion here.

27. See the "moving image of eternity" as Plato has it in *Timaeus* 37c–38c, taken up by Thomas Aquinas and critically addressed in the work of Franz Brentano.

28. Differing from understanding time as a moving image of eternity, these thinkers still considered time a universal dimension of human existence. Even if, as these thinkers see it, time stems from the imminence of the future, it continues to control the entirety of human existence, including the past, subjugated, as it therefore must be, to time. The second position differs from that view, seeing the past and the future as two different dimensions of human existence and therefore affording true *metanoia*, even after the fact.

29. John Poulakos, "From the Depths of Rhetoric: The Emergence of the Aesthetics as a Discipline," *Philosophy and Rhetoric* 40, no. 4 (2007): 335–352.

30. Poulakos's map of the relationships between rhetoric, aesthetics, philosophy, and poetry is helpful precisely because it includes Kant's aesthetics. The latter proves crucial for interpreting Losev's construction of ancient aesthetics, as informed as it arguably is, if only heuristically, by philosophy after Kant. As a post-Kantian thinker, Losev heuristically departs from Kant, even if he lands in the radically different realm that he calls late ancient aesthetics. By extension, the rabbinic aesthetics in the Talmud would belong to the same construction. Poulakos's map will therefore help tracing that movement in Losev, and open up a new, broader vista, on the aesthetics in the Talmud as well.

31. Poulakos, "From the Depths of Rhetoric," 345.

32. Ibid.

33. Kant, *Critique of Pure Reason*, A141.

34. Kant, *Critique of Judgment*, 351–353.

35. Provisionally, in a sense that I can only signal in this inquiry, workings of the judgment of beauty are different from what Benjamin conceived as law-creating and law-preserving nature of violence. The latter two work by way of affect, the display of blood. The former, being a subjective universal, is indefinite in terms of whether it is an invitation a subject sends to the others to accept the subject's judgment of beauty; is it instead an expectation, which is much stronger then an invitation can be, or is it in fact an imposition? Interpreters of Kant explored all and did not finally privilege

any of these possibilities, which suggests a built-in indeterminacy in how the subjective universal is structured. Much more important for the argument in this book, it also suggests that subjective universal is politically suitable to rather different and even mutually exclusive political regimes and/or forms of power, from democratic to dictatorial, for even the dictatorial regime cannot function without connecting its subjects one with another on the impossible shaky grounds of a mere "I like."

36. Poulakos, "From the Depths of Rhetoric," 346.

37. I am borrowing from Eric Auerbach here.

38. Poulakos, "From the Depths of Rhetoric," 347.

39. Ibid.

40. As another post-Kantian thinker, Carl Schmitt, would have it, it would be a bond of a group of friends against their foes or enemies.

41. Poulakos, "From the Depths of Rhetoric," 348.

42. I in no way argue, however, that invoking the transcendental formal element of Kant's aesthetics undermines Poulakos's derivation of Kant's aesthetics back to "the depth of rhetoric," nor is my primary goal to highlight how Kant emerges "from the depths of rhetoric" in a radically new way, introducing, as he does, the formal element of "exacting agreement from everyone" rather than employing the allegedly commonly shared sense ("common sense"). I instead emphasize the emergence of the formal element of "This is beautiful" as opposed to the content element of the commonsensical "I like it" in order to create a room for the Talmudic aesthetics on the Poulakos map.

43. See, for example, Richard Hidary, "Classical Rhetorical Arrangement and Reasoning in the Talmud: The Case of Yerushalmi Berakhot 1:1," *AJS Review* 34, no. 1 (April 2010): 33–64; Saul Lieberman, *Greek in Jewish Palestine; Hellenism in Jewish Palestine* (New York: Jewish Theological Seminary of America, 1994). I have also contributed to that discussion in *What Is Talmud? The Art of Disagreement* (New York: Fordham University Press, 2009).

44. However, the aesthetics of the Talmud is not foreign to rhetoric as a tradition of thinking. One reason for that is that rhetoric not only appeals to emotions and affects, but, as Rodolphe Gasché argues in *Un arte muy fraìgil: Sobre la retoìrica de Aristoìteles*, trans. Pablo R. Oyarzuìn (Santiago: Ediciones Metales Pesados, 2010), rhetoric is a tradition of judging the past (forensic rhetoric), the present (aesthetic, demonstrative rhetoric), and the future (deliberative rhetoric) along the lines of what is possible, as opposed to what is necessary or impossible. In that sense, rhetoric in general and rhetoric in the Talmud in particular are heavily grounded in the power of formal rational argument, rather than in affectivity and emotion, even when the beautiful is involved. In that sense, as well, classical rhetoric, at least in

Aristotle's version of it, remains congruent with Kant's transcendentalist aesthetics of subjective universals.

45. Immanuel Kant, *The Critique of Judgment*, 51, cited in at Poulakos, "From the Depths of Rhetoric," 345.

46. In Hermann Cohen, who thought about the "fundamental" in terms of sources and origins.

47. In Martin Heidegger's version of fundamental ontology.

5. APODICTIC IRONY AND THE PRODUCTION OF WELL-STRUCTURED UNCERTAINTY: *TOSAFOT GORNISH* AND THE TALMUD AS THE POLITICAL AFTER KANT

1. Here I both refer to and interpret Daniel Boyarin's view of Talmudic dialectics.

2. I borrow Chayim N. Bialik's characterization of *aggadah* or the homiletic part of the Talmud as having a smiling face and apply that characterization more broadly, to the Talmudic discussions at large. Chapters 6 and 7 will help us see the necessity of and the source of the resistance to that broader application of Bialik's view.

3. The traditional, Boethian, view of rhetorical syllogism as a truncated and thus imprecise logical syllogism is at work here, as well as a more general component of that view, a sense that rhetoric is inferior to logic in precision, even if it is superior to logic in persuasion.

4. A possible objection to my analysis of the *Gornish* commentary is that it is not only far from synchronic, but it is also not diachronic. What is more, it even is not hermeneutic in the sense of using later and simpler texts, however complex they might still be, to explain earlier and even more complex ones. Instead, the analysis here reclaims the importance of the earlier text for a current discussion, in this case, in the discussion of the political, using the lens of that discussion to read the earlier text in a new light. That would be dismissible as an anachronism.

My answer to that is that any synchronic or diachronic critique of a text must already imply a certain understanding of its meaning, uncritically taken as though must be, at least initially. Having to rely uncritically on such an initial understanding, either the synchronic or diachronic modes of criticism at best explain the genesis of the text thus understood. That means these approaches leave no room for asking a question about the genesis of the understanding from which they start. Furthermore, the hermeneutical approach does question the initial understanding of a text and in that differs from either the synchronic or diachronic approaches. I therefore remain closer to the hermeneutic approach. An important difference remains, however. The hermeneutic approach moves backward in time, assuming that later texts and interpretations are comparatively simpler than the earlier texts they interpret. Without challenging that assumption, the route I take here essay goes in both directions: from later to earlier, to use the modern theoretical lens to reread earlier texts, and from earlier to later to enrich the modern discussion of the political by reengaging the earlier corpora of text sand thought as contributors to current discussions.

5. Paul W. Franks, *All or Nothing: Systematicity, Transcendental Arguments, and Skepticism in German Idealism* (Cambridge, Mass.: Harvard University Press, 2005).

6. *Critique of Judgment* 258.

7. See, for example, Kant's characterization of the "*jüdische Glaube*" as "*ein Inbegriff bloß statutarischer Gesetze*" (*Die Religion* B 185, 186; A 176), that is, "Jewish faith" as a "sum of merely statutory laws." Immanuel Kant, *Religion within the Bounds of Bare Reason*, trans. Werner S. Pluhar (Indianapolis: Hackett, 2009), 139. As Chapters 6 and 7 will show, that position of Kant prompted Jewish adepts and/or critics of his philosophy to reevaluate Jewish Law so as to prove its transcendental rather than positive nature, thus making it possible to include "Jews" as Jews within the subject of reason without having to deprive the Jews of the "Jewish law." Hermann Cohen and R. Joseph Dov Soloveitchik would be representative of that move. A problem with that approach was that it was defensive of Jewish Law but uncritical of Kant's opposition between positive law and transcendental law. That meant the neo-Kantian adepts of the Jewish Law (1) subscribed to the dogmatism versus skepticism dilemma, even if only as a starting point; (2) embraced the opposition between transcendental and positive as the only way out of the dilemma; and (3) did no more and no less than change the placement of "Jewish law" from positive to transcendental. That meant not only subscribing to the positive-versus-transcendental divide but also accepting the classification of the Jewish tradition as "law" in Kant's sense, no matter whether it is positive or transcendental.

8. Daniel Boyarin, *Socrates and the Fat Rabbis* (Chicago: University of Chicago Press, 2009).

9. Ibid.

10. The modern part of the task in this chapter therefore involves calling into question the shared assumption of Schmitt and Rancière. That means not only putting Schmitt's and Rancière's shared negative assumption about disagreement in question by juxtaposing them to the broader tradition of the Talmud and commentary, which approaches disagreement as a goal necessitating a discourse, rather than an unwelcome circumstance of discussion. There is an even higher stake involved here. The approach to disagreement as a goal in the Talmud is only an entrance into a crucial but

carefully suppressed dimension of the political that is a genuine counter-example to both Schmitt's and Rancière's understandings of the role of disagreement in the political.

11. See Israel M. Ta-Shma, *Ha-Sifrut ha-parshanit la-Talmud be-Eropah uvi-Tsefon Afriḳah: ḳorot, ishim ṿe-shiṭot* (Jerusalem: Magnes Press of the Hebrew University of Jerusalem, 1999); Boyarin, *Socrates and the Fat Rabbis.*

12. See Franks, *All or Nothing.*

13. I render Kant's terms "*vernünftige Wesen überhaupt*" (*Critique of Judgment*: 15, 410) and "*jedes vernünftige Weltwesen*" (*Critique of Judgment*: 422), which are interpretable as "a worldly entity (in general) who thinks according to reason," of which Mensch is the only known example, which entity thinks and acts within the limits of reason, as a *subject of reason*, for the purposes of this chapter.

14. Carl Schmitt and G. L. Ulmen, *Roman Catholicism and Political Form* (Westport, Conn: Greenwood Press, 1996).

15. *Critique of Judgment* 257–258 (212–213).

16. Ibid., A146.

17. *Critique of Pure Reason* A141.

18. Ibid., 137–147 (112–121).

19. See Chapter 5, specifically the discussion of Kant and Poulakos in relation to rhetoric.

20. To clarify, under the name of "positive law," Kant may have been referring only to the "Old Testament," yet by implications both made and resisted by Jewish neo-Kantian thinkers, for example, by Herman Cohen and Joseph Soloveitchik (whom the next chapter addresses) "positive law" applies to rabbinic legal codes, as well including what these thinkers saw as foundations of the medieval codes of Rabbinic laws in the late ancient text of the Talmud. In response, these thinkers defended Jewish law as transcendental rather than positive, thereby never leaving the parameters of discussion defined by Kant. Kant also prompted Jewish adepts and/or critiques of his philosophy to reevaluate Jewish Law, proving its transcendental rather than positive nature, thus making possible to define "Jews" as Jews into the subject of reason without having to deprive Jews of "Jewish law," an approach that defended Jewish Law, but was uncritical of Kant's opposition between positive law and transcendental law. That meant that neo-Kantian adepts of the Jewish Law subscribed to the dilemma dogmatism versus skepticism dilemma, even if only as a starting point, embraced the opposition between the transcendental and the positive as the only way out of the dilemma, and simply redefined "Jewish Law" as transcendental. That meant not also accepting the classification of the Jewish tradition as "law" in Kant's sense, no matter whether positive or transcendental.

21. See Boyarin, *Socrates and the Fat Rabbis.*

22. See Chaya T. Halberstam, *Law and Truth in Biblical and Rabbinic Literature* (Bloomington: Indiana University Press, 2010). Halberstam developed the notion of uncertainty as such, whether well structured or not, in the context of late ancient texts of the Talmud.

23. At stake for the viewer is what the real interest of the judges is: Is it to attain as much certainty as possible about what indeed happened by asking as many questions as possible about it, or is it to be precise in not taking sides by either defending the weaknesses in the witness at the expense of the defendant or letting the defendant(s) go at the expense of dismissing a valid witness against him, her, or them.

24. In this context, "knew of the *ibbur*" takes precedence over "understood in *ibbur*," with *ibbur* meaning transitioning to the new month, as opposed to declaring the new month on the thirtieth (not the twenty-ninth) day of the current one.

25. The term refers to proving a certain witness was not present at the time when, as the witness describes, the event in question occurred, which means the witness is hostile to the defendant, which the term *hazzamah* literally suggests.

26. These witnesses must have missed the transition from a short month and counted starting from the month before, which was full, but one of them wrongly assumed it was short, too.

27. While Maimonides dismissed the rhetorical form of refuting and defending in the Talmud and sought to eliminate the ambiguities of homonyms in discerning essences referred to in Scripture (or the matters discussed, as opposed to things described), and while rhetoric, for Maimonides, had to give way to philosophically apodictic knowledge, the Tosafist commentary thus takes a different, although no less rationalist path, which Gornish both amplifies and in part, takes returns to the realm of logical apodictic thinking. The Tosafists often promote the rhetorical harmonization of the Talmud by making sure that any argument that a character in the Talmud makes is not dissonant with any other potentially relevant argument of that character. The Tosafists achieve that result through the refutations with which they attack any given fragment of Talmudic discussion based on its purported incoherence if juxtaposed with another relevant place in the Talmud. That comes with a satisfactory counterrefutation, thereby proving the intellectual coherence of the Talmud as a whole. Aiming to make all discussions in the Talmud cohere with one another, the Tosafists cannot afford there being any case of a refutation without a counterrefutation, or the Talmud as a whole would no longer cohere.

In contrast, the Gornish commentary takes an apodictic approach to each move in refutations and counterrefutations in the Tosafot. That involves articulating many questions about the apodictic grounds of the analysis of the Tosafists. However, in the *Gornish* commentary, that does not always have to result in answering every such question. Entering the space of apodictic thinking proves more important to the *Gornish* commentary than having covered all grounds there. The Gornish commentator therefore would feel comfortable formulating questions without worrying about immediate answers. Rather, as in the case in mathematics, as well, the concern would be to formulate the problems in apodictic terms, regarding each move of refuting and defending that they address in the Tosafot commentary, or if necessary to that end, in the Talmud. Most important is that an attack or a refutation must be apodictically sound, no matter what defense or counterrefutation counters it.

28. According to Rodolphe Gasché's recent reinterpretation of the political dimension of Aristotelian rhetoric in his *Un arte muy fraìgil*, rhetorical and political discourses take place only where "pure affect" (or, as it were, the irrational representation of the first order, prior to mimesis) no longer (or not yet) executes its irrational power and does not yet provide the foundation for Schmitt's "political form." Instead, as Gasché argues, the foundation of rhetoric comes from the formal (in Kant's sense) element (*stocheion*) of rhetorical *argumentation* (as opposed to affect), which, as Gasché shows, is the discussion of the "possible" as opposed to the "either impossible or necessary." As should be already clear, with some modification, Gasché's interpretation applies to the political dimension in the *Gornish* commentary as well. Crucially, the judges' treatment of the possible in terms of refutable and counterrefutable is not oriented toward knowing the past, and thus grants no direct application of Gasché's reading of Aristotle to Gornish. Yet, an extension and/or reformulation of Gasché's reconstruction of Aristotelian version of the political in terms of action based on refutability and defensibility clearly applies. As such application suggests, the Gornish commentary looks for and finds the apodictic grounds for treating the "possible," thus creating a distinct version of the "political form" that does not coincide with Schmitt's political form. Put differently, the rhetorical and by extension political dimension in the *Gornish* commentary arises from but does not fully coincide with Gasché's reconstruction of Aristotelian understandings of the rhetorical-political form, at least to an extend at which the possible, due to its ontological orientation, does not fully map on refutable and counterrefutable. Rodolphe Gasché, *Un arte muy fraìgil: Sobre la retórica de Aristóteles*, trans. Pablo R. Oyarzún (Santiago: Ediciones Metales Pesados, 2010).

29. Israel Ta-Shema's interpretation bypasses the dimension of apodictic irony in the Gornish commentary. Such a reading sees the *Gornish* commentary as "fragments," to borrow either Walter Benjamin's or Ta-Shema's term. The alternative demonstrated here, however, accounts for apodictic rhetoric in the *Gornish* commentary as not simply a series of fragmented examples, but rather as a sequence of well-orchestrated moves through which Gornish moves her implied readers. What otherwise would be disparaged as fragments becomes a coherent sequence of readings that help the implied reader ascend from empirical fragments to apodictically coherent and pedagogically well-designed conclusions. Yisrael M. Ta-Shema, *Ha-Sifrut Ha-Parshanit la-Talmud Be-Eropah Uvi-Tsefon Afrikah: Korot, Ishim Ve-Shiot* (Jerusalem: Magnes, 2003), 130–131.

30. The Babylonian Talmud text is, if not satiric then at the very least genuinely ironic. In contrast, the *Gornish* commentary, is not genuinely ironical, but only depends on the irony in the Talmud, which it subjects to logical scrutiny. The Gornish commentary does no more than look for and supply apodictic grounding for the Talmud's irony, thus taking the latter seriously, indeed, mathematically.

31. A possible objection at this point concerns the notion of aporetics, or formulating legitimate problems that which are proven to have no solution. The philosophical tradition embraces and even welcomes uncertainty, for example the aporetic dialogues of early Plato, or on the other end of the spectrum, Kant's antinomies. So: Are not well-structured uncertainty and apodictic irony just versions of philosophical aporetics, a thinking that is well known and well established in the tradition of philosophy from Plato to Kant?

My answer is that a carefully constructed philosophical aporia or antinomy advances apodictic certainty about what is impossible to solve, thereby maintaining an aporia. This differs from the form of apodictic uncertainty, or specifically in the *Gornish* commentary, the apodictic irony of (de) selection, which the rabbinic notion of the possible as refutable and counter-refutable implies. The aporetic tradition of philosophy aims at achieving certainty on ontological grounds, even if that means being sure that such certainty cannot be attained (Kant's antinomies, and Rancière's disagreement are good examples). In contrast, the tradition of apodictic irony cultivates uncertainty as its goal, attempting to put the apodictic analysis of (de)selection at the service of that cultivation.

6. FORMALLY HUMAN (JEWISH RESPONSES TO KANT I)

1. My interest in these moves is of course not historical. Rather, I am interested in seeing how the modernist rethinking of rabbinic tradition and Jewish existence post-Kant both attempts and fails to recover the effacement

of the interpersonal in the intersubjective. Just as the notion of formal man in this chapter, so too the notion of implicit in the following one becomes the site where such an attempted recovery is taking place.

2. See Theodor Adorno, *Aesthetic Theory* (Minneapolis: University of Minnesota Press, 1997).

3. For the purposes of my argument here, it will suffice to say that while, as many scholars have suggested, Maimonides drew on Aristotelian idea of the inclusion (and therefore translatability) of rhetoric in philosophy, his modern interpreters took a Platonic view in which rhetoric must be excluded from philosophy altogether, unless, as I will explain in the essay, one takes a transcendentalist position in which one can indeed be both a philosopher and a Talmudist.

4. Moshe Halbertal, "What Is the *Mishneh Torah*? On Codification and Ambivalence," in *Maimonides After 800 Years*, ed. Jay M. Harris (Cambridge, Mass.: Harvard University Press, 2007), 81–113.

5. Even if and precisely because the question of the self-declared intent of Maimonides is ambivalent, scholars have continued to address the question of the relationship between the Talmud and the MT. As Shamma Friedman highlights, Maimonides's contemporaries asserted without doubt that he sought to replace the Talmud with his code, at least for the purposes of both studying and practicing Jewish law. In their view, Maimonides had certainly proposed replacing learning the Talmud with studying his code, a proposal that they consequently either endorsed or opposed. Shamma Friedman, "The Talmud of Maimonides," in *Dinei Israel: Studies in Halakhah and Hebrew Law*, vols. 26–27 (Hebrew) (Tel Aviv: Tel Aviv University; New York: Yeshiva University, 2008–2009), 221–239. Scholars of the modern period, however, considered such an interpretation mistaken. Instead, they presented different explanations of Maimonides's position, interpretations in which the code culminates the study of the Talmud as an intellectual pursuit but does not replace it. That scholars have been divided on these issues is indicative of complexity in Maimonides's thinking about the Talmud. Most readily, as Friedman helps us to see, Maimonides understands the Talmud in two ways: as a literary corpus (content), which he does not dismiss, and as a literary-intellectual form, which he does seek to replace with the more systematic form of the code. However, this dualism of content and form needs to be understood in terms of the broader context and greater nuance of Maimonides's work in order to shed light on the tacit work of constructing the Talmud as an object of either critique or defense during and after Maimonides's time.

To clarify the relationship between the Talmud and the code in Maimonides, modern scholars often appealed to the philosophical

Maimonides of the *Guide of the Perplexed* or more broadly to the philosophical foundations of his thinking. In that context, they asked how and on what grounds Maimonides the philosopher and Maimonides "the Talmudist" could coexist in one person. Many scholars of that period argued that the MT can tell us about Maimonides the philosopher in light of his jurisprudence, legal sensibility, and philosophical systematization. However, as we will see, the Brisker Rav stands out by highlighting what the MT can indicate about how Maimonides approached the Talmud.

6. Maimonides, "Introduction" to *Mishneh Torah*, MT Intro. 23–27. Translation of *Mechon Mamre*, amended.

7. With respect to time, in an apologetic exercise, ideas come from the interpreter and go backward to their place in the genealogy of authorities, which means that "clarification" does not have to do with historical time, but only with the genealogical rank of the authorities for any given idea, which may translate into history but does not have to do so.

8. Maimonides, "Introduction" to *Mishneh Torah*, MT Intro. 41. Translation of *Mechon Mamre*, amended.

9. This does not prevent Maimonides from requiring or even privileging the study of "Talmud" in the primordial sense of the word, as exegesis or inference in the *Mishneh Torah*, "The Book of Knowledge," "Laws of Studying the Torah" 1:11–12. Having portrayed the style in "the Talmud" as unnecessary in the introduction, in the *Book of Knowledge*, in contrast, he thus does not demote studying the *gemara* or "Talmud," that is, reasoning about the matters from their principles, deducing matters from matters, comparing matters, contemplating the rules of interpreting the Scripture until one knows the principle of the rules, how the permitted and the forbidden had been deduced, and similar things learned from the tradition. This issue is called, in varying versions of the text, either *gemara* or Talmud, and *gemara* or Talmud is thus an intellectual discipline, which, as the introduction suggests, does not necessarily include refutations and counter-refutations, but instead follows the rules of systematic thinking, the one Maimonides demonstrates in the MT.

10. See, for example, Shamma Friedman, *Talmud Aruckh: Perek ha-Sokher et ha-Umanin* (New York: Jewish Theological Seminary of America, 1996).

11. According to both modern scholars and their medieval predecessors, this principle of triple coincidence both regulates the dynamics of refutations and defenses and frames the divergences in positions between masters (*amoraim*) in their arguments with each other and with the sages of the Mishnah. One practical implementation of the principle of triple coincidence is that a master of the Talmud cannot diverge from a teaching of a sage in the Mishnah unless this master identifies his position with the authority of

another sage. As a result, not only the people named in the Talmud but also the ideas and teachings ascribed to them follow the principle of triple coincidence. The pattern of refuting, defending, and disagreeing also follows that principle.

12. "Memory" might mean both the mechanical memory for words and the intellectually advanced memory for things, including ideas and other matters behind these words, as ancient manuals of rhetoric would have it, as well as memory in relations to other rhetorical techniques—invention, example, and delivery, not to mention refutation. For an analysis of these notions in the history of rhetoric, see Frances A. Yates, *The Art of Memory* (Chicago: University of Chicago Press, 2001). To access this programmatic aspect of discussion, I would need not only and not primarily to juxtapose the Talmud with the manuals of rhetoric of the same period—specifically, with what these manuals have to say about memory and refutation—but also to isolate the literary-ontological form of Talmudic argumentation: to address the question of what kind of human performance and, in particular, what kind of existence transpires from the form of discussion in the Talmud, separate from any thematic in-text references to that existence, which goes well beyond the scope of this essay. I attend to this task elsewhere.

13. *Inventions of Rabbenu Chayim Ha Levi: Inventions and Elucidations on Maimonides* (Hebrew) (Brooklyn: Z. Berman, 1985–86).

14. Ibid., 1.

15. Ibid.

16. By implication, because you do not protect one life at the expense of an equal life, it should not be a factor in "commit adultery or die," either. This argument represents an attack on the Tosafists' reading in the Brisker Rav's attempt to explain why Maimonides does not accept their point of view.

17. Notably, a more general distinction found in the Brisker method of Talmud study lies between a *hafza* (object) and a *gavra* (person). This distinction was at work in the analysis above, as well—acting as a person (*gavra*) in the situation of active murder and as an object (*hafza*) or an instrument in the passive situation—and it recalls the Kantian distinction between man as a goal and man as means.

18. Needless to say, conceptual transcendental a priorism is a way to read texts—in this case Rabba's dictum about blood in the Talmud—by making them into *sources* (in the strictest sense Hermann Cohen will give to that concept) for a rhetorical, or natural-ontological, or even transcendental understanding of the concept of life.

19. Highlighting with the Brisker Rav the philosophical foundation of Maimonides's modus operandi as a Talmudist allows approaching the old

question of the relationship between Maimonides the philosopher and Maimonides the codifier of the law in a new light. The question is not only what connection, if any, exists between Maimonides of the *Guide* and Maimonides of the *Mishneh Torah*, but also, as Isadore Twersky highlights, the methodological or metalegal component of the *Mishneh Torah* per se. See Isadore Twersky, *Introduction to the Code of Maimonides (Mishneh Torah)* (New Haven: Yale University Press, 1980), and his *Studies in Jewish Law and Philosophy* (New York: KTAV, 1982). He identifies that component with philosophy as a general theory of law, however, thereby reenacting Maimonides's reduction of the Talmud to law, while the Brisker Rav demonstrates the role of philosophical thinking in legalistic thinking in action, that is, in the ways in which Maimonides thinks in the areas of applying the law, which for him, and even more clearly for R. Joseph Soloveitchik, is a question of thinking in general, implemented in law in particular. Twersky, however, explains the relationship between philosophical and legalistic aspects in the code to identify the metalegal with the philosophical at the expense of the rhetorical.

20. That poses the question of how philosophical notions work not only and not primarily in the *Guide*, but also and perhaps in a greater degree in seemingly nonphilosophical legalistic areas of the code of the *Mishneh Torah*.

21. As Soloveitchik highlights, the question of where questions come from is not discussed, because it has nothing to do with the current question: What is the origin of lawful behavior in thinking? See his *Das reine Denken und die Seinskonstituirung bei Hermann Cohen* (1930; Berlin: Schoen Books, 2005).

22. See ibid., 40–41.

23. The difference is that in philosophy, as opposed to a courtroom, the law is not already known and is yet to be established.

24. Soloveitchik, his *Das reine Denken und die Seinskonstituirung bei Hermann Cohen*, 43.

25. Ibid.

26. This also speaks to the conception of the Talmud as a form of legalistic, refutation-driven way of thinking, a conception that Maimonides both constructs and dismisses. In the historically long debate about the relationships between the MT, the Talmud, and philosophy in Maimonides, Shamma Friedman has claimed that Maimonides dismissed the Talmud as a form of thinking but preserved the Talmud as a literary work. Though helpful, this claim raises a further question. Why, in the face of such an obvious solution, were scholars divided on the issue in first place? Remarkably, Friedman is no exception. He, too, chooses sides and disagrees with

Maimonides's dismissal of the Talmud, even if only as a literary-intellectual form.

Friedman has argued that Maimonides never gave up the content of the Talmud, while he did indeed dismiss the rhetorical-refutational form of it. Soloveitchik's notion of pure thinking helps to discern the basis of that dismissal: Maimonides's allegiance to pure thinking. (Remarkably, that assumes thinking done in the Talmud as a "literary work" could not have been pure by Cohen's standards.) What that means, however, is that the framework of discussing Maimonides the philosopher versus Maimonides the Talmudist needs to change, and the question needs to be asked about Maimonides as neither a philosopher nor a Talmudist but as a thinker.

7. MIS-TAKING IN *HALAKHAH* AND *AGGADAH* (JEWISH RESPONSES TO KANT II)

1. This analysis was initiated in part by Gilles Deleuze's *Le pli*, which redefined the implicit from one of the most general and self-evident logical concepts to something very specific, related to the notion of a very specific conceptual formation, and by Jean-François Lyotard's "Emma," which emphasized the trend toward considering the implicit as something that actually exists, that is "ready-made" and just waiting for time to be "excited," that is, to be brought, as it were, from the basement to the kitchen, from the shelf to the table, from storage to the light—in other words, from the implicit to the explicit. In this essay, I try to say that there are instances when bringing from the darkness of storage to the light modifies things drastically or even destroys them, making the very bringing to light problematic. See Gilles Deleuze, *Le pli: Leibniz et le baroque* (Paris: Editions de Minuit, 1988); Jean-François Lyotard, "Emma," *Nouvelle revue de psychoanalyse* 39 (Spring 1989): 43–70. In a shorter and differently framed version, materials in this chapter appeared in "Rethinking the Implicit: Fragments of the Project on Aggada and Halakhah in Walter Benjamin," in *Words: Religious Language Matters*, ed. Ernst Van Den Hemel and Asja Szafranec (New York: Fordham University Press, 2016), 249–269.

Thus, in Chaim Nachman Bialik's approach, *aggadah* seems to be included in this wide category of substantial literary forms. Compare it with Bialik's definition of *aggadah* in "Le Knusah Shel Ha-Aggada": "The Hebrew written *aggadah* is a fundamental literary form that dominated for several hundreds of years in the world of folk and personal liberal creativity of the Israeli nation." Bialik further defines "form" in terms of subject, shape, and style. See Bialik, "Halakhah ve-Aggada," in *Koll kite Ch. N Bialik* (Tel-Aviv: Devir, 1962), 220, available in English as "Halakhah and

Aggadah," trans. Leon Simon, in *Revealment and Concealment: Five Essays* (Jerusalem: Ibis Editions, 2000), 46–47.

2. Franz Clemens Brentano, *The Theory of Categories*, trans. Roderick M. Chisholm and Norbert Gateman (The Hague: Martinis Inhofe, 1981), 169–170.

3. Within the project of language, the implicit cannot be the same as the *indirect*. Brentano's critique allows us to try to think about the implicit in terms of what is being thought of *in obliquo*.

4. Brentano, *The Theory of Categories*, 169.

5. Ibid., 171.

6. Because the grammatical importance of *Sein* (being, as opposed to nonbeing, or in this context, existence as opposed to nonexistence) is complicated by Brentano and thereby displaced from its central position in grammar, Brentano's results can be applied to expressions that are not subject to grammatical rules of *Sein*. This includes the texts of the Talmud, which organizes expressions around legal topics and speakers who make rulings or who discuss rulings about rulings, rather than confining the narration to predications describing (or even prescribing) allegedly existent matters of fact. In Brentano's terms, the Talmud treats determinations in the Mishnah as relative determinations, because, in the Talmud, the speakers presume the Mishnaic sages had thought of something "indirectly." For instance, the speakers in the Talmud and later interpreters of it discover a mental disposition wherein this or that utterance in the Mishnah takes place. It is the indirect character of this determination that makes Talmud, the process, not the text, an experience of discovery and invention, rather than one of explanation and commentary.

7. Walter Benjamin, *The Origin of German Tragic Drama*, trans. John Osborne (London: NLB, 1977).

8. An affinity between Max Kadushin's and Walter Benjamin's approaches is worth highlighting here. The former, in his "conceptual" approach to the rabbinic exegetical tradition of Midrash, follows a similar line of thinking: what Kadushin calls "concept-values" organize what he calls the "rabbinic mind." Neither approach is fully present as explicitly fully defined or locally definable concepts. See Max Kadushin, *The Rabbinic Mind* (New York: Bloch, 1972), and *A Conceptual Approach to the Mekilta* (New York: J. David for the Jewish Theological Seminary of America, 1969).

9. This treatment of "predications" is similar to Brentano's critique of using the grammatical notion of predication for thinking about either thinking or existence.

10. Walter Benjamin, "Letter to Gershom Scholem on Franz Kafka," trans. Edmund Jephcott, in *Selected Writings, Volume 3, 1935–1938*, ed.

Howard Eiland and Michael W. Jennings (Cambridge, Mass.: Harvard University Press, 2002), 327.

11. See Benjamin to Gershom Scholem, August 11, 1934, in *The Correspondence of Walter Benjamin, 1910–1940*, ed. Gershom Scholem and Theodor W. Adorno, trans. Manfred R. Jacobson and Evelyn M. Jacobson (Chicago: University of Chicago Press, 1994), Letter 240, 452–454.

12. In the history of the Mishnah's reception, however, the Mishnah increasingly becomes understood as a normative document telling how things shall be rather than how the conflicts are to be resolved if and, alas, as often as common sense proves not to work. In that sense, not only the Talmud but also the Mishnah becomes effaced. This process, however, is beyond the scope of inquiry in this book.

13. Bialik, "Halakhah ve-Aggada," 228; "Halakhah and Aggadah," 81.

14. Bialik, "Halakhah ve-Aggada," 228; "Halakhah and Aggadah," 83.

15. Benjamin, "Letter to Gershom Scholem on Franz Kafka," 326.

16. Ibid.

17. Ibid.

18. Franz Kafka, *Parables and Paradoxes* (New York: Schocken, 1958), 11.

19. Nor true failures can be forgiven, like sins can. Sin is similar to failure and dissimilar to mistake, for mistakes can be corrected, while sins and failures cannot. Sins, however, can and should be forgiven; failures, by contrast, need to be maintained. This notion of failure thus both invokes and erases the Talmudic notion of failure, as I will soon explain.

20. In Benjamin and Kafka's case, but not in the case of the interpersonal in the Talmud, where it is not abandoned by the subject but cultivated in another subject as a way to restrain that subject's position, not to abandon it, let alone to arrive to a universal intersubjectivity.

21. Jill Robbins, "Kafka's Parables," in *Midrash and Literature*, ed. Geoffrey H. Hartman and Sanford Budick (New Haven: Yale University Press, 1986), 265–284.

22. Kierkegaard's hermeneutics of interpretation in *Fear and Trembling* does not require misapprehension. Kierkegaard recognizes only that Abraham defies any interpretation of his actions and thoughts in terms of universal ethics and is instead the "knight of faith." Kierkegaard does not see Abraham undergoing an experience of misapprehension or, for that matter, undergoing any describable experience. Kierkegaard's method of interpretation concerns readers, not Abraham. Kierkegaard demands that readers of the story understand the problem of the inexplicability of Abraham's actions in terms of universal ethics, which in turn circumscribes him and the readers of the story in a hermeneutic circle. An emblem of that circle and the way to break it is Abraham as a "knight of faith," who

exists—that is, finds his salvation from nonbeing—precisely because he escapes any universal understanding of his actions or motives. The hermeneutical circle of reading is very different from the way in which the time machine of misapprehension works. The former involves only the readers of the story, while the machinery of misapprehension describes the trajectory of the characters in the story, as well.

In Kierkegaard's hermeneutics of interpretation, that is to say, the implicit is directly explicable in an interpretation, at least in principle. This means it is not actually implicit in Benjamin's or Kafka's terms, but rather is only "implied." For Kafka, the implicit does not became any explicable, "implied" sense, because the time machine of misapprehension guarantees that the implicit remains implicit as the only way in which one can deal with it.

23. Nor is what is implicit in the divine utterance a case of the gap between signifier and signified. That Abraham mistakes it reveals the utterance as standing outside signification and related to signification only indirectly. What is implicit in the utterance is not clarified at the beginning of the story, and even at the end it remains oblique, not explicit.

Two major considerations stand in the way of reducing the implicit to the positive terms of a gap between signifier and signified. One comes from Benjamin's perspective, the other from Brentano's. According to the former, a mistake is productive only because it is never known in advance to be a mistake. In this process, time is of essence. The time of mistaking, however, is not controllable from any subject position—not by the character at the beginning of the story nor by the already wise subject at the end. At the end of the story, the mistake is already understood as a mistake and thus is no longer productive. Looking back from the end of the story, the character, Abraham realizes that he made a mistake. This realization neutralizes the mistake, which was not seen as such at the beginning. At the end of the story, Abraham is the same subject as before, but he can never assume the same subject position he had in the beginning. He can no longer mistakenly interpret the divine command, nor need he make any interpretation at all, because the productive ambivalence of the command is now fully articulated and thereby totally lost. At the end of the story, its subject, Abraham is the same, but he can never repeat his movement from the beginning to end, even though the story does so over and over again as different readers encounter it. But this is only because the time of the story is not the time of its reading. Again, as Benjamin puts it, the characters lose "in parable," but win "in reality." In the time of the story, no subject goes through it unchanged—there is no self-identical, atomlike subject who lives through, controls, or knows the story in advance, from beginning to end, or even from end to beginning. Abraham at the end cannot understand, explain, or interpret Abraham at the beginning. Rather, the story, and in particular, mistake making, has its own time, and this time is neither reversible nor is it retraceable. The time of mistaking, in other words, is not time traversed by any self-identical subject. Rather, time is a device that makes mistaking both possible and productive, with no unified subject to control it. The way that the time machine works makes the mistake ambivalent—that is, establishes the possibility that is not a mistake—at the beginning of the story. Benjamin's position is that every mistake contains an element of irreversible misapprehension of the inconceivable. But misapprehension is still an apprehension: it approaches the inconceivable without ever revealing it. The inconceivable utterance of G-d thus remains inconceivable even at the end of the story, and its meaning remains as implicit as it was in the beginning. The only difference is that toward the end of the story, both Abraham and the readers of the story know that they deal with an implicit that cannot be conceived or fully explicated, yet something with which Abraham nevertheless had to deal.

Brentano's approach to the implicit is symmetrically the opposite of Benjamin's. Whereas Benjamin begins from the implicit and argues for its independent existence, which makes it irreducible to any explication or interpretation, Brentano begins from the multiplicity of mutually exclusive interpretations and from there arrives at thinking of the inexplicability of the implicit without any claims about its existence or nonexistence. From Benjamin's standpoint, the utterance "bring him [Isaac] to sacrifice" proves to be inconceivable and thus similar to what he posits as ideas. The inconceivable remains implicit and therefore resists apprehension. What gives the implicit power to remain implicit despite all attempts at explication is the power of its existence, as opposed to nonexistence. To remain implicit, the implicit must exist. But the existence or nonexistence of the implicit is irrelevant for Brentano. For him, the implicit is what is thought of, not what either exists or does not exist. That is why he begins from multiple explications or interpretations. You cannot think directly of the divine utterance "bring him to sacrifice" and bypass at least one of its different and competing interpretations. From that point of view, as we have seen, sticking with either of these interpretations destines Abraham to make a mistake. It is via that experience of misapprehension that, by the end of the story, Abraham and readers think of the utterance as exceeding any of its interpretations and therefore think of it as implicit—again, whether existent or not.

What this means, however, is that in both Brentano's and Benjamin's views, the only way to speak about the implicit in terms of signifier and signified would be to define the implicit as a gap between one signified ("slaughter") and another ("bring to the altar.") Both signifieds would then have the same signifier, the divine utterance. However, possessing a shared signifier cannot explain the gap in signification. This is why the linguistic theory of signification, or for that matter, the project of language as an object of linguistics, provides no sufficient reading.

Can one overcome this limitation of the purely linguistic approach to reading the story? Beyond the narrower scope of linguistics, the notion of a gap between a signifier and another signifier belongs to Lacan's theory of psychoanalysis, which still is considerably dependent on the model of language as the object of linguistics. However, in Lacan's theory of psychoanalysis, the subject position plays a more prominent role than it does in pure linguistics. The gap can be discovered from a specific subject position, that of the analyst. Thereupon it becomes noticeable from another subject position, that of the patient. The patient, of course, does not assume the position of the analyst, but rather gets access to the gap by means of the patient's relationship to the analyst, which in most cases is that of transference. Is Abraham the analyst, and the reader or even G-d the patient? That suggestion does not help. The machinery of mistaking neither requires disclosure nor dismisses transference. Rather, its mode of work is closer to the Freud's topology of the evident and hidden content of dreams than it is to Lacan's reformulation of Freud's theory in the linguistic terms of signification and of gaps between signifiers.

24. b. Gittin 43a.

25. b. Gittin 41ab.

26. Ibid.

27. The discrepancy between the explicit theme of discussion, a half-slave marrying a free woman, and its meaning in the context of discussing the *tanna* in question, where the discussion must focus on a half-free woman only, indicates that even the main stage is a citation from another possible stage where the discussion between the anonymous characters happens without relationship to this particular *tanna*.

28. b. Gittin 43a.

29. In the original, there is a slight difference between Raba Bar Rav Huna's logical conclusion and Raba's citation of it, which shows Raba's attempt to use it for his own current discourse, where the expression "has not any [approved] betrothal" is used rather than "is not betrothed." Raba does this because he uses it as a symmetrical analogy for a man who is half-slave, who semantically cannot "*be betrothed," he only can "*have an approved or unapproved betrothal."

30. Isaiah 3:6.

31. b. Gittin 43a.

32. Rashi's medieval commentary *ad locum* explains the structure of misapprehension as follows. "This ruin"—with these words, "the Bible says 'this ruin is in your hands'" applies to the people of Jerusalem, who lost their access to learning Torah, and they were asking their fellows [all Torah questions] saying "You have your garment, let you be our officer and let this ruin be under your hands," meaning tell us the hidden things that are hard to explain, for they are like your garment [which you miraculously have when we do not]: you have an intimate knowledge of the Torah, because the garment is owned intimately by its owner, so you tell us those hidden things and let you be our teacher, and this ruin, that is, the matters of Torah, will be under your hand, because no one can hold the words of Torah without failing in them. That is, a man cannot understand the truth of the words of the [oral] Torah until he will fail by teaching them with mistakes, and he is corrected, and he accepts and understands. [Thus Rava Bar Rav Huna said to Rav Hisda:] They are under your hands, Oh Rav Hisda, and I failed." This explanation lets the readers decide whether Rava Bar Rav Huna was ironical or not. Or else, following the larger framework of the Talmud, it assumes that he was certainly ironical, both based on the explanation ("What was the reason etc.") and on the general tactic of failing proofs in the sequence.

33. For some readers, in particular for those looking from the point of view of the main stage, the double-edged sword of silence explained through the irony of failing in order to fail one's opponent sheds some light on Rabba's position about the case with "survivors" of a half-slave killed by the animal as well. Rabba's final proposal, "The fine is payable to the descendants, if there were any," can be understood as equally ironical, too. It looks like it is defending the case as helpful, but in reality it shows the absurdity of its consequences for the question of the legality of half-a-slave marriage. That irony means that using Rabba's pronouncement to defend against a countercase for the Mishnah is not effective, either.

34. In particular, they then recall a teaching of another named rabbi, Rav Shesheth, that yielded yet another option for them—that marrying a half-slave man to a half-slave woman is omitted because it is definitely illegal. That would mean there is no aporia at hand. Yet the characters could not rely on that alone, because that would render the "forgetful omission" justifiable in the name of one of the rabbis only and in full dependence on memory about that rabbi only. They of course want to cover as many possible grounds as they can, and so the discussion continues with further refutations and counterrefutation in play.

35. See Haim Zalman Dimitrovsky, Daniel Boyarin, Marc G. Hirshman, and Shamma Friedman, *'Aṭarah lḤayyim: meḥqariym basiprwt hatalmwdiyt*

wharabaniyt likbwd prwpeswr Ḥayyim Zalman Diymiyṭrwbsqiy (Jerusalem: Hebrew University of Jerusalem Magnes Press, 2000); Daniel Boyarin, *Ha-'Iyun ha-Sefaradi: le-farshanut ha-Talmud shel megorshe Sefarad* (Jerusalem: Mekhon Ben-Tsevi le-ḥeḳer ḳehilot Yisra'el ba-Mizraḥ, Yad Yitsḥaḳ Ben-Tsevi ṿeha-Universiṭah ha-'Ivrit bi-Yerushalyim, 1989); Sergey Dolgopolski, *What Is Talmud? The Art of Disagreement* (New York: Fordham University Press, 2009).

36. Notably, the role of mistaking and failing is different for Benjamin and in the Talmud. For the former, there is a subject who has to go through the experience of mistake to get closer to the ideas, even if never getting them in any concept. In the latter, the characters cause other characters to go through the experience of failing, and even when a character assumes a role of a subject who failed, it is done only ironically as a way to show to another character—through a reduction to absurdity—that the failure was of that of the other character.

37. We now see more clearly the difference between the Talmudic form of mistaking and Benjamin's form of the tractate as two simultaneously divergent and convergent ways to approach what Benjamin calls "ideas." Benjamin's understanding of the form of the tractate treats the machinery of mistaking as a product of wisdom's decomposition, which is the decay of *aggadah* that occurs along with dismissing the truth, or *halakhah*. However, if, unlike Benjamin, and like the Talmud story, we understand the working of take the machinery of mistaking positively, we can contemplate the Talmud as a project wherein *halakhah* and *aggadah* are not juxtaposed, as they were in the whole project of Jewish modernism, including, in Benjamin's reading, by Kafka. In the Talmud, the machinery of mistaking longer involves the decay of *aggadah*, but simply is a normal device among other rhetorical devices in the Talmud. In terms of Benjamin's philosophy, the Talmud would then turn out to be a kind of tractate, rather than a traditional source of irrationally separated *aggadah* and *halakhah*.

In Benjamin's perspective, the Talmudic story thus proves to be a prose form that uses the time machine of mistaking to sustain itself constantly in the implicit, both for the rabbis who read the story while being part of it and for readers who come to it later. Because of the crisis of modernity signaled by the sense of an unbridgeable split between *aggadah* and *halakhah*, between the inconceivable and what can be said about it, between the implicit and the explicable, in Benjamin's account of the form of the tractate, a utopian image of the Talmud is lurking. In this image, the split does not take place. The revised theoretical idea of the implicit seems to be one of the adequate tools to grasp this image in theory.

38. Bialik and Benjamin clearly diverge in their more specific defenses of the Jewish Law against Kant's critique of the positive law. For Bialik, the political power of the implicit manifests in the poetic form of the *aggadah*, restraining, as it does, the explicit—and thus positive "truth"—the *halakhah*. Benjamin, both in his capacity as a reader of Kafka and beyond, does not locate the "truth" on the side of the *halakhah*. Rather, the allegedly positive and explicit law—"Jewish" or general—only seems to be explicable, let alone explicit. That law belongs to and comes from the power of the implicit, which is always misapprehended through "positive" concepts but cannot be accessed in any other way. For both thinkers, limitations of the positive *halakhah* call for the counterpower, which is the *aggadah* for Bialik or the power of mistake and misapprehension for Benjamin. The *aggadah* puts its "mighty paw" on the positivity of the *halakhah* or its "truth," and misapprehension restrains one's submission to the explicit regulations the *halakhah* imposes on its subjects. Any positive, prosaic, rhetorical, technical, comprehension of the law is always also a misapprehension of that law. Yet, most dramatically, despite their different defenses of "Jewish Law" against Kant's critique of the positive law, both thinkers share Kant's assumption that the *halachah*, or Jewish Law, is a positive law. Their defense of the "Jewish Law" therefore tacitly inherits Kant's starting point—the construction of the rabbinic tradition of the Talmud as that of the "Jewish" and "Law." For Kant, the direct reference of the "Jewish Law" might be limited to Old Testament, yet these thinkers extend the notion to include the rabbinic tradition as well.

39. Needless to say, they do not opt for any irrational concepts either, following in this Kant, too, who fought adamantly against the irrational or "mystical," in particular in his criticism of the "spirit seer" See Immanuel Kant and John Manolesco, *Dreams of a Spirit Seer, and Other Related Writings* (New York: Vantage Press, 1969).

40. Rashi *ad locum*: "Bring him up [to the sacrifice] (Gen. 22: 2) He [G-d] did not tell Abraham 'to slaughter' Isaac, because the Holy One, Blessed be He, did not desire to have Isaac slaughtered, but only to have him brought up to the mountain for his preparing for the sacrifice [the original is ambiguous about whose preparing—Isaac's to being sacrificed or Abrahams's to do a sacrifice] When he brought him up, [G-d] ordered him to take him down." (The translation is mine.) For medieval controversy about reading this passage, see Devorah Schoenfeld, *Isaac on Jewish and Christian Altars: Polemic and Exegesis in Rashi and the Glossa Ordinaria* (New York: Fordham University Press, 2013).

41. I allude to Erich Auerbach's argument in *Mimesis*, where, at least on my reading, he argues that because the account of the story comes from the

past as past, that is not from the past in the sense of *present historicum*, the reader cannot suspend disbelief or entertain the story as real but not in full. Instead, the reader must choose between these options: (1) The story accounts for the implicit and distant past that can have no explicit description, or (2) The story results from political manipulation of priests.

8. THE EARTH FOR THE OTHER OTHERS

1. In that respect, the steady darkness of the night is not radically different from the steady light of the day, for both are slow. Only the speedy glimpse of lightning can bring the being of the things all together in view, alas, at the same moment as all things disappear from the view in either completely disorienting darkness of the night or in no less blinding bright light of the day.

2. Rodolphe Gasché, *Geophilosophy: On Gilles Deleuze and Felix Guattari's "What Is Philosophy?"* (Evanston, Ill.: Northwestern University Press, 2014).

3. For the purposes of my argument in this chapter, I leave any consideration of Heidegger's sense of the earth as *Erde* for another occasion. Instead, I focus on Deleuze's notion of the earth in relation to Heidegger's *Sein*, or being, in Gasché's reading and beyond.

4. That question extends beyond the question of mapping the relationships between the Talmud and philosophy, for the very possibility of a map, however complex, now is also part of the question.

5. Gilles Deleuze and Félix Guattari, *What Is Philosophy?* (New York: Columbia University Press, 1991).

6. In Rancière's terms, what is at stage is the question of whether the Talmud competes with philosophy in providing the discourse of justice, without which the political, as Rancière understands it, would not be possible, or in supplying the discourse of justice, does the Talmud include philosophy within a larger discourse of memory and remembering as the foundation of the justice and thus of the political. If the latter, then the ontology and theology of justice would be no more than a possible, but not formally necessary part of the discourse of justice. The task of the discourse of justice would therefore be the task of thought to remember the past, rather than to attend to what is, what was, or even to the being versus nonbeing.

7. Of course, this explanation of the Lascaux paintings follows, at least in part, the logic of totemism: A "human" identifies with a totem, the bull. Yet a stipulation is due. Before that "identification," there is no "human," or more precisely, there is no "presence." In contrast, any identification would imply two preexisting units, the identifier and the identified, colliding in

one. This is why the rubric of totemism, including the notion of identification that it entails and that is entailed by it, does not fully suffice to grasp what Bataille's interpretation articulates.

8. bBM 84a. See the analysis of that story in Daniel Boyarin, *Unheroic Conduct: The Rise of Heterosexuality and the Invention of the Jewish Man* (Berkeley: University of California Press, 2000), 127ff. For an analysis of a relevant composition on Resh Lakish in bGittin 47a, see Zvi Septimus, "Three Ways of Understanding Talmud Authorship" (manuscript, June 2016).

9. Gilles Deleuze and Félix Guattari, *A Thousand Plateaus: Capitalism and Schizophrenia*, trans. Brian Masumi (Minneapolis: University of Minnesota Press, 1987), 56, 69–70.

10. Babylon is also referred to as connected to the "Land/Earth of Shinar," yet the reference is by way of a synecdoche indicating an area that is a part of or adjacent to Babylon as a political territory, which implies no more equation between Shinar and Babylon than the Land of Goshen can imply equation with Egypt.

11. Extending Levinas's analysis of these notions.

12. Notably, "political" is not on the list of relative deterritorializations and reterritorializations. Does that suggest that for D&G the political or its possibility would belong to Earth-Thought?

13. Schmitt's *nomos* of earth is an attempt of thinking in this direction, even if, perhaps that Earth remains a geometrical object for him.

14. This leaves and even reinforces the possibility of pseudocausality, a notion Deleuze developed in *Logic of Sense*. See Gilles Deleuze, *The Logic of Sense*, ed. Constantin V. Boundas, trans. Mark Lester and Charles Stivale (New York: Columbia University Press, 1990).

15. In a way, the noncausal nature of the Earth as absolute deterritorialization resembles how Cohen thinks the "origin" in the "pure thought" as discussed in Chapter 6.

16. See Edmund Husserl, "Foundational Investigations of the Phenomenological Origin of the Spatiality of Nature," trans. Fred Kersten, in Edmund Husserl, *Shorter Works* (Notre Dame, Ind.: University of Notre Dame Press, 1981), 222–233.

17. At work here is Deleuze and Guattari's "*survol*," which Rodolphe Gasché attempts rendering as "survey" in English.

18. Hannah Arendt's distinction between humankind, a biological entity, and humanity, a community of those who are judging and therefore acting humanly, does not apply here, even if it proves relevant in other inquiries. Because humanity as an ability to judge rather than follow rules, for example in Kant, is not limited to humankind, even if the latter is the only known

example of it, the universality of the earth, rather than land, is not limited to humankind in the first place, and the notion of humanity does not fully apply for the same reason: No example is ever universal enough.

19. Gasché, *Geophilosophy*, 116.

20. Cf. the opening pericope in Perek Chelek, b. Sanhedrin 90ab.

INDEX

www.ingramcontent.com/pod-product-compliance
Lightning Source LLC
Chambersburg PA
CBHW032119020426
42334CB00016B/1004

9780823280193